Provo's
TWO TEMPLES

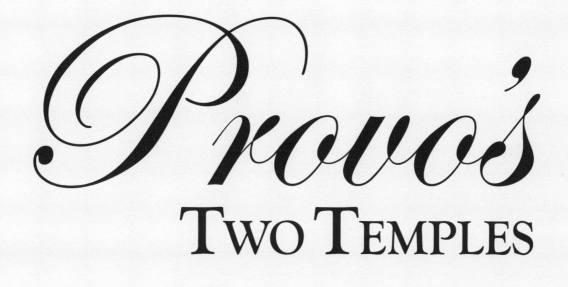

Provo's
Two Temples

Richard O. Cowan & Justin R. Bray

RSC
BYU

DESERET
BOOK

Published by the Religious Studies Center, Brigham Young University, Provo, Utah, in cooperation with Deseret Book Company, Salt Lake City.
Visit us at rsc.byu.edu.

Printed in the United States of America by Sheridan Books, Inc.

DESERET BOOK is a registered trademark of Deseret Book Company.
Visit us at DeseretBook.com.

Cover design and interior layout by Juliana G. Cox and Madison Swapp.
Front cover photo by Brent Nordgren and Lee R. Cowan. Spine photo by Julie Cannon Markham. Back cover photo by Reinhard Franz. Front flap photo by Reinhard Franz. Back flap photo by Lee R. Cowan. Chapter one opener photo courtesy of Provo City Library. Provo Temple chapter opener photo by Reinhard Franz. Provo City Center Temple chapter opener photo by Brent Nordgren.

ISBN 978-0-8425-2965-5
US Retail: $29.99

Library of Congress Cataloging-in-Publication Data

Cowan, Richard O., 1934- author
 Provo's two temples / Richard O. Cowan and Justin R. Bray.
     pages cm
 Includes bibliographical references and index.
 ISBN 978-0-8425-2965-5
 1. Provo Utah Temple. 2. Provo City Center Temple. 3. Provo (Utah)–Church history. I. Bray, Justin R., author. II. Title.
 BX8685.P76C69 2015
 246'.9589332–dc23
                         2015021409

Contents

Preface

After publishing other books on Latter-day Saint temples, Richard O. Cowan began planning a work on the Provo Utah Temple. Not only was it his local temple, which he had witnessed being built and which he had attended for over four decades, but it had a distinctive place among the Church's growing family of temples. It had a unique design and had gained the distinction of being the most productive temple in the Church.

In September 2011, Richard invited Justin Bray to become a coauthor on this project. Only two weeks later, Church President Thomas S. Monson announced that the Provo Tabernacle, nearly destroyed by fire the previous year, would be rebuilt into Provo's second temple. The authors immediately decided to expand the scope of their project to include both of Provo's two temples. The new temple would also be distinctive, constructed in the red-brick shell of the older building.

The two authors bring different backgrounds to this project. After earning his doctorate in history at Stanford University in 1961, Richard O. Cowan taught courses in religion at Brigham Young University for over fifty years. His research focus has been on the Doctrine and Covenants and on Latter-day Saint history during the twentieth century. He has authored more than a dozen books related to these topics, including three about Mormon temples. As a student at BYU, Justin Bray served as Dr. Cowan's research assistant for two years. Following graduation, he joined the staff at the Church History Department in Salt Lake City. Among other things, he has been assigned to conduct oral history interviews with general Church leaders. Bray has authored several articles related to LDS history and religious practice and coedited two books on historian Andrew Jenson's missionary travels. He is completing work on a master's degree in history at the University of Utah.

An important feature of this book is the large number of insightful photographs, particularly related to construction of the new Provo City Center Temple. The authors are grateful to Lee R. Cowan, Richard's son, who has worked tirelessly to document key steps in the construction. The authors are also indebted to Julie

Cannon Markham, who maintained a richly illustrated blog recording the story of how the new temple was built and who made many of her photos available to be included in this book.

Several individuals have provided vital information needed for this work. These include former presidents of the Provo Utah Temple and Kurt Jensen, the temple's recorder. John Emery, project manager for Jacobsen Construction, and James Hansen, the Church's site manager, have kept the authors up to date on developments as the Provo City Center Temple has been built.

The following individuals at Brigham Young University's Religious Studies Center (RSC) have made important contributions as well. Thomas Wayment, publications director, has provided counsel and encouragement regarding this project. Devan Jensen, executive editor, kindly answered repeated questions regarding style and form. Brent Nordgren, production supervisor, directed the design and generously provided technical assistance and photos. Juliana Cox is the capable graphic designer of this book, with the assistance of Madison Swapp. We express thanks to editing interns Austin Ballard, Alison Brimley, Shanna D'Avila, Rebecca Bird, Hadley Griggs, Rachel Gessel, Rebekah Weaver, and Leah Welker.

Appreciation is also due to a group of Brigham Young University students who have provided important help to Richard Cowan with this project. Rachelle Price has spent many hours helping research, collect, organize, and evaluate the materials used in this work. Madison Thornberg and Ashley Logan have helped with many details. Under the direction of Patty Smith, the staff in Religious Education's faculty support center have provided assistance in various ways. Reg Beales, for example, produced several of the maps and schematic drawings we have used. Without their help, this project could not have been accomplished.

The authors hope that you will find this book to be interesting. In addition to information about the history of Provo's two temples, we hope you will gain insights that will enrich your service in these or any other latter-day temples.

CHAPTER 1

Beginnings

1776   Spanish explorers praise Utah Valley

1830   Church of Jesus Christ organized in New York State (April 6)

1836   First LDS temple dedicated at Kirtland, Ohio

1840   Baptisms for the dead inaugurated at Nauvoo

1849   Fort Utah established

1877   Endowments for the dead inaugurated at St. George Temple

1893   Salt Lake Temple dedicated (April 6)

1940   Latter-day Saint population in Utah Valley reaches nearly 45,000

1956   Los Angeles Temple (largest in the Church) dedicated

1964   Oakland Temple (last before Ogden and Provo Temples) dedicated

1966   Latter-day Saint population in Utah Valley number passes 107,000

*T*he story of Provo's two temples has roots going back to the early nineteenth century in the state of New York. In 1820, Joseph Smith—a young man fourteen years of age—was confused by the conflicting claims of the different churches in his area. Western New York has been called the "burned-over district" because of the revivalist fervor that prevailed there. In the midst of his confusion, young Joseph turned to the Bible for help. He was moved by a New Testament promise: "If any of you lack wisdom, let him ask of God, that giveth to all men liberally, and upbraideth not; and it shall be given him" (James 1:5). Joseph knelt to pray in a beautiful grove of trees that would be made sacred because of what happened there. Joseph reported that, in response to his fervent prayer, God the Eternal Father and His Son, Jesus Christ, appeared to him. Joseph recalled that their "brightness and glory def[ied] all description" (Joseph Smith—History 1:17). He was instructed to join none of the churches but was promised that he would be instrumental in restoring the true faith to the earth.

This was only the first in a series of divine manifestations. Three years later, an angelic messenger named Moroni came to Joseph and told him that "the preparatory work for the second coming of the Messiah was speedily to commence; that the time was at hand for the Gospel, in all its fullness to be preached in power, unto all nations that a people might be prepared for the Millennial reign."[1] To emphasize the importance of this preparation, Moroni cited several

Joseph Smith. Portrait by Alvin Gittins.
© Intellectual Reserve, Inc.

Temples have served two major functions: first, they have been places where heaven and earth meet . . . and second, places where sacred ceremonies or "ordinances" have been performed by which the faithful enter into covenants with God.

biblical passages, including the last two verses of the Old Testament (Malachi 4:5–6), which he paraphrased as follows: "Behold, I will reveal unto you the Priesthood, by the hand of Elijah the prophet, before the coming of the great and dreadful day of the Lord. And he shall plant in the hearts of the children the promises made to the fathers, and the hearts of the children shall turn to their fathers. If it were not so, the whole earth would be utterly wasted at his coming" (Doctrine and Covenants 2; see also Joseph Smith–History 1:37–39). Thus, the first divine communication following the visit of the Father and the Son—even before restoration of the priesthood or organization of the Church—informed the Prophet about Elijah restoring the priesthood keys that would unite children and fathers.

Moroni also told Joseph about a record written on gold plates that included the religious history of the ancient inhabitants of America. Translated "by the gift and power of God" (D&C 135:3), this record was published as the Book of Mormon, named for one of the ancient historians who was primarily responsible for its compilation. Among other things, it relates how Jesus Christ visited the Western Hemisphere following his Resurrection and Ascension to bless his "other sheep" in the New World (see John 10:14–16). Thus the Book of Mormon has been designated as "Another Testament of Jesus Christ."

In 1829, John the Baptist—a resurrected being—bestowed the authority of the lesser, or Aaronic, Priesthood upon Joseph Smith. Then the three chief ancient Apostles—Peter, James, and John—restored the higher, or Melchizedek, Priesthood. All these events led to the formal organization of The Church of Jesus Christ of Latter-day Saints at Fayette, New York, with six official members on April 6, 1830. Hence Latter-day Saints regard their church as a restoration of New Testament Christianity, or the "primitive church" (see Articles of Faith 1:6).

A Temple-Building People

Almost from the beginning, Latter-day Saints have been a temple-building and temple-attending people.[2] For them, temples are more

than ordinary meetinghouses; each temple is truly the "House of
the Lord." Since Old Testament times, temples have served two
major functions: first, they have been places where heaven and earth
meet—a place of revelation between God and man—and second,
places where sacred ceremonies or "ordinances" have been performed by which the faithful enter into covenants with God. Holy
instructions and promises connected with these ordinances testify of
humankind's ultimate eternal destiny.

At Kirtland, Ohio, the Latter-day Saints overcame poverty
and persecution to build their first temple in the mid-1830s. Their
sacrifice surely brought forth the blessings of heaven. As the temple

Kirtland Temple. Photo by Craig James
Ostler.

neared completion, the Saints enjoyed a rich outpouring of spiritual gifts, including prophecy, speaking in tongues, and visions of angels. Joseph Smith declared that "this was a time of rejoicing long to be remembered."[3] These events climaxed with glorious experiences during the day-long dedication of the temple on Sunday, March 27, 1836. One week later, on April 3, the Prophet recorded that Jesus Christ appeared in glory to accept the temple, and that Elijah the prophet, in fulfillment of Malachi's prophecy, restored the sealing keys that were "to turn the hearts of the fathers to the children, and the children to the fathers" (see D&C 110; Malachi 4:5–6). Within a few years, the first genealogical societies were organized in both Europe and North America. Latter-day Saints often refer to this interest in ancestors as "the spirit of Elijah." Clearly the first function of temples—a place of revelation—had been restored. The Kirtland Temple, however, had no facilities for temple ordinances—the second

Nauvoo Temple. Courtesy of Louis R. Hill.

function of temples. Instead, the building consisted primarily of two large meeting halls, one above the other.

Sacred ordinances were unfolded while the second temple was being built at Nauvoo, Illinois. In 1840, Joseph Smith taught the Saints that they could be baptized on behalf of deceased individuals (compare 1 Corinthians 15:29). They eagerly went into the Mississippi River to perform this ordinance, thus making gospel blessings available to their loved ones who had died without this opportunity. In 1842 the Prophet presented the endowment, which was a "course of instructions" describing the path which leads back into the presence of God.⁴ Joseph recorded that on May 4 he had "spent the day" with a select group, "instructing them in the principles and order of the Priesthood, attending to washings, anointing, endowments, and the communication of keys pertaining to the Aaronic Priesthood, and so on to the highest order of the Melchizedek Priesthood" and teaching all the "principles by which any one is enabled to secure the fullness of those blessings" and be prepared to dwell in the presence of God "in the eternal worlds."⁵ Soon couples were also being "sealed," or married, making solemn covenants "for time and for all eternity" (see D&C 132:7–20). When completed, the Nauvoo Temple repeated the pattern of two large meeting rooms but added a font in the basement and facilities for other ordinances on its uppermost floor. Children could also be linked to their parents through sacred ceremonies performed by priesthood authority.

Unfortunately, the forces of religious bigotry climaxed with the murders of Joseph Smith and his brother Hyrum in 1844. As anti-Mormon persecution continued, the Saints in Nauvoo—under the leadership of Joseph's successor, Brigham Young—made their well-known trek across the plains to new homes in the Rocky Mountains.

Although Brigham Young selected the site for a temple within a few days of arriving in the Salt Lake Valley, it would not be completed for another forty years. While the Salt Lake Temple was under construction, three others—all in Utah—would be dedicated. The first of these, which was in St. George (1877), followed the basic pattern of the Kirtland and Nauvoo Temples. At this time, endowments for the dead—not known in the

St. George Temple; note the original short tower.

first two temples—were inaugurated in the St. George Temple and quickly became the major component of the Saints' temple service. Speaking at the time that the St. George Temple was being completed, several Church leaders indicated that the design of future temples would more specifically meet these new needs. In 1879 Elder Orson Pratt pointed out that the Church by then had tabernacles and other buildings for the Saints' regular meetings. Therefore, temples could be designed especially for more "sacred and holy purposes"—for ordinances associated with "the Priesthood of the Most High God." Therefore "by and by," Elder Pratt concluded, "we will have Temples, with a great many things contained in them which we now have not."[6]

The decade and a half following the dedication of the St. George Temple witnessed a dramatic acceleration in temple construction. Not just one, but three of these sacred edifices were under construction at the same time. Two—Logan and Manti—were dedicated during the 1880s, and the Salt Lake Temple was finally dedicated in 1893. These three temples retained the large upper assembly room but included in the lower half beautiful rooms with murals on their walls where sacred temple ordinances were received. The temples also included a cafeteria for the convenience of temple patrons and workers who often needed to be in the temple during mealtimes, as well as laundries where rented temple

Salt Lake Temple. Courtesy of Craig James Ostler.

clothing was cared for. In the 1930s, the St. George Temple would be remodeled to include similar facilities.

Four more temples were built during the first half of the twentieth century—in Hawaii, Alberta, Arizona, and Idaho—reflecting the Church's expansion beyond Utah. These temples omitted the large upper assembly room, retaining only the facilities for performing endowments, sealings, and other ordinances. However, the Los Angeles Temple—dedicated in 1956 and the largest built by the Church up to that time—did include the large assembly room on its upper floor.

The 1950s also brought the Church's first overseas temples. These smaller buildings were dedicated in Switzerland, New Zealand, and England. California's second temple was then dedicated at Oakland in 1964. Thus, by the later 1960s, thirteen temples were located in widely scattered places around the world. However, three-quarters of a century had passed since the last temple had been dedicated in Utah. Still, Church membership along the Wasatch Front—including Utah Valley—was growing rapidly.

Temples in the Western United States, 1964

Temples in the Western United States. Created by Think Spatial BYU.

The Latter-day Saints in Utah Valley

For centuries, Utah Valley had been the home of American Indian tribes, particularly the Ute nation. Their settlements clustered around

Utah Lake, where they were close to their sources of food. Perhaps the first European men to see the valley were Francisco Atanasio Domínguez and Silvestre Veléz de Escalante, two Spanish priests who were seeking a better route from Santa Fe to Southern California in 1776. These men recognized the "very good farmland" throughout the valley and later gave favorable descriptions of the area.[7] Their cartographer, Don Bernardo de Miera, even called Utah Valley "the most pleasing, beautiful, and fertile site in all of New Spain."[8] Furthermore, John C. Frémont—a nineteenth-century American explorer—surveyed the region in the 1840s and similarly gave a glowing report of the valley's fertile soil. His belief that the area would make "an excellent locality for stock farms" likely influenced Mormon settlement in the Great Basin just a few years later.[9]

Soon after the Mormon pioneers entered the Salt Lake Valley in 1847, Brigham Young sent scouts north and south to locate possible sites for additional settlements. Fort Utah was established on the Provo River in 1849 as a defense against early conflict with the local Ute Indians. After about a year, Mormons began building homes outside the fort, expanding their settlement.

For a time, it seemed possible that Provo—named after fur trader Etienne Provost—might become a rail hub, even exceeding Ogden in importance. During the 1880s, a Union Pacific subsidiary passed through

Monument to Dominguez and Escalante in Spanish Fork City Park. Courtesy of Richard Cowan.

Provo on its way to southern Utah, and the Rio Grande connected
Utah Valley with Salt Lake City and with Denver. Other rail schemes,
however, did not materialize, and when the main connection to
Southern California was completed just after 1900, Provo was
bypassed. Thus Utah Valley remained a largely agricultural and pre-
dominantly Latter-day Saint area, with about a 95 percent Mormon
population. In this environment, such key institutions as Brigham
Young University and the Missionary Training Center flourished.

By 1940, Church membership in Utah County had reached
only 44,730. However, the coming of Geneva Steel and other indus-
tries to the area during World War II launched a period of significant growth. During the early 1960s, total membership passed the
100,000 mark; it stood at 107,666 in 1966. Not only were numbers
growing, but the area had one of the highest levels of activity anywhere in the Church. Elder Dallin H. Oaks, a native of Provo and
member of the Quorum of the Twelve Apostles, later asserted that
Utah County was "one of the most important centers" for the Latter-
day Saints.[10] With this growth in population, many wondered if the
time for a temple in Utah Valley had come at last.

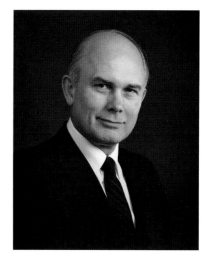

Dallin H. Oaks. © Intellectual Reserve,
Inc.

Notes

1.   Karen Lynn Davidson, David J. Whittaker, Mark Ashurst-McGee, and
      Richard L. Jensen, eds., *Histories, Volume 1: Joseph Smith Histories, 1832–1844*,
      vol. 1 of the Histories series of *The Joseph Smith Papers*, ed. Dean C. Jessee,
      Ronald K. Esplin, and Richard Lyman Bushman (Salt Lake City: Church
      Historian's Press, 2012), 494–95.

2.   For a discussion of Latter-day Saint temples, see James E. Talmage, *The House
      of the Lord* (Salt Lake City: Bookcraft, 1962); Boyd K. Packer, *The Holy Temple*
      (Salt Lake City: Bookcraft, 1980); and Richard O. Cowan, *Temples to Dot the
      Earth* (Springville, UT: Cedar Fort, 1997).

3.   History, 1838–1856, volume B-1 [1 September 1834–2 November 1838],
      The Joseph Smith Papers, josephsmithpapers.org/papersummary/
      history-1838-1856-volume-b-1-1-september-1834-2-november-1838.

4.   Talmage, *House of the Lord*, 99–100.

5.   *Teachings of Presidents of the Church: Joseph Smith* (Salt Lake City: The Church of
      Jesus Christ of Latter-day Saints, 2007), 414.

Opposite: Photo by Reinhard Franz.
Section start: Courtesy of Michael Jolley.
Following: Courtesy of Jordan Hogenson.
Photo edited.

6. Orson Pratt, May 20, 1877, in *Journal of Discourses* (London: Latter-day Saints' Book Depot, 1878), 19:19–20.

7. Ted J. Warner, ed., *The Dominguez-Escalante Journal: Their Expedition through Colorado, Utah, Arizona, and New Mexico in 1776* (Salt Lake City: University of Utah Press, 1995), 70.

8. As cited in Richard V. Francaviglia, *Believing in Place: A Spiritual Geography of the Great Basin* (Reno, NV: University of Nevada Press, 2003), 99.

9. As cited in D. Robert Carter, *Founding Fort Utah: Provo's Native Inhabitants, Early Explorers, and First Year of Settlement* (Provo, UT: Provo City Corporation, 2003), 23.

10. Richard Neitzel Holzapfel, *A History of Utah County* (Salt Lake City: State Historical Society, 1999), 376n38.

PART 1

A Temple on the Hill

CHAPTER 2

The Long-Anticipated Announcement

1860s   Brigham Young and others prophesy of a temple on a hill north of Provo

1911   BYU's Maeser Building dedicated on Temple Hill

1950s   Proposals for training missionaries at BYU revive idea of temple in Provo

1967   First Presidency announces plans to build Ogden and Provo Temples, would follow Swiss pattern (August 14)

Provo Temple site announced (September 2)

*T*he rapid growth of Church membership in Utah Valley following World War II stimulated speculation that a temple might be built there in the near future. Still, the idea of a temple was not new. It dates back to pioneer times.

Brigham Young. © Intellectual Reserve, Inc.

Anticipating a Temple

For decades, Provo residents had referred to what would become the southwest corner of Brigham Young University's upper campus, which overlooked the town to the south, as "Temple Hill." This tradition stemmed from a prophecy believed to have been made by Brigham Young sometime in the late 1860s. After he and his party "ascended to the summit of this beautiful hill," Brigham purportedly declared, "You are now standing on holy ground, and the day will come when a magnificent temple will be erected here to our God."[1] As a result, this high ground became known as Temple Hill, and members of the Church anxiously anticipated a temple in Utah Valley.

In 1871, Abraham O. Smoot, president of the Utah Stake and mayor of Provo, addressed the local Saints and revealed, "We have been told to build up a temple here yet we are making haste to get rich."[2] Furthermore, according to the diaries of L. John Nuttall, who was then secretary to the First Presidency, Church leaders acquired property in Provo for a "Temple Block" in 1874.[3] Interestingly, this initial property was neither part of Temple Hill on BYU campus nor where the temple now stands. It was located at the present southwest corner of 900 East and University Parkway—the field just east of BYU's Harmon Building. However, nothing came of it—perhaps due to financial constraints of the Church at the time. Ten years later—in 1884—Abraham O. Smoot, still president of the Utah Stake, lamented, "I look forward to the time when other temples will be completed throughout the valleys of these mountains, and one on the beautiful plateau north of this city."[4] Similarly, a speaker in an 1888 meeting in the Provo Tabernacle referred to a prophecy given by Elder Parley P. Pratt during the

Abraham O. Smoot.

Early Provo and Temple Hill

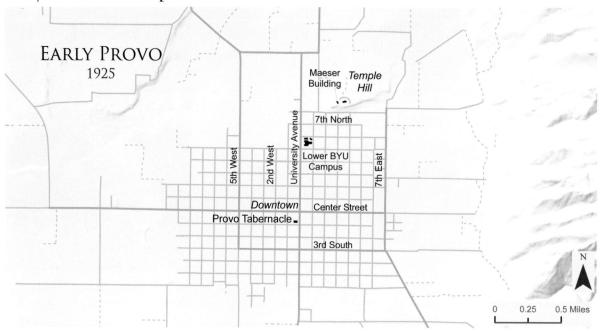

EARLY PROVO
1925

Early Provo and Temple Hill. Created by
Think Spatial BYU.

Maeser Building on Temple Hill.
Courtesy of Lee R. Cowan.

"early days of Provo" that "a temple would be built about a mile and a half" north of the town."[5]

At the turn of the century, BYU officials aggressively expanded campus atop the hill by erecting a building in honor of Karl G. Maeser, the school's first permanent principal. At its 1911 dedication, Elder John Henry Smith, a member of the Quorum of the Twelve, noted that although the grounds had been "rendered sacred to many of us from our earliest childhood in the thought that a temple someday would be erected upon this hill," the building would instead become a "temple of learning." Following the dedication of the Maeser Building, the idea of a temple on what had become the BYU campus faded. Still, members of the Church remained hopeful that a house of the Lord would be built nearby.

With proposals during the 1940s and 1950s for teaching languages to missionaries at Brigham Young University, the idea of a temple in Provo revived. In 1952, BYU president Ernest L. Wilkinson wrote to the First Presidency, "We do not, of course, have a temple adjacent to our campus. We would welcome one when in your wisdom the time has arrived." He "treasured" Brigham Young's prophecy that a temple would be built on "Temple Hill," now occupied by the BYU campus. He concluded that with the construction of a temple on or next to the campus, "all of the missionaries' training could be accomplished here."[6] The need for a temple nearby was further affirmed as university enrollment soared from 4,510 in 1950 to 10,305 in 1960 and the first student stake was organized in 1956; however, another decade would pass before these ideas became a reality.

About this same time, Ben E. Lewis, who was serving as president of the East Sharon Stake just northeast of the BYU campus, related the following experience:

Ernest L. Wilkinson. Courtesy of Cowan MTC Archives.

BYU campus in 1940. Provo Temple was yet to be built. Courtesy of Provo City Library.

The General Authority turned to me and said, "Brother Ben, if the Church ever decides to build a Temple in Provo, we will let you know." That took care of that.

One day I had a call from one of our Bishops in the Oak Hills area, saying one of the members of his Ward, a Brother Leichty who owned a sizable piece of property in the Ward, had come to him and told him of a dream he had the night before in which he had witnessed the construction of a Temple on his property, and that if the Church wanted to build a Temple there he would donate his land for that purpose. This call came just three days before we were having our quarterly Stake Conference to which a General Authority had been assigned to come. Back in those days we had two conference sessions, one in the morning and one in the afternoon. In between these sessions we would take the General Authority to one of our homes for dinner. It was our turn to host the General Authority for the Sunday dinner which was held in the Family Room of our home which sat on a hill overlooking the valley. The room had large pane glass windows, and we could look from that room and see the location of the Leichty property. This provided an opportunity for me to put in a "plug" for a temple in Provo. When I brought the General Authority into our Family Room I took him over to the window where we could look out and see the Leichty property, and told him about Brother Leichty's dream, and that he had expressed his willingness to donate the property to the Church if they wanted to build a temple on it. The General Authority turned to me and said, "Brother Ben, if the Church ever decides to build a Temple in Provo, we will let you know." That took care of that. Barbara called, "It's time to sit down for dinner."[7]

A Special Announcement

As early as the 1950s, President David O. McKay had discussed the possibility of constructing new temples on the Wasatch Front, but other building projects—such as the large Los Angeles Temple and the first three overseas temples—had consumed available Church funds. But by the later 1960s, this situation had improved.[8]

Emil B. Fetzer had become Church architect and a member of the Church Building Committee on July 1, 1965. One of his duties was to inspect temples periodically "to ascertain that they would always be in proper condition to be worthy houses of the Lord.

This entailed the responsibility to make certain that all necessary and required repairs, modifications and up-grading were promptly and properly accomplished." He personally reported the results of these inspections to the First Presidency. In 1967, he informed the Presidency that the Logan and Manti Temples were "drastically and urgently in need of extensive upgrading, reconditioning, remodeling and refurbishing." He estimated that these repairs would require the temples to be closed for at least two years.[9] Another problem was that the Logan, Manti, and especially Salt Lake Temples were seriously overcrowded. In the light of this information, Church leaders considered what would be the best course to follow.

Noting that BYU students traveled to Manti in great numbers, Mark B. Garff—chairman of the Church Building Committee—suggested the possibility of building "a small temple in Provo and one in Ogden." President McKay directed him to investigate the matter further and then make a report. On Tuesday, August 8, 1967, leaders of the Building Committee met with the First Presidency. Garff indicated that the overcrowding in the Logan and Manti Temples was "becoming so acute that it becomes necessary either to remodel those temples or build new ones." He recommended building new ones "if for no other reason than economics," because "remodeling the old temples would cost nearly twice as much as building the new ones." His assistant, Fred Baker, pointed out that the Salt Lake Temple's workload in 1966 was two and a half times as great as it had been in 1950, so this temple particularly would need to be remodeled to expand its capacity.

Architect Fetzer presented various options. The Presidency approved the concept of building the temples in Ogden and Provo and directed Garff and the Building Committee "to go forward and make provisions for the location of the new temples, prepare their plans, and so far as possible have the same plan for both temples."[10] Brother Fetzer felt sure that even before he made his report on the Logan and Manti Temples, "the First Presidency clearly had in mind to build the new Temples in Ogden and in Provo."[11]

Without any delay, presidencies of the twenty-eight stakes in the Provo area were invited to a special meeting, which would be held

Top: Logan Temple. Courtesy of Kenneth R. Mays. *Middle:* Manti Temple. Courtesy of Kenneth R. Mays. *Bottom:* Salt Lake Temple. Courtesy of Craig Ostler.

Mark B. Garff and Fred A. Baker at meeting where Provo Temple was announced. Originally printed in *Church News*, August 19, 1967, 3.

only six days later on Monday morning, August 14, 1967. They gathered at the Park-University Ward Chapel on Eighth North and Sixth West. A similar meeting was held that afternoon in Ogden. Presiding at these gatherings were Hugh B. Brown and N. Eldon Tanner, counselors to David O. McKay in the First Presidency. Also in attendance were Mark B. Garff and Fred A. Baker of the Church Building Committee.

President Tanner announced plans for the two new temples and explained that they were needed to "relieve pressure on the Salt Lake, Logan, and Manti Temples." In 1966, some 52 percent of all temple ordinances were performed in these three temples. The Brethren explained that enlarging the Logan and Manti Temples "would cost between three and four million dollars and would destroy the architectural value of the two buildings." The two new temples, on the other hand, could be built for an estimated $2.5 million each (over $15 million today) and would significantly cut down required travel. The Church leaders also pointed out that the two new temples would cut the load on the Logan Temple by about one-half, the Manti by about one-third, and the Salt Lake Temple by about one-fourth.

The Brethren indicated that Latter-day Saints living in the temple district would be asked to raise a substantial portion of the total cost, the exact amount to be determined later. All these plans were accepted enthusiastically by the stake presidencies attending this exciting meeting.[12]

"Benefits can come through location of a temple here," Provo's newspaper, the *Daily Herald*, noted. "From the standpoint of those of the church in this area who do temple work, the benefits are obvious by way of convenience and saving in time and

Adjusted Temple Districts

Temple Districts in 1967	Proposed Temple Districts
Logan: 159,614	Logan: 80,638
	Ogden: 115,780
Salt Lake: 493,473	Salt Lake: 370,969
	Provo: 115,891
Manti: 93,466	Manti: 60,771

transportation. From a community and monetary standpoint, the temple will attract many people to Provo. Visitors mean economic stimulation and growth."[13]

The Chosen Site

At the meeting on August 14, 1967, possible sites for the temple were discussed. The sites under discussion included the downtown park adjacent to the Provo Tabernacle, as well as other properties the Church owned—particularly on the east bench at the foot of the mountains. Stake leaders quickly discouraged the downtown site because it was small and parking would be a problem. Richard O. Cowan, counselor in a married-student stake presidency, suggested that the temple be located within walking distance of Brigham Young University so students could participate conveniently.

A committee of five stake presidents was appointed to select the specific site to recommend to the First Presidency. President Lewis recalled the following:

> President Tanner said that a site had not been selected for the Temple, and turning to me he asked if I would be willing to serve as the Chairman of the site selection committee. My response was that I would be happy to serve. A favorable vote was given to that proposal. President Tanner said to the Presidents it would be necessary to have a chairman for the fund raising for the Temple. Turning to me again, he said, "Since you have already indicated your willingness to be the chairman of the Site Selection Committee, would it be all right if we asked you to be the chairman of the Fund Raising Committee?" My answer was "yes."[14]

President Lewis visited briefly with President Tanner to get his instructions and counsel.

"I brazenly told President Tanner it was not necessary to have a Site Selection Committee because I knew about a piece of property we had purchased for the University just below the mouth of Rock Canyon that would be an ideal spot for the Temple. He responded by suggesting there was wisdom in having a committee

Stakes included in the proposed Provo Temple District

- Alpine
- American Fork
- BYU First–Eighth
- East Provo
- East Sharon
- Kolob
- Lehi
- Nebo
- Orem
- Orem West
- Palmyra
- Provo
- Sataquin-Tintic
- Sharon
- Springville
- Spanish Fork
- Timpanogos
- Utah
- Wasatch
- West Sharon
- West Utah

recommendation, with which I agreed. How wise he was."[15] Other committee members were also stake presidents: G. Marion Hinckley of the West Utah Stake, Fred. L. Markham of the Utah Stake, Clyde Sandgren of the BYU Third (singles) Stake, and Wayne B. Hales of the BYU Sixth (married student) Stake.

The committee considered several possibilities. President Lewis recalled:

> We went to look at a number of potential sites, but kept coming back to the site I had showed them and told them about, at the mouth of Rock Canyon, which we had purchased from the Leichty Brothers for the University. The advantage of this site was that it was on a hill, where it could be seen from many different places in the valley, and those who came to the Temple could look out and get a panoramic view of the valley, Utah Lake, and the Oquirrh Mountains beyond. The Committee members were unanimous in favor of the site and authorized me to get in touch with President Tanner to let him know of our recommendation.

Members of the Church's building committee, however, proposed that the temple be built next to the downtown tabernacle, as was being done in Ogden. "It was then I learned the wisdom of having a site selection committee," President Lewis conceded. The First Presidency called a meeting in which each group would present reasons for its recommendations. President Lewis continued:

> I was invited to come to present our Committee's reasons for our recommendation, the principal argument given by the Church Building Committee was that the Ogden and Provo Temples were to be constructed at the same time, and should be treated in the same way. I pointed out that the available land in Ogden was substantially greater than in Provo, that there was not enough land for the building itself in Provo, and no land available for parking. After hearing the arguments on both sides, the First Presidency ruled in favor of the recommendation made by our Site Selection Committee, and told the Building Committee to authorize the Architect to proceed with the plans for the Temple to be built on the site our Committee had recommended.[16]

Members of the Church's building committee . . . proposed that the temple be built next to the downtown tabernacle, as was being done in Ogden.

Just two weeks after the original meeting in Provo, President David O. McKay officially announced the specific site: "The Provo site is a property on the northeast bench overlooking the city and the beautiful Brigham Young University campus. This property is bounded on the north by 2320 North and extends from about 800 to 1200 East streets. On the southeast is Rock Canyon Road. It is an easy access from several major highways."[17] Architect Fetzer was grateful that the broad side of this pie-shaped site looked out over the valley and that it was "within easy walking distance, two blocks, of the great Brigham Young University with large faculty, faithful student body, excellent facilities and innumerable support services."[18]

Alan Barnett, a Provo native who had received a master's degree in architectural history at the University of Utah, contrasted the Provo site with the one in Ogden. In Ogden, the temple shared a ten-acre block in the center of the city with the Ogden Tabernacle. In Provo, on the other hand, the more spacious site "gave the Provo Temple plenty of breathing room and allowed it to be viewed alone and from some distance, like a piece of sculpture or a crown jewel."[19]

The site chosen for the Provo Temple has an interesting geological background. Prehistoric Lake Bonneville had an original elevation of about 5,100 feet. Waves washing up along its shoreline created a bench along the mountains known as the Bonneville level. Later—after much of the water had drained out from the lake—a second bench, known as the Provo level, was formed at an elevation of about 4,750 feet. These two levels can be seen as two distinct lines along the mountains when viewed from the center of the Utah, Salt Lake, and adjacent valleys. The temple site—at an elevation of about 4,850 feet—is between these two levels. It sits on an alluvial fan formed by material eroded from adjacent Rock Canyon. The nearby houses that overlook the temple are on the Bonneville level, while the BYU campus, overlooked by the temple, is situated on the Provo level.[20]

The area of the Provo Temple site was well known and important as a refuge to the American Indians who lived in Utah Valley. In February 1850, following a battle with a militia sent from Salt Lake Valley, a band of Ute Indians escaped through deep snows into Rock Canyon. "A small number of these retreating Utes tied on snowshoes

The more spacious site "gave the Provo Temple plenty of breathing room and allowed it to be viewed alone and from some distance, like a piece of sculpture or a crown jewel."

of their own hasty manufacture, laboriously trudged upward to the head of the canyon, and descended northward through Pole Canyon to the Provo River," which they followed clear to the Kamas Valley.[21]

Before subdivisions surrounded the site where the temple was to be built, the area was covered with farms and orchards. Among those living in this area were Palestinian immigrants Moses and Aishe Kader and their large family. One Provo resident, Jerry Bell, recalls how his father, Junius, had a barber shop in downtown Provo. During the aftermath of the Great Depression, when money was scarce, he remembers Moses bringing his children into town for haircuts. Moses then invited the Bells to come out and pick pears, peaches, apricots, berries, asparagus, and other produce in exchange for the barber's service. Lucille Bell bottled the fruit. Her daughter Bonnie recalled that their goal was 365 jars—enough for one each day of the year. Thus the Kaders' fruits and vegetables helped keep the Bell family alive during those difficult years. Jerry's family therefore

Finished Provo Temple and the view of the valley. Courtesy of Don LaVange, edited.

regarded the land where the Kaders lived with reverence—almost as being sacred—because of the food they obtained there.[22] Interestingly, one of the Kaders' sons, Omar, went onto a distinguished career that included service as an assistant dean at Brigham Young University.

Dale T. Fletcher, a professor in Brigham Young University's art department, and his family lived in northeast Provo. The Fletchers enjoyed sketching typical scenes of "meadows, barnyards, and countryside. The children, armed with pencils, crayons, and paper, were motivated by their parents to look closely and record their impressions." Therefore, when Brother Fletcher learned that the Provo Temple would be built across the street from his home, he concluded to submit a painting of this sacred spot to the first Festival of Mormon Arts at Brigham Young University in 1968: "I waited for a day and a half out there, looking for the temple through an empty picture frame without ever touching my large white canvas. Silly, sitting among sego lilies, waiting for angels to come and pose. Faithless and impatient, I gave up and tried to paint what I saw." He imagined that he could see "light descending from heaven, cleaving the mountains, hallowing, redeeming grass, baptizing unto newness of leaf, working atonement, eternal marriage, achieving godhood, with all the angels hymning in the wild wheat."[23]

Area Surrounding Temple Site

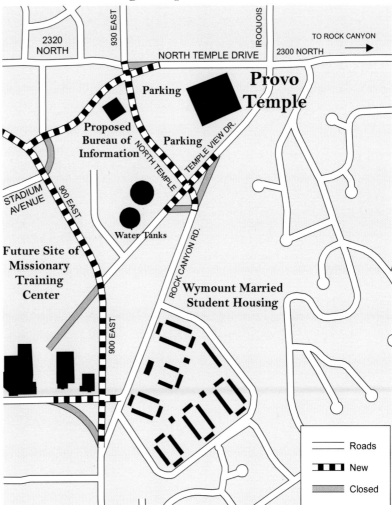

Area surrounding temple site. Created by Think Spatial BYU.

Notes

1. Benjamin H. Bullock, affidavit, 1952, Church History Library, Salt Lake City.

2. Excerpt from School of the Prophets Meeting in Provo, December 16, 1887, L. Tom Perry Special Collections, Harold B. Lee Library, Brigham Young University, Provo, Utah.

3. Jedediah S. Rogers, *In the President's Office: The Diaries of L. John Nuttall, 1879–1892* (Salt Lake City: Signature Books), 319. See also Ernest L. Wilkinson and W. Cleon Skousen, *Brigham Young University: A School of Destiny* (Provo, UT: Brigham Young University Press, 1976), 94–95.

4. Provo Utah Central Stake general minutes, May 31, 1884, Church History Library.

5. "Sunday Services," *The Daily Enquirer*, September 11, 1888, 1.

6. Ernest L. Wilkinson to the First Presidency, August 7, 1952, BYU Archives.

7. Ben E. Lewis, "I Remember, 1988–2000," MSS 2203, L. Tom Perry Special Collections, 25–26.

8. Gregory A. Prince and William Robert Wright, *David O. McKay and the Rise of Modern Mormonism* (Salt Lake City: University of Utah Press, 2005), 269.

9. Emil B. Fetzer, *Completed Writings of Emil Baer Fetzer: Husband, Father, Grandfather, Architect, Church Architect of Holy Houses of the Lord, Chronology of His Life Journey*, 1, M270.1 F421f 2003, Church History Library.

10. Prince and Wright, *David O. McKay and the Rise of Modern Mormonism*, 269.

11. Emil B. Fetzer, "The Sacred Twin Temples: Ogden Temple, Provo Temple," in *Completed Writings of Emil Baer Fetzer*, 3.

12. Henry A. Smith, "2 New Temples Planned," *Church News*, August 19, 1967, 3–4; see also "Church to Build Two New Temples," *Improvement Era*, September 1967, 16.

13. "Temple Slated for Provo Area," *Daily Herald*, August 15, 1967, 1.

14. Lewis, "I Remember," 13:26.

15. Lewis, "I Remember," 13:26.

16. Lewis, "I Remember," 13:27.

17. "Temple Sites Are Outlined," *Church News*, September 2, 1967, 5.

18. Fetzer, "Sacred Twin Temples," 2.

19. Alan B. Barnett, "Temple Architecture for a Modern Age: The 40th Anniversary of the Provo Temple" (Provo Founders Day Lecture, April 2,

2012, given at the L. Tom Perry Special Collections, BYU), typescript in possession of the authors, 4.

20. Richard O. Cowan, conversation with Morris S. Peterson, September 2011.

21. D. Robert Carter, *From Fort to Village, Provo, Utah, 1850–1854* (Provo, UT: Provo City Corporation, 2008), 1.

22. Richard O. Cowan, conversation with Jerry Bell, September 2011.

23. Floyd E. Breinholt, "Temple Site," *Relief Society Magazine*, June 1970, 447, 450; see also Dale T. Fletcher, "A Note on 'Provo Temple Site, 1968,'" *BYU Studies* 10, no. 4 (Summer 1970): 455–56.

Photo by Bruce Nordgren.

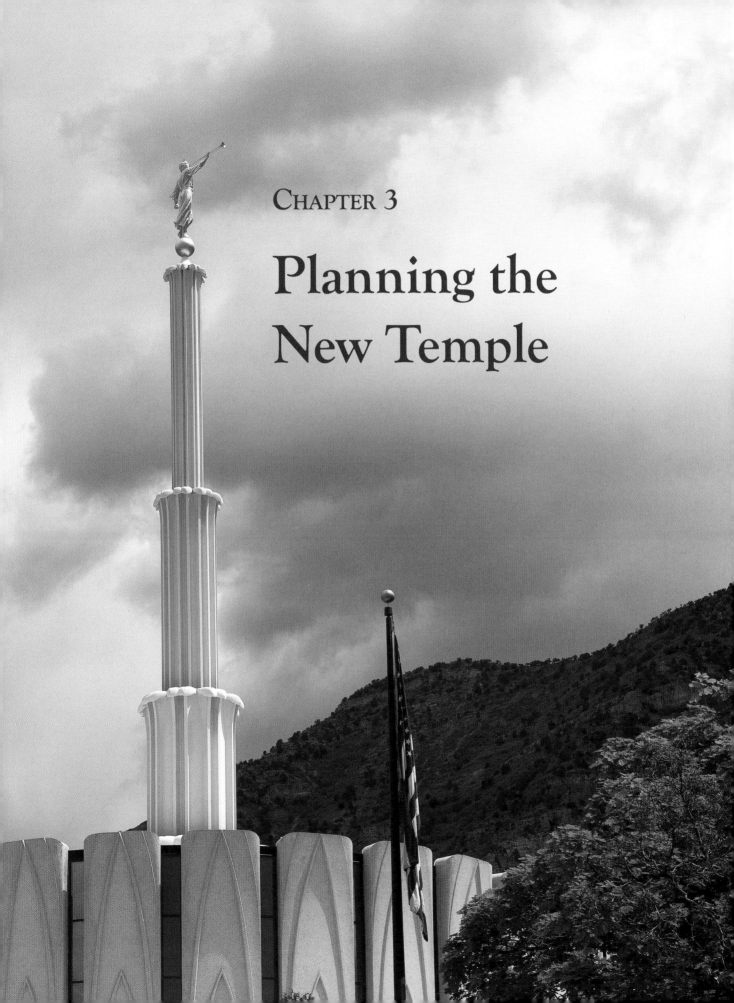

CHAPTER 3

Planning the
New Temple

1955   Swiss Temple presents endowment in one room using film

1965   Emil Fetzer becomes Church architect (July 1)

1967   First Presidency announces plans to build Ogden and Provo Temples, would follow Swiss pattern (August 14)

Fetzer appointed to design Ogden and Provo Temples

During his flight, Fetzer envisions arrangement of temple rooms (August 30)

1968   First Presidency approves temple design (January 24)

1969   All stakes raise their allotted funds (by August)

One of the main functions of temples is to provide a suitable setting for presenting sacred ordinances that have an eternal impact on our lives. Because the endowment requires more time than any other ordinance to complete, there are more people engaged in this activity than any other in the temple at any given moment.

Presenting the Temple Endowment

In his oft-quoted book *The House of the Lord*, Elder James E. Talmage described the endowment as a course of instruction that teaches us the path that leads back into the presence of God. He affirmed that it embodies "certain obligations on the part of the individual," including a "covenant and promise to observe the law of strict virtue and chastity, to be charitable, benevolent, tolerant and pure; to devote both talent and material means to the spread of truth and the uplifting of the race; to maintain devotion to the cause of truth; and to seek in every way to contribute to the great preparation that the earth may be made ready to receive her King—the Lord Jesus Christ."[1]

Elder Talmage's description was echoed by Elder John A. Widtsoe: "The temple endowment relates the story of man's eternal journey, sets forth the conditions upon which progress in the eternal journey depends, requires covenants or agreements of those participating to accept and use the laws of progress, gives tests by which our willingness and fitness for righteousness may be known, and finally points out the ultimate destiny of those who love truth and live by it."[2]

"To endow is to enrich," taught Elder Boyd K. Packer, also of the Quorum of the Twelve, "to give to another something long lasting and of much worth." He explained that temple ordinances endow one with divine power, with eternally significant knowledge, and with marvelous promises and challenges.[3]

The endowment requires approximately an hour and forty-five minutes to be received. In early temples, it was presented in a series of rooms that had murals on the walls. Beginning with the Creation

Top: Swiss Temple. Courtesy of Alexander Baugh. *Bottom:* Gordon B. Hinckley. Courtesy of Cowan MTC Archives.

of this earth, these murals and the instructions of the endowment depicted the successive stages in our quest to return to God's presence. In 1953, however, when President David O. McKay announced the first "overseas temple"—which would be built in Switzerland— he indicated that "the Church could bring temples to these people by building smaller edifices for this purpose and more of them."[4]

Harold W. Burton—a Latter-day Saint architect then living in Southern California—recalled how the year before, Howard McKean—then chairman of the Church Building Committee—had wanted to discuss with him President McKay's challenge to find a less costly way to build temples. Burton realized that it would be necessary to reduce the size of these sacred structures without diminishing their "functional capacity." His experience in the motion picture industry a decade earlier led him to a possible solution. "It was my opinion that if the first four temple ordinance rooms could be combined, and with picture projection substituted for mural paintings to create a proper setting pertaining to the Creation, the Garden, and the World, very substantial reduction in the size of the Temple could be effected." Although some felt this idea was "too revolutionary," it was adopted for the Swiss Temple.[5]

Using modern equipment such as motion pictures made it possible to present the endowment in a single ordinance room, in more than one language, and with far fewer than the usual number of temple workers. The film was produced under the supervision of Elders Joseph Fielding Smith and Richard L. Evans of the Quorum of the Twelve Apostles and architect Edward O. Anderson. Gordon B. Hinckley, secretary of the missionary committee (not yet a General Authority), had the prime responsibility for creating the film. "It was a charge of enormous significance," Brother Hinckley's biographer declared. "The ramifications of this project were enormous, as they would extend far beyond the temple in Switzerland." In the fifth-floor room of the Salt Lake Temple where Elder Talmage had completed his monumental book *Jesus the Christ*, Brother Hinckley spent many evenings, Saturdays, and some Sunday mornings outlining ideas. Although other members of the committee were helpful, Hinckley soon found himself working personally with President McKay.[6] Together they spent considerable time reviewing the temple ceremonies and praying for divine guidance. President McKay later remarked, "There is no other man in the church who has done so much in assisting to carry this new temple plan to the Saints of the world as has Brother Hinckley."[7] Elder Harold B. Lee insisted that "there was no difference" between the endowment instruction given formerly "and that which was later given in temples except as to the method." He believed that the use of films to present the "teachings of the holy endowment" had come "under inspiration to our President."[8]

The Swiss Temple—dedicated in 1955— set the pattern for the New Zealand and London Temples, which opened three years later. Originally, each of these newer temples had only one presentation room, meaning that a new session could begin only every two hours. The Oakland Temple—dedicated in 1964—had two large endowment rooms, enabling a new session to start every hour or so. Designs for the new Ogden and Provo Temples would bring an even greater improvement.

Designing the Provo and Ogden Temples

At the August 14, 1967, meeting where the Ogden and Provo Temples were announced, Church leaders explained that these new temples "will be of the smaller type," following the pattern developed for the first overseas temples, "but so designed to have a high capacity."[9] They decided to build both temples from the same basic plan in order to expedite construction and to economize. Efficiency

President McKay later remarked, "There is no other man in the church who has done so much in assisting to carry this new temple plan to the Saints of the world as has Brother Hinckley."

Emil B. Fetzer. Courtesy of Utah State Historical Society.

"I was in shock. I never had the slightest inkling nor gave it any thought that I would ever be given an assignment to design a temple."

and convenience were prime concerns.

A few days after this meeting, officials of the Church Building Department were summoned to visit with President David O. McKay and his counselors in his Hotel Utah apartment. After some preliminary discussion about the new temples, President McKay turned to Emil B. Fetzer, the Church architect, and declared, "Brother Fetzer, I would like you to design the new temples for Ogden and for Provo. Rather than building huge monumental buildings as has been the custom of the past, I would like these two temples to be functional and economical with temple quality. In the coming years, many temples will be built. Of necessity, these temples must be functional in design and cost so that they may accomplish their sacred purposes and be blessings to the Church membership."[10] Specifically, the prophet instructed them to use the "same architectural plan for both temples," include no solemn assembly room, have only "a single spire rather than multiple spires," not place an angel Moroni atop the spire, and not include any unnecessary "footage" or "cubage."[11]

As Brother Fetzer and the others left the meeting and walked down the hall to the elevator, he recalled, "I was in shock. I never had the slightest inkling nor gave it any thought that I would ever be given an assignment to design a temple. Yet, it had indeed happened. The Prophet of the Lord had given me the assignment to design not one but two temples. This was a major emotional high point to last a lifetime and longer—an exciting moment to cherish and remember forever."[12]

Emil Baer Fetzer was born January 4, 1916, in Salt Lake City, Utah, and received his degree in architecture from the University of Southern California in Los Angeles in 1943. He then went to work for a firm composed of his father and brother, who were also architects. He later became Church architect on July 1, 1965. He served in this capacity until 1986, during which time he would design over twenty temples, the first being those at Ogden and Provo. Others would include the Jordan River Temple and temples in Atlanta, Georgia; São Paulo, Brazil; Tokyo, Japan; Mexico City, Mexico; and Freiberg, Germany. He later was also the architect for the Kimball Tower on BYU campus. He passed away on November 2, 2009.[13]

Emil Fetzer worked closely with Mark B. Garff and Fred A. Baker, chairman and vice-chairman respectively of the Church Building Committee. In the new temples, they envisioned presenting the endowment in the traditional way. At a meeting with the First Presidency on October 29, however, Baker was told that the temple should use films rather than having companies progress from room to room. This surprised him. Architect Fetzer was not at this meeting because he was in Southern California on business.

The following day, Fetzer and Baker needed to fly to Europe on Building Committee matters. They met in the Kennedy airport in New York before boarding a Pan-American DC-8 jet for the overnight trans-Atlantic flight. After dinner, Baker shared the First Presidency's instructions with Fetzer, and they proceeded to discuss the "grand assignment" to design the two temples. As they attempted to work at their seats, a stewardess offered them the use of a table in the galley where they could spread out their papers. Brother Fetzer recalled:

> After we had discussed temple design for some time, all of a sudden I felt as though I were walking through a temple building. I described to Brother Baker what I was seeing in my mind as I was walking through the temple—the temple recommend desk in the main entrance foyer, the inner foyer, the offices and ancillary spaces and facilities on the ground floor. On the second floor I saw and described the chapel and sealing rooms. However, the most important of all that I was seeing was the unusual plan configuration of the third floor. There was a large, beautiful, center room (celestial room) surrounded by a cluster of six rooms (ordinance rooms) which completely surrounded the celestial room. A broad, circular hallway went completely around the six rooms

This "unique and fundamental modification of temple design concept was more than my own thinking. It was a direct inspiration given to me by the Holy Spirit."

Provo Temple Third Floor

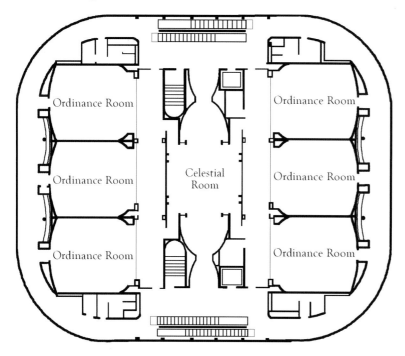

Provo Temple, third-floor plan. Map created by Reginald Beales.

with access to them from this hallway. It was a wonderful concept and a very unique and distinctive plan arrangement.

Before they knew it, it was daylight, and the plane was landing in Frankfurt. They had been discussing the temple "all night long."[14]

Fetzer later reported that the idea for this outside hallway came from a park in Copenhagen, which was completely surrounded by a roadway in the form of an elongated ellipse. He called this a "Danish ellipse," and "a modification of this idea was adapted to be exactly what I needed to accommodate the rooms and corridors of the upper two floors."[15] Still, he insisted, this "unique and fundamental modification of temple design concept was more than my own thinking. It was a direct inspiration given to me by the Holy Spirit."[16]

Mark B. Garff, chairman of the Church Building Committee, explained that "most monumental structures have been designed with first emphasis on the outside appearance, with the interior fit to the outside design." In contrast to this pattern, he noted that Fetzer "gave first consideration and emphasis to the needs of the interior and then designed the exterior to enclose the areas." Hence the outside walls of the temple's main upper portion followed the rounded course of the third-floor hallway. "The exterior of the temples," Fetzer later insisted, "is designed without pretense or sham but rather to simply and honestly reflect the plan of the interior."[17]

Architectural historian Alan Barnett placed these temples as part of the Modernist movement. Clearly, their design exemplified the maxim "form follows function" of famed architect Louis Sullivan. When asked if he were a Modernist, Emil Fetzer replied, "I think that probably rather than being a very traditionalist, I was modern, but not ultra modern. I think that I held a very moderate course on trying to keep up with the newer design motifs. Function was very important to me, how a plan worked and how a plan functioned. And then the clothing of that plan in a logical manner, using the materials that are available.[18]

Barnett pointed out that the temple's rounded corners fit into an architectural trend of the time. Rounded buildings of the era included the circular Salt Palace in nearby Salt Lake City. Barnett believed that "the formality, elegance, optimism, and spage-age feeling of New Formalism are evident in the appearance of the Ogden and Provo Temples." Still Fetzer blended his modernist design with a very traditional form—the pointed Gothic arch—which pointed "steadfastly toward heaven" and gave a feeling of "upward motion" to the temple's wall panels.[19]

Emil Fetzer envisioned the temple having "four fronts" rather than just one. The main floor would be rectangular, while the upper two floors would have elliptical corners. Since the 2nd floor is recessed below the 3rd floor and since gold glass windows of the 2nd floor are continuous full height panels," Fetzer explained, "it gives an appearance that the 3rd floor is floating above the temple base." He continued, "This is the effect that I desired—that the sacred ordinance rooms and the celestial room would appear to be above and separated from the mundane and wordly aspects of life. This design is especially noticeable at night when the continuous band of gold glass windows are lighted from inside. The third floor appears to be floating directly above and apart from the building base.[20]

The Ogden and Provo Temples were to be identical in their basic plan. "They are essentially identical," the architect explained, "but with minor modifications in design details to establish individual identifications."[21] He continued, "Even though, at a first look, the exteriors of the two temples appear to be the same, a closer study, especially of the upper floors, would indicated distinct variations of design." The large cast stone panels of the Ogden Temple are fluted, while those on the Provo Temple feature a series of bas-relief "inverted tear drop designs." The Ogden has metal grillwork over the third-floor

"This is the effect that I desired—that the sacred ordinance rooms and the celestial room would appear to be above and separated from the mundane and worldly aspects of life."

Original Ogden Temple. Note the differences from the Provo Temple in the tower and window designs. Courtesy of John Livingstone.

There was a very audible and distinct gasp. I did not know what they expected to see but this was not it.

windows, while the Provo Temple does not. The tower design of each temple reflects the pattern of the cast stone panels below.[22]

Even though Fetzer believed that the concept of these two temples came through inspiration, he explained that it still "required carefully planning, thinking through . . . the relationships of the various plan elements, drawing it to scale and bringing it all into a coordinated plan." He needed to fit together and draw to scale major rooms plus such building components as structural supports, stairways, mechanical and electrical systems, foyers, and restrooms. "Since I had walked through the temple in my mind I knew, in a general configuration, the major plan elements. It was necessary to plan, refine, size and perfect the designs," he concluded.[23]

In order to make the temples as functional as possible, Fetzer consulted with temple presidents and workers, members of the Genealogical Society, the Building Committee, other Latter-day Saint architects, and even General Authorities. The "basic premise of the temple design," he believed, "is to provide for ease of use by both the temple patrons and temple workers." Therefore, he provided not only elevators, but escalators, which were "never before planned in temples" and would afford "easy, safe, and efficient movement of large numbers of temple patrons and workers"—particularly the elderly or handicapped—from floor to floor. Fetzer further explained that the continuous hallways around the perimeter of the second and third floors would make it impossible to get lost; all a person would need to do is keep walking and he or she would be brought back to the point of starting.[24]

With the assistance of his brother, Henry P. Fetzer, Emil prepared perspective drawings of the temple exteriors. He then contracted with Architectural Arts of Los Angeles to produce large color renderings of the Provo and Ogden Temples in their respective settings. Fetzer next showed the floor plans and architectural renderings to his close associate, Fred A. Baker, who was vice chairman of the Church Building Committee. "He studied them and gave his full approval with great enthusiasm." They then took these materials to Mark B. Garff, chairman of the Church Building Committee. Fetzer recalled, "After studying the plans and with my explanation, he was very complimentary and approved them. However, when he saw the perspectives with the unusual and unique designs, he was somewhat taken back and was surprised. He said 'Are you sure?' I said that I was sure. The designs are different from any other temple designs of the past."[25]

Finally, on January 24, 1968, Fetzer presented his design to the First Presidency. Once again, they met in President McKay's apartment. Brother Fetzer recalled that ninety-five-year-old President McKay "was quite feeble in body . . . but very alert, vigorous and keen of mind with a kindly sense of humor. He also spoke quite softly and it was necessary to listen carefully to what he was saying."[26] The architect first showed the Presidency a series of plans for each of the temples' floors. "They were all very complimentary of them and expressed their pleasure on the function and operation of the Temple according to these plans and explanation." When Fetzer next placed the large color rendering of the temple design on the easel, "There was a very audible and distinct gasp. I did not know what they expected to see but this was not it," Fetzer remembered. One of President McKay's counselors asked him, "Does this design offend you?" A "deathly silence" followed this question. "I began to consider how I could change the design so that it would look like the Salt Lake Temple," Fetzer nervously reflected. After what must have seemed like an eternity, "President McKay, with a loud and firm voice said, 'No! I like it very much.' At that moment, I was on the side of the majority. It did not matter what others may think, the Prophet of the Lord had approved my designs."[27]

Public Announcement of the Design

After architectural drawings and plot plans for the two new temples had been approved by the First Presidency and the Quorum of the Twelve, they were released to and approved by local Church

Top: Mark B. Garff, Emil B. Fetzer, and Fred A. Baker present Ogden Temple rendering in meeting with First Presidency. *Church News*, February 3, 1968, 3. *Bottom*: First Presidency examines temple rendering (left to right: David O. McKay, N. Eldon Tanner, Joseph Fielding Smith, and Hugh B. Brown). *Church News*, February 3, 1968.

Emil Fetzer's rendering of the Provo Temple. Courtesy of L. Tom Perry Special Collections, Harold B. Lee Library.

leaders. On February 3, 1968, the *Church News* reported that "design and floor plans show a new and modern concept of temple construction." The temples would have four levels—a basement, and three upper floors. The ground floor would be square while the two upper floors would be "modified oval in shape. The exterior of each temple will be of white cast stone, gold-anodized aluminum grilles and

PROVO TEMPLE
THE CHURCH OF JESUS CHRIST OF LATTER DAY SAINTS
EMIL B. FETZER CHURCH ARCHITECT

bronze glass panels." A spire in the center of the building of anodized aluminum, golden in color, would reach a height of about 185 feet. Interestingly, the architect's rendition showed a statue of the angel Moroni surmounting the tower, facing west toward the building's main entrance.[28] (The figure of Moroni would not actually be added to the Provo tower until 2003.)

Garff noted that the design was "a combination of utility, beauty, comfort, convenience and efficiency," while "at the same time the spiritual atmosphere so typical of temples of the Church has been retained." He emphasized that the design was very efficient: "Provision is made for convenient, unhurried and uncrowded use of the temples by large numbers of patrons with a minimum of lost time for waiting or other delays."

The hillside slope in Provo would be contoured to provide parking west of the temple. The entire site would be surrounded by "a decorative fence consisting of wrought iron and cast stone panels." Plans also provided for a possible future visitors' center to be constructed on the site.[29]

Over the years, various symbolic meanings have been read into the Provo Temple's design. Upon looking at the building with its rounded corners and tower (which originally was colored gold), many local Church members believed it was designed to symbolize the cloud and pillar of fire that led the ancient Israelites during their wanderings in the desert. Some people believe that President McKay had instructed the architect that this be the temple's symbolism.[30] However, Fred Baker, who worked closely with Emil Fetzer in designing the temple, recalled, "We didn't have any symbolism in mind. . . . The truth is that we were so focused on what happened inside the temple, it never entered our mind [that there should be any symbolism outside]. . . . What happened on the inside was so magnificent, it overcame everything."[31]

Probably with tongue in cheek, some Brigham Young University students imagined that the temple could represent a wedding cake with a candle on top, as though to encourage eternal marriage. While individuals might have read their own meanings—perhaps insightful— into particular features, their ideas were unofficial, so of course were not authoritative or binding.

Even though the basic design of the temple had been released, months of painstaking effort were still needed to prepare the plans before actual construction could begin.

Fund-Raising

At the 1967 meeting where the First Presidency had announced plans to build the Provo Temple, President N. Eldon Tanner had announced, "Brethren, the Lord has directed us to build a temple in Provo. We will need a million dollars from you brethren for your share of the project. General church funds will pay the balance. Will you give this priority and let your other building projects go for the time being and raise this money as fast as possible."[32]

The assembled stake presidents received this word with great enthusiasm. "The pledges of support and cooperation were made by the stake presidencies"[33] with the anticipation that their Saints would be eager to assume a major share of the construction cost.

The stake presidencies eagerly turned to members of their stakes requesting funds. For example, in the Spanish Fork Stake, fund-raising was well under way for a total of $320,000 needed for a new stake center and for a new chapel in Salem. With the announcement of a temple, these plans were temporarily set aside. "It seemed that every heart was touched," stake president Joseph Toronto gratefully noted. The stake's share for the temple was fifty-six thousand dollars, but "we raised over seventy-five thousand dollars, the easiest money we ever collected because of the great willingness of both young and old to sacrifice," President Toronto affirmed. "For example, children would say, 'Grandpa, we can't have an ice cream cone, go to the movie, or go on that vacation. We are sacrificing to build the temple.' There were many sacrifices from our faithful members. The Saints not only paid their allotments for the temple in record time, but also their allotments for the stake and ward buildings. And the tithing increased also."[34]

Fund-raising throughout the rest of the temple district was equally successful. In August 1969, President Ben E. Lewis, chairman of the fund-raising committee, reported that all stakes in the district had "contributed one hundred percent or more of their quota toward the construction costs of the new temple."[35] The Saints now could look forward to the groundbreaking and the start of actual construction.

Children would say, "Grandpa, we can't have an ice cream cone, go to the movie, or go on that vacation. We are sacrificing to build the temple."

Notes

1. James E. Talmage, *The House of the Lord* (Salt Lake City: Bookcraft, 1962), 100.

2. Widtsoe, *Program of the Church* (Salt Lake City: Church Department of Education, 1937), 178.

3. Boyd K. Packer, *You May Claim the Blessings of The Holy Temple* (Salt Lake City: Bookcraft, 1980), 153.

4. *Church News*, July 23, 1952, 2; *Church News*, July 30, 1952, 1; *Church News*, April 11, 1953, 7.

5. Harold W. Burton, "Architectural Features of the Oakland Temple of The Church of Jesus Christ of Latter-day Saints," 6, MS 4235, folder 1, Church History Library.

6. Sheri L. Dew, *Go Forward with Faith: The Biography of Gordon B. Hinckley* (Salt Lake City: Deseret Book, 1996), 176–77.

7. David O. McKay, Dedication Proceedings, New Zealand Temple, April 20–23, 1958, quoted in Richard O. Cowan, *Temples to Dot the Earth* (Springville, UT: Cedar Fort, 2011), 177.

8. Harold B. Lee, "Preparing to Meet the Lord," *Improvement Era*, February 1965, 122.

9. Henry A. Smith, "2 New Temples Planned," *Church News*, August 19, 1967, 4.

10. Emil B. Fetzer, "The Sacred Twin Temples: Ogden Temple, Provo Temple," in Emil Fetzer and June Fetzer, *Completed Writings of Emil Baer Fetzer* (self-published, 2003), 3.

11. Fred Baker to Justin Bray, May 17, 2012.

12. Fetzer, "Sacred Twin Temples," 3.

13. "Emil Baer Fetzer: Beloved Father, Architect," *Deseret News*, November 4, 2009, B7.

14. Fetzer, "Sacred Twin Temples," 3.

15. Fetzer, "Sacred Twin Temples," 4; see also Doyle L. Green, "Two Temples to Be Dedicated," *Ensign*, January 1972, 6–11.

16. Fetzer, "Sacred Twin Temples," 4.

17. Fetzer, "Sacred Twin Temples," 5.

18. Emil B. Fetzer, interview, March 25, 1987, quoted in Alan B. Barnett, "Temple Architecture for a Modern Age: The 40th Anniversary of the Provo Temple" (Provo Founders Day Lecture, April 2, 2012, given at the L. Tom Perry Special Collections, BYU), typescript in possession of the authors, 10–12.

19. Barnett, "Temple Architecture," 15, 17–18.

20. Fetzer, "Sacred Twin Temples," 5.

21. Fetzer, "Sacred Twin Temples," 1.

22. Fetzer, "Sacred Twin Temples," 5–6.

23. Fetzer, "Sacred Twin Temples," 4.

24. Fetzer, "Sacred Twin Temples," 5.

25. Fetzer, "Sacred Twin Temples," 6.

26. Fetzer, "Sacred Twin Temples," 7.

27. Fetzer, "Sacred Twin Temples," 8.

28. Jack E. Jarrard, "New Utah Temples' Drawings Win Okay," *Church News*, February 3, 1968, 3, 8; see also "Ogden and Provo Temple Plans," *Improvement Era*, March 1968, 14; "The LDS Scene," *Improvement Era*, April 1968, 77.

29. Jarrard, "New Utah Temples," *Church News*, February 3, 1968, 8.

30. Merrill J. Bateman to Richard O. Cowan, e-mail, August 20, 2012.

31. Fred Baker oral history, interviews by Justin R. Bray, 2012.

32. Quoted in Joseph Young Toronto, *Forever and Ever: The Life History of Joseph Young Toronto* (Provo, UT: BYU Press, 1996), 171.

33. Smith, "2 New Temples Planned," 4.

34. Toronto, *Forever and Ever*, 171.

35. Quoted in "Provo Temple Rites Set," *Church News*, August 30, 1969, 3.

Photo by Ricketyus. Photo edited.

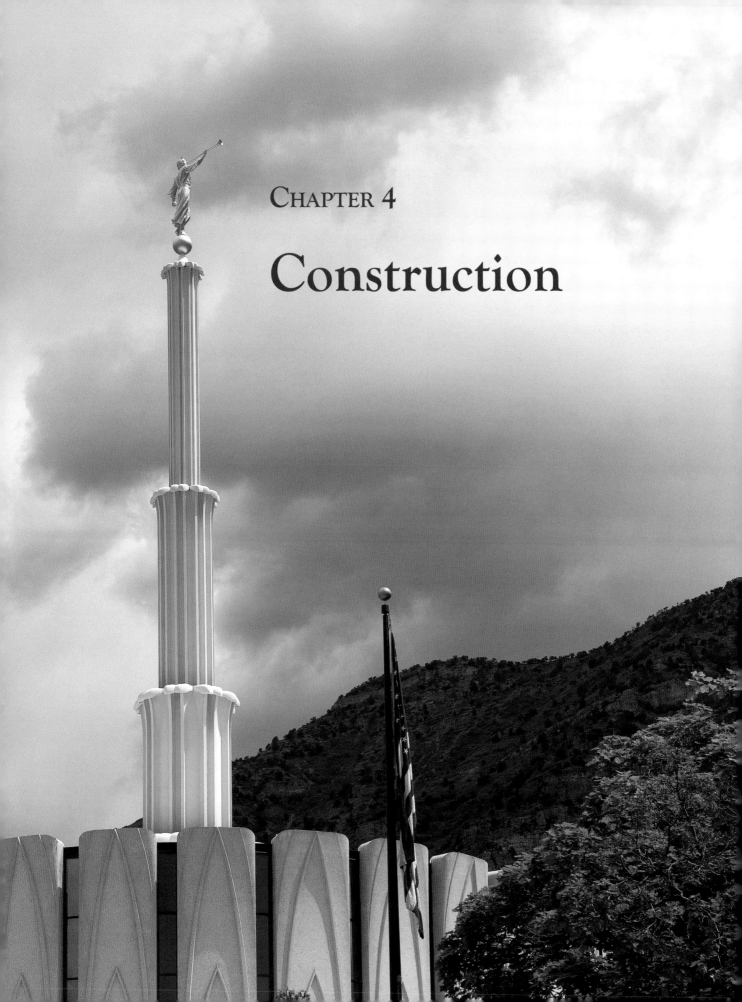

CHAPTER 4

Construction

1969   Ground broken by President Hugh B. Brown
(September 15)

Hogan and Tingey submit low bid (October)

1970   Ground-floor walls and higher steel framework completed
(by October)

1971   Cornerstone laid and temple presidency announced
(May 21)

Tower completed (July)

*W*hen the basic design for the Ogden and Provo Temples was announced early in 1968, the architect, Emil B. Fetzer, indicated that preparing the detailed plans would require at least a year. Therefore, by the summer of 1969 there was a growing interest to see the temples' construction get under way. Finally, ground was broken for the Ogden Temple on September 8 of that year. The same inaugural ceremony took place in Provo just one week later.

Groundbreaking

The afternoon of Monday, September 15, 1969, was overcast but pleasant as about twelve thousand excited persons gathered on the gently sloping site where the Provo Temple would stand. Many were accommodated in bleachers or chairs set up for the occasion, but thousands of others stood or sat on the nearby hillside.

Eleven General Authorities attended—including Presidents Hugh B. Brown and N. Eldon Tanner, First and Second Counselors in the First Presidency; Presidents Joseph Fielding Smith and Alvin R. Dyer, who at this time were additional counselors in the First Presidency; Elders Ezra Taft Benson, LeGrand Richards, and Gordon B. Hinckley of the Twelve; Elders Elray L. Christiansen, Henry D. Taylor, and James A. Cullimore, assistants to the Twelve; and Eldred G. Smith, Patriarch to the Church. President Tanner conducted the service. Presidents Smith and Dyer offered the opening and closing prayers.

A priesthood chorus under the direction of A. Harold Goodman—president of the BYU Fifth Stake and member of the Brigham Young University music faculty—sang "The Spirit of God," which had been written for the Kirtland Temple dedication. A Primary children's chorus under the direction of Bishop Lewis Rawlinson sang "When He Comes Again."

In the main address, President Brown praised the Utah Valley Saints for their willingness to contribute funds for the temple. He recounted his own contributions to the Church both in time and money and then concluded that "the Church owes me not one cent.

I have received more than I have ever given." He suggested that the temple-building fund would not be the last opportunity to contribute. His promise that the Brethren would most certainly provide other opportunities in the future prompted good-natured laughter from the assembled crowd. "Participation is the very soul of growth," he insisted. President Brown concluded with his testimony and then reaffirmed, "The Lord owes me nothing, I owe him everything."[1]

President Tanner brought greetings from President David O. McKay, who was not able to attend because of poor health. (He would pass away four months later.) He described the assembled throng as "a great sight." He also expressed appreciation for donations to the temple fund, particularly acknowledging the contributions made by BYU students.

Mark B. Garff, chairman of the Church's Building Committee, acknowledged "the hard work and long prayers" of his committee in carrying out the instructions they received from the First Presidency. Particularly, "he paid tribute to the work of Emil Fetzer."[2]

Stake president Ben E. Lewis recalled how as a boy he had planted pennies, hoping that "a beautiful penny plant would blossom forth full of pennies." When his desire remained unfulfilled, his father wisely counseled him that if he planted his pennies in the garden of the Lord, they would grow. "As a temple committee,"

President N. Eldon Tanner speaks at groundbreaking. *Church News.*

Lewis continued, "we invited every man, woman and child to contribute and plant their funds in the temple of God. We can now announce that we raised the million dollars we were asked to contribute, and you people have contributed more. You have gone the second mile."[3]

President Hugh B. Brown officially turned the first shovel of dirt; the other General Authorities followed. Next, the stake presidents and then the bishops in the temple district had their turns. Finally, others who were present were able to participate by wielding the gold-colored shovels to turn over some of the soil.

Construction Begins

The final set of plans for the temple—prepared under the direction of architect Emil B. Fetzer—consisted of 135 large pages. These "included plot plans; landscape layouts; architectural plans and detailed engineering drawings for structural, mechanical and electrical disciplines; equipment and furniture layouts. A large, written book of specifications clearly and specifically detailed construction requirements."[4]

Several construction companies were invited to study these plans and submit a formal bid. "Contractors were selected based on their past construction performances and on the size of projects that they had successfully completed commensurate to the size, cost, scope and finish of the temples," Emil B. Fetzer explained. "Due to the sacred character of the temples, selected contractors were required to be temple worthy members of the Church."[5] In late October, just a few weeks after the groundbreaking, the bids were formally opened by President N. Eldon Tanner and read by

Top: President Hugh B. Brown (left) breaks ground with President Joseph Fielding Smith (middle) and Elder Gordon B. Hinckley (right). Courtesy of L. Tom Perry Special Collections, Harold B. Lee Library. *Bottom*: Richard and Dawn Cowan at groundbreaking. Courtesy of Richard Cowan.

Top: Concrete columns for temple's lower floors. Courtesy of Church History Library. *Bottom:* Temple walls rising. Courtesy of Church History Library.

Emil B. Fetzer. The low bid of $4,275,000 was submitted by Hogan & Tingey Construction Company of Centerville (a community just north of Salt Lake City). Interestingly, this winning bid was only $4,000 less than that submitted by Okland Construction Company, which had received the contract to build the similar Ogden Temple. A "letter of intent" was handed to the winning contractors so that construction could commence immediately.[6] As the process of building got under way, builders rushed their work "against an early deadline."[7]

Because the stainless steel baptismal font was so large, it needed to be put into place in the temple's basement before the concrete for the main floor was poured overhead. Wrapped in heavy plastic, the font was protected from damage as construction proceeded all around it. By the end of April 1970, support columns, rebar, and walls of the first floor began to rise above the ground.[8] By October, the outer walls of the ground floor were completed, and structural steel for the upper floors was in place.[9]

Cornerstone Laying

Temple cornerstones are reminders of Paul's describing the Church as being "built on the foundation of the apostles and prophets, Jesus Christ himself being the chief cornerstone" (Ephesians 2:20). Over six thousand interested spectators gathered at 12:15 p.m. on Friday,

Crowd at cornerstone ceremony.
Courtesy of L. Tom Perry Special
Collections, Harold B. Lee Library.

May 21, 1971, to witness the laying of the Provo Temple's cornerstone.
At this time, the temple's walls were mostly completed. When temples
were built of large hewn stones, placing the cornerstone had marked
the beginning of construction, such as at Kirtland, Nauvoo, or Salt
Lake. When reinforced concrete became the norm, as was the case with
Provo, cornerstone layings became purely symbolic and were conducted
during construction after the walls surrounding the cornerstone area
were sufficiently completed. Later, beginning in the early 1980s, this
ceremony would become part of the dedication proceedings held after
the temple is finished. Hence, over the years, the placing of cornerstones shifted from the beginning to the conclusion of construction.

The ceremony in Provo was planned by the newly appointed
Provo Temple Advisory Committee, which was chaired by Fred A.
Schwendiman, president of the BYU Third Stake. Committee mem-
bers included three other stake presidents—Alma P. Burton, Sharon
Stake; L. Flake Rogers, Provo East Stake; and Joseph Y. Toronto,
Spanish Fork Stake. Other members of the committee were Ben E.
Lewis—former president of the Sharon East Stake and chairman
of the fund-raising committee—and Harold Glen Clark, who was
recently appointed Provo Temple president.

Left: President Joseph Fielding Smith speaking. Photo by Maxine Cameron. *Right:* First Presidency at cornerstone laying. From left to right: Harold B. Lee, Joseph Fielding Smith, N. Eldon Tanner. *Church News.*

Twenty-two General Authorities were in attendance, including all three members of the First Presidency. President Harold B. Lee, First Counselor in the First Presidency, conducted the impressive ceremonies. The opening and closing prayers were offered respectively by President Spencer W. Kimball and Elder Marion G. Romney of the Quorum of the Twelve Apostles. Music was provided by the Brigham Young University Chorale.

In his remarks, President Joseph Fielding Smith recalled how the Prophet Joseph Smith taught that the prime purpose of the gathering was to build temples, so as "to enable the saints to gain the blessings in these holy houses." He cited the fact that we are responding to the Lord's commandment to build temples and that the fact that we "go forward in this labor of love is one of the great evidences of the divinity of this work in which we are engaged." He insisted that "the Lord has given us every power, every key, every truth, and every ordinance necessary to gain salvation and exaltation in His kingdom. The fullness of the gospel consists of the fullness of these truths, powers and ordinances needed to enable men to gain the fullness of reward in the celestial kingdom." He emphasized that the highest ordinances and blessings of the gospel are available only in temples and that "there is no other place where the fullness of the blessings of the priesthood, of the Church, and of the gospel can be gained." He described eternal marriage as "the crowning ordinance of the gospel, the crowning ordinance of the temple." In temples, we "may enter into those ordinances

Opposite: Top: Left to right: Exiting the stand are Harold B. Lee, Joseph Fielding Smith, Ben E. Lewis, N. Eldon Tanner, and Gordon B. Hinckley. *Bottom:* Exiting the stand are Gordon B. Hinckley, Marion G. Romney, Hugh B. Brown, Thomas S. Monson, and Boyd K. Packer. Photos by Maxine Cameron.

which lead to eternal life," and "through vicarious ordinances, it is our privilege to offer to our dead ancestors all of the blessings which have come to us." President Smith was grateful for his witness that "through obedience to the Lord's laws, which includes taking upon ourselves the ordinances of His house, we may have peace in this life and eternal life in the world to come." In conclusion, he challenged Church members "to use the new temple to the fullest extent as soon as its facilities are available."[10] The level of activity in the Provo Temple during coming decades would show how completely Utah Valley Saints accepted and carried out President Smith's challenge.

President N. Eldon Tanner introduced the recently appointed temple presidency—Harold Glen Clark, Joseph Y. Toronto, and O. Wendle Nielsen. He acknowledged the contributions made by many to the construction of the temple. As a counselor in the First Presidency, he had been intimately connected with this project from the beginning. He then explained what significant artifacts had been placed in the cornerstone box: photographs of Church leaders; a

Cornerstone inscription. Photographer unknown.

group picture of stake presidents in the temple district; Church literature, including the standard works; current issues of the *Ensign*, *New Era*, and *Friend*; a copy of the August 19, 1967, *Church News*, which announced plans to build the Provo and Ogden Temples; a list with signatures of donors to the Provo Temple–building fund; copies of current daily and weekly newspapers from the local area; brochures describing Temple Square, other temples of the Church, and the purpose of temple activity; and photographs showing the groundbreaking and various stages of construction of the Provo Temple.[11]

Ben E. Lewis, chairman of the temple fund-raising committee, also spoke. He reported that the Saints had contributed "nearly twice" the one million dollars they had been asked to raise.[12]

Space was left in the wall near the northeast corner of the temple to place the sealed copper box containing this historical memorabilia. The commemorative plaque of white marble was then placed over the opening, under the direction of President Joseph Fielding Smith. The gold-leafed lettering announced, "ERECTED A.D. 1969–71, DEDICATED A.D. 1972." President Smith's first counselor, Harold B. Lee, applied the mortar to the cornerstone before setting it into place.

President Harold B. Lee placing cornerstone plaque. *Church News.*

Construction Completed

When the 118-foot spire was put into place during July 1971, the temple's exterior appeared to be finished. The spire was anchored to a steel base and was sheathed by four tiers of fiberglass. "The last four feet of the spire is a metal spike which will serve as a lightning rod. A three-fourths inch thick copper cable runs down through the roof, through the building, and into the ground."[13]

By the fall of 1971, construction was drawing to a close. As exterior landscaping and interior furnishing were completed, the temple was ready for its open house and dedication.

Notes

1.　Stephen W. Gibson, "A New Temple Begins," *Church News*, September 20, 1969, 3.

2.　Gibson, "New Temple," 3.

3.　Gibson, "New Temple," 3.

4.　Emil B. Fetzer, "The Sacred Twin Temples: Ogden Temple Provo Temple," in *Completed Writings of Emil Baer Fetzer*, Emil B. Fetzer and June S. Fetzer (self-published, 2003), 9.

5.　Fetzer, "Sacred Twin Temples," 9.

6.　"Low Bid on Provo Temple," *Church News*, November 1, 1969, 7.

7.　"Church in Action: Provo Temple Rises Rapidly," *Church News*, May 2, 1970, 13.

8.　"Church in Action: Provo Temple Rises Rapidly," 13.

9.　"Church in Action," *Church News*, October 17, 1970, 13.

10.　Dell Van Orden, "Provo Temple Cornerstone Laid," *Church News*, May 29, 1971, 3.

11.　Dell Van Orden, "Cornerstone Rites at Provo Temple," *Church News*, May 15, 1971, 3.

12.　Van Orden, "Cornerstone Rites," 3.

13.　"Church in Action," *Church News*, July 24, 1971, 13.

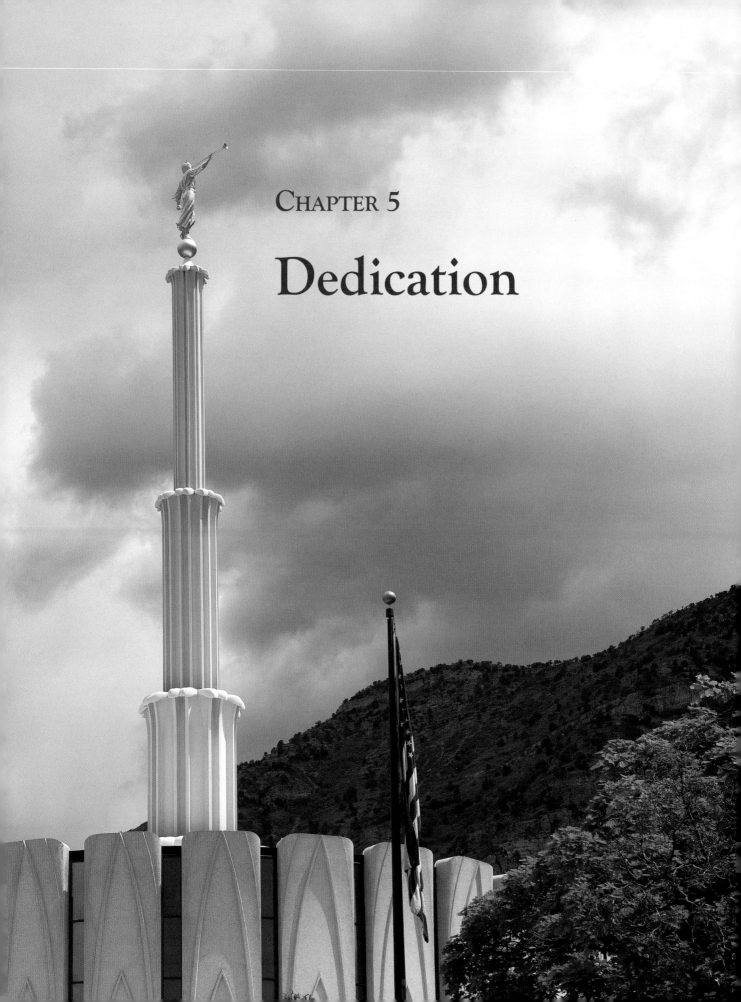

CHAPTER 5

Dedication

1972   Public open house held (January 10–29)

Temple dedicated (February 9)

*N*ow that construction was completed, the Provo Temple was ready for its dedication. The Provo Temple Advisory Committee—which had been formed to plan the cornerstone laying, open house, and dedication—included temple president Harold Glen Clark and stake presidents Fred Schwendiman, Alma P. Burton, L. Flake Rogers, Ben E. Lewis, and Joseph Y. Toronto.[1]

Provo Temple District

- American Fork Region (five stakes)

- Brigham Young University Region (ten stakes)

- Coalville Region (one stake)

- Orem Region (three stakes)

- Payson Region (three stakes)

- Provo Region (four stakes)

- Provo North Region (three stakes)

- Spanish Fork Region (three stakes)

The Open House

Ever since 1893, when community leaders not of the Latter-day Saint faith were invited to walk through the Salt Lake Temple the evening before its dedication, the Church has used temple open houses as an opportunity to share the gospel with others.

In November 1971 the First Presidency had announced dates for the Ogden and Provo Temples public open houses.[2] In Provo, this event took place from Monday, January 10, through Saturday, January 29, 1972. Representatives of the press, as well as local Church leaders from the temple district and their wives, were invited to a special preview on Saturday, January 8. Some 10,000 people visited the temple that day.[3]

Tours were conducted from 9:00 a.m. to 9:00 p.m. each day except Mondays, when they ended at 4:00 p.m. so as not to interfere with family home evenings, and Sundays, when the temple was

Tents at open house, January 1972.
Church News.

closed. To shelter visitors during the winter weather, a large heated tent—seating 1,600—was set up in the parking area immediately west of the building. While waiting for their turn to enter the temple, visitors could read explanatory displays about temple work and other facets of the gospel. An enclosed walkway leading from the tent to the temple's front entrance not only shielded the visitors from winter weather, but also helped ensure that their shoes would be relatively clean as they entered the temple.[4] To provide a more even flow of visitors, individual stakes were assigned days when they were especially invited to come to the temple. Because the temple visit was to be a sacred occasion, the tours were conducted silently; preschool children were not invited, and children under fourteen were to be accompanied by an adult.[5]

On one Monday evening, temple president Harold Glen Clark was escorting his own family through the temple after the regular tours were over. They heard a knocking on the front door. "The Truman Madsen family was standing at the door, not aware that the temple was closed early on Mondays. This family had held four family home evenings to prepare their children for the temple dedication. This Monday night was to be the climax, and the family had come in the spirit of fasting and prayer, showered and dressed in their Sunday best for the children to have their first temple experience. Truman and Ann had prayed for a special experience in the temple for their children, only to find that it was closed. Truman wrote, 'We learned an unexpected lesson from this experience. There we were, all scrubbed, clean, excited, and expectant. But the door was locked; it was a Monday. What a letdown. But the lights were all on so I went to look inside, pressing my nose against the glass. There was the temple president, showing his own family through the temple. Seeing us, and having compassion, he invited us to join them. We knew for a moment how it felt to be denied entrance to the temple. And just as suddenly, we experienced more joy than we had prayed and planned for.'" Of the incident, Ann Madsen said, "In Isaiah it is written, 'Before they ask, I will answer' and President Clark's invitation was an answer to our fervent prayers."[6]

Special tours were conducted for groups with unique needs. For example, a group of people who were visually impaired enjoyed a personal tour conducted by the temple president, who provided vivid descriptions of what the temple looked like. Members of this group were permitted to step down into the area beneath the baptismal font so they could examine the form of the oxen by touch.

A total of 246,201 persons visited the temple during its open house.[7] Most were from within the temple district, but others traveled hundreds of miles to attend. Most came individually or as families, but some came on chartered buses with seminary or institute classes.

Those participating in the open house felt a special spirit as they visited the temple. The Church's *New Era* magazine published a number of responses from the youth and young adult readers: "I had such a wonderful feeling while inside the temple, I didn't want to leave"; "After coming 600 miles to see the house of the Lord, then having the experience, I realized it was worth traveling around

There we were, all scrubbed, clean, excited, and expectant. But the door was locked. . . . We knew for a moment how it felt to be denied entrance to the temple.

the world for"; "The whole temple seemed to be a part of heaven"; "The spirit there was unbelievable, and it is not even dedicated yet"; "I think it has caused me to have a new outlook on life. Now I look forward to the future instead of fearing it"; "This was the most completely peaceful twenty minutes that I have ever experienced."

Some visitors were particularly prompted to get more involved in family history research and performing ordinances in behalf of the dead: "I got a deeper feeling of love when I looked at the font and realized that our Father in Heaven has inspired his servants to construct such a room so that everyone can enjoy the lifesaving ordinance of baptism"; "I couldn't help but think about the countless number of souls who are waiting to have their work done."

Some were particularly impressed with the sealing rooms: "When I saw the sealing rooms, I knew that I truly wanted a temple marriage"; "The mirrors give such a beautiful representation of eternity."

For others, reaching the celestial room was the climax of their tour, and it led them to set significant goals: "When I got to the celestial room, I suddenly realized that this building isn't like the rest of the buildings in the world; it is the house of the Lord. Now I have no doubt where I want to be married"; "As soon as I entered the celestial room, I had the feeling that I must never settle for anything lower than the celestial kingdom"; "The moment I turned the corner and viewed the celestial room for the first time, I was hit by one of those shock waves that start at your toes and work their way up. It made me realize that I have a long way to go to obtain celestial glory."[8]

One Provo High School student returned on several days after school. Each day she would start for home but would end up in the temple. It was like a magnet to her. After going through the normal tour, she would sit in the celestial room as long as they would let her, "just to feel the presence of the Lord, to pray, to commune."[9]

Because of the heavy traffic through the temple during those three weeks, just over a week was set aside afterward for cleaning the temple before its February 9 dedication.

On Sunday evening, February 6—just three days before the temple's dedication—temple president Harold Glen Clark spoke at the regular BYU ten-stake fireside. He emphasized that we must know that the spirit "is as real and specific in personality as the body. That though the body dies, the spirit never dies. You can only understand temple work when you believe and know that the spirit is a literal child of our Heavenly Father." He taught that our spirit came from our Heavenly Father, and that temple ordinances provide the only way for us to return to His presence. He specifically spoke about one aspect of temple ordinances that was particularly relevant to his student audience; "When you plan to marry, [the temple] will teach you that you not only size up a body of a sweetheart, but the spirit. You marry a spirit as well as a body and [of] the two, the beauty of the spirit—the integrity of the spirit—comes first." He insisted that "a noble spirit in a handicapped body is better than a mediocre spirit in a perfect body." In conclusion, President Clark counseled, "Students should not be sad because they cannot work in the temple or receive their endowments. You are preparing yourselves by going to school. The time will come. And when you do take promises in the temple you will do so with real understanding."[10]

The Temple Dedicated

The dedications of these sacred houses of the Lord have always been eagerly anticipated spiritual events. To dedicate something means to set it apart as holy or devote it to sacred purposes. "Dedicate" is often linked to "consecrate" from the Latin *cum* (together) plus *sacrare* (to make sacred). When a temple is dedicated, it is specifically given to the Lord whose house it is to be.

> *When a temple is dedicated, it is specifically given to the Lord whose house it is to be.*

In Old Testament times, temple dedications were special occasions. When the Tabernacle of Moses was completed, "a cloud covered the tent of the congregation, and the glory of the Lord filled the tabernacle." These manifestations of God's accepting presence were so powerful that even "Moses was not able to enter" (Exodus 40:34–35).

The dedication of Solomon's Temple in the promised land was a similar spiritual occasion. Countless animals were sacrificed as the ark was taken into the temple and placed in the Holy of Holies. Once again a cloud of the Lord's glory "filled the house of the Lord"

(1 Kings 8:4–11). In his prayer of dedication, King Solomon petitioned, "The Lord our God be with us, as he was with our fathers: let him not leave us, nor forsake us: That he may incline our hearts unto him, to walk in all his ways, and to keep his commandments, and his statutes, and his judgments, which he commanded our fathers" (1 Kings 8:57–58). At the conclusion of the days of dedication the people left—as would the faithful in later dispensations—"joyful and glad of heart for all the goodness that the Lord had done" for them (1 Kings 8:66). In the present dispensation, the dedication of the Kirtland Temple climaxed a season of remarkable spiritual outpourings.[11]

Temple dedications have been scheduled in different ways over the years. The pattern of having more than one dedicatory session was established at the outset in Kirtland, when a second session was scheduled four days afterward for those who could not get into the initial dedicatory meeting. The Nauvoo Temple was dedicated piecemeal— separate dedications being conducted for the baptismal font and the attic facilities as they were completed. This pattern was repeated at St. George. Then, at the Nauvoo and Manti Temples, a private dedication was conducted before the public dedication because of fears that there might be disruptions during times of persecution. The Salt Lake Temple's thirty-one dedicatory sessions extended over nineteen days. Portions of the Mesa and Swiss Temple dedications were broadcast by radio. Proceedings of the Los Angeles Temple's dedicatory sessions were carried by television from the large upper assembly room into several other rooms inside the temple. The 1964 dedications of the Oakland Temple were the first time the proceedings were carried into a different building—the adjoining interstake center—by television.

In later years, further variations would continue. At the Bountiful Temple dedication, a total of 200,000 Saints were able to attend the twenty-eight sessions inside the temple itself or at one of five other locations. Dedications of the Palmyra, Winter Quarters, and Nauvoo Temples were made available by satellite transmission to stake centers throughout North America. Beginning with the Helsinki Temple, dedications of overseas temples were carried by satellite to selected locations in the Salt Lake area for the benefit of

Saints who had emigrated from those places or for missionaries who had served there.

The dedication of the Ogden Temple continued over three days, with proceedings being carried to overflow gatherings in the adjacent Ogden Tabernacle. On the other hand, only two sessions were required for the dedication of the Provo Temple on February 9, at 2:00 p.m. and 7:00 p.m., because of the large overflow venues available nearby. The dedicatory services were conducted in the temple's celestial room and were carried by closed-circuit color television to other areas in the temple, even in hallways. About 3,500—less than 10 percent of the total attending—were able to witness the proceedings within the temple itself. Several overflow locations were available in large auditoriums in nine buildings on the Brigham Young University campus. The largest of these were the recently opened 21,000-seat Marriott Center and the 7,500-seat George Albert Smith Fieldhouse; in each of these locations, large see-through screens

Inscriptions on the east facade of the temple. Photo by Lee R. Cowan.

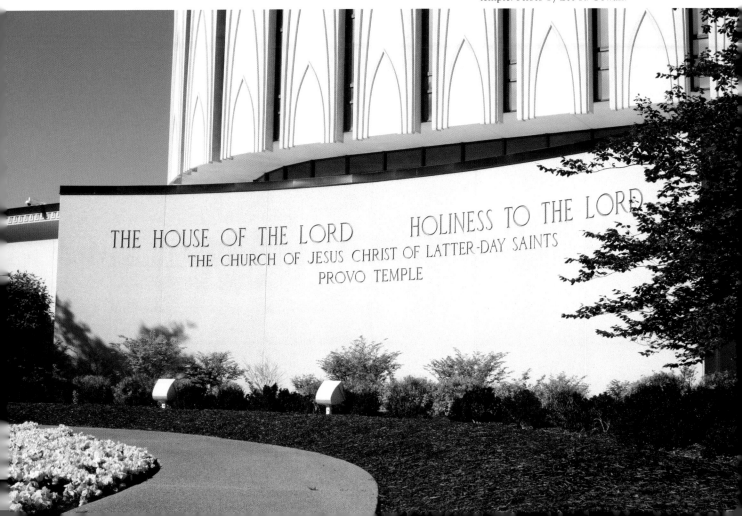

enabled people sitting on both sides of the auditoriums to witness the proceedings (although those sitting behind the screen would be seeing a reversed image). Other locations included the Joseph Smith Building auditorium and several large halls or theaters in the Harris Fine Arts Center. In each location, one of the area stake presidents was assigned to act as the host. A total of 74,000 persons attended, 37,000 in each of the two dedicatory sessions. BYU security personnel helped direct parking around these venues. President Fred A. Schwendiman, chairman of the Temple Advisory Committee, felt that this was "the largest assembly of Latter-day Saints ever held on one day in one city." He also noted that the combined total of nearly 75,000 was nearly one and a half times the population of Provo, which stood at 53,131 persons according to the 1970 census.[12]

Those attending the Provo Temple's dedication needed to be Church members in good standing who were at least twelve years of age. Following an interview with their bishop, they were given an invitation or ticket to attend a specific session of the dedication in either the temple or a designated overflow location.

General Authorities attending the dedication included the entire First Presidency–Joseph Fielding Smith, Harold B. Lee, and N. Eldon Tanner. Upon their arrival at the temple, they were greeted by members of the temple presidency and Temple Advisory Committee and escorted to the beautiful celestial room on the temple's third floor, where the temple's dedicatory services would be conducted.

The two dedicatory sessions followed the same basic outline, including musical numbers and remarks by Church leaders. Two specially selected choirs provided music for the dedicatory sessions—one in the afternoon, and the other in the evening. The conductors in the afternoon were Leila Matheson, Lawrence Sardoni, Tom Biesinger, and Darrell Stubbs, with Janice Burton as organist. In the evening, the choir was conducted by Robert Downs, Brandt Curtis, Barbara Latham, and Leslie Rees, with Robert Manookin at the organ. Several of these musicians were members of the BYU music faculty.

President Joseph Fielding Smith shared the same prepared message in each of the two sessions. He greeted those present in the celestial room or in one of the overflow locations. He prayed that "the

Lord [would] pour out His Spirit upon us in great abundance." He observed that his grandfather, Hyrum Smith, had been born on this date—February 9—in 1800, and that it was fitting that this anniversary was being marked by the dedication of another temple "wherein those keys and powers, held jointly by him and the Prophet Joseph Smith, may be used for the salvation and exaltation of many of our Father's children." President Joseph Fielding Smith testified that the decision to build this temple had come through inspiration. "It is now our purpose to present it to the Lord, as one of His holy houses, as a place where His Spirit may dwell in the hearts of all those who come here to worship Him in spirit and in truth. In this holy house we are entitled to receive revelation and guidance from on high. The Lord is anxious to reveal His mind and His will to us, and to give us counsel and direction and doctrine as rapidly as we are able to receive them. We believe all that God has revealed, all that he does now reveal, and I testify to you that there are many great and important things yet to be set forth in the days that are ahead."

In conclusion, he prayed that "we shall use this holy temple for the performance of the ordinances of salvation and exaltation, for both the living and the dead; that the saints in this area will come here to find peace and the spirit of inspiration; and that through our work here many more souls shall be saved in our Father's kingdom. I ask the Lord to bless and prosper all who have contributed in any way to the construction of this temple and that He will bless those who labor in it for the salvation of the children of men. When we dedicate a house to the Lord, what we really do is dedicate ourselves to the Lord's service, with a covenant that we shall use the house in the way He intends that it shall be used."[13]

In the afternoon session, President N. Eldon Tanner challenged his listeners to make use of the temple "in the way it has been set apart to be used," and admonished parents to set a good example and teach their children "to look forward to the spiritual blessings they would receive there." Elder Thomas S. Monson of the Quorum of the Twelve Apostles spoke of how the teachings received in the temple provide direction for our lives: "It is only when we lose our eternal perspective that we founder in darkness."[14]

The Dedicatory Prayer

The highlight of each session was the dedicatory prayer. In these prayers, President Smith explained, "We present the temple to the Lord as one of His houses on earth. Our other public prayers are simple and short and offered as guided by the Spirit of the Lord." In contrast to prayers generally offered in Church meetings, which tend to be brief, "dedicatory prayers for temples . . . are formal and long and cover many matters of doctrine and petition."

The dedicatory prayer of the Kirtland Temple, given by revelation (Doctrine and Covenants 109), set the pattern for the prayers at subsequent temple dedications. The Prophet Joseph Smith prayed "that thy glory may rest down upon thy people, and upon this thy house, which we now dedicate to thee, that it may be sanctified and consecrated to be holy, and that thy holy presence may be continually in this house" (Doctrine and Covenants 109:12). He also prayed for "the nations of the earth" and their leaders and for the gathering of Israel (Doctrine and Covenants 109:54, 61). The Prophet Joseph concluded his prayer of dedication by asking the Lord to bless the General Authorities and their families and to help His work roll forth in preparation for His glorious Second Coming (Doctrine and Covenants 109:68–76).

Subsequent temple dedicatory prayers have included ideas similar to those revealed by the Lord at Kirtland. Petitions for protection are typical.[15] For example, the prayer in earthquake-prone Guatemala sought protection from the "tremblings of the earth."[16] Other prayers have noted unique local developments. The prayers at Palmyra, Nauvoo, and Winter Quarters all referred to the significance of earlier events at those historic sites.

All dedicatory prayers have been given "by the spirit of inspiration," President Smith testified, "and have then been read by such of the Brethren as have been appointed to do so. The prayer I have prepared for the dedication of this Provo Temple is no exception." Perhaps one reason why these prayers are written out and then read is so that they can be given word for word—the same in each of the dedicatory services. President Joseph Fielding Smith requested that his first counselor, Harold B. Lee, read the dedicatory prayer, which he had composed, for the Provo Temple. After giving praise to God and expressing thanks for the Savior's great Atonement and for the latter-day restoration of the marvelous gospel plan, the prayer specifically offered gratitude that "Thou didst reveal unto us Thy priesthood, even the sealing power, by the hand of Elijah the Prophet, so that in this temple, and in all Thy other holy houses, Thy faithful saints may be endowed with power from on high; and may enter into those everlasting covenants which open the door to the receipt of all of the blessings of Abraham, Isaac, and Jacob and all the holy prophets." As "we turn our faces to this holy house," we "plead with Thee to make us worthy to inherit the fullness of those blessings found only in Thy holy temples—even those blessings found which grow out of the continuation of the family unit forever. Acknowledging that we desire these blessings not only for ourselves but for those who have gone before, "we plead for Thy guidance and directing light as we go forward in this work—one of the greatest ever revealed to the children of men in any age of the earth."

Provo Temple viewed from the southwest. © Intellectual Reserve, Inc.

The prayer lamented the evil conditions prevailing in the world but expressed gratitude for the divinely inspired Constitution. It petitioned, "Wilt Thou bless the executive, legislative and judicial branches of our government, that each may function wisely and courageously in its respective field, for the preservation of our constitutional form of government." Acknowledging that Church members are increasingly found in many nations of the earth, the prayer stated, "We pray that the rulers of all people, under the guidance of Thy Holy Spirit, may be constrained to adopt forms of government which will assure to all men those freedoms which rightly belong to them and which are justifiable before Thee."

The prayer particularly asked the Lord to bless the youth of Zion that they might be protected from evil. "Preserve them, O our God; enlighten their minds and pour out upon them Thy Holy Spirit, as they prepare for the great work that shall rest upon them." Specifically, the prayer petitioned, "Let that great temple of learning—the Brigham Young University . . . be prospered to the full. Let Thy enlightening power rest upon those who teach and those who are taught . . . May those who teach and study in all academic fields have their souls enlightened with spiritual knowledge, so they will turn to Thy house for blessings and knowledge and learning that surpass all that may be found elsewhere."

After expressing gratitude for the privilege of building the temple, the prayer continued, "We dedicate it as a house of baptism, a house of endowment, a house of marriage, a house of righteousness, for the living and the dead. We humbly pray that Thou wilt accept this edifice and pour out Thy blessings upon it as a house to which Thou wilt come and in which Thy spirit will direct all that is done, that it may be accepted unto Thee. Let Thy spirit and blessings attend and guide all who officiate herein, that a feeling of holiness will prevail in every room of this, Thy holy house. May all who enter have clean hands and pure hearts, and may they be built up in their faith and depart with a feeling of peace, and praising Thy holy name."

After asking for blessings on all parts of the temple and grounds, the prayer concluded, "And now finally, we dedicate this temple as an abode for Thee and Thy Son and Thy Holy Spirit and ask that Thou wilt place Thy ratifying seal of approval upon this dedicatory ordinance, and upon all that we have done and shall do in this, Thy holy house, which we now give unto Thee, the Lord."

Looking to the future, President Smith acknowledged that "we look forward to the day, O our God, when Thou wilt reveal unto Thy servants where other temples shall be built, in all the nations where Thy Saints increase in numbers and serve Thee in righteousness."[17] The Provo Temple was the fifteenth operating temple in the Church. In less than three decades, the total number of temples would exceed one hundred.

Dedicatory prayers are followed by the sacred "Hosanna Shout"—an expression of joyous praise. The word "hosanna" literally means "save, we pray." In ancient times, this shout typically was given out of doors and included the waving of leafy tree branches. On the occasion of the Savior's triumphal entry into Jerusalem, for example, the faithful waved pond fronds as they shouted "Hosanna" in praise to Him (John 12:13). In modern times, white handkerchiefs have been substituted, as the Hosanna Shout is typically given indoors. The Hosanna Shout has been a regular part of every temple dedication and has been rendered on a few other occasions—including the 1892 placing of the Salt Lake Temple capstone, the 1930 centennial general conference, and the 2000 dedication of the Conference Center adjacent to Temple Square. The shout is also reflected in the chorus of "The Spirit of God." This hymn has been sung at the dedication of every temple, often in conjunction with a choir singing the "Hosanna Anthem," which was composed for the Salt Lake Temple's

Provo Temple looking east. Photo by Jaren Wilkey, courtesy of Mark Philbrick.

dedication by Evan Stephens. It proclaims, "The House of the Lord is completed . . . May our off'ring by him be accepted. Amen, Amen. Rejoice, oh, ye Saints, whose patient faith and labor have reared this house wherein today ye stand; rejoice, ye blest departed saintly spirits, behold, your temple, finished, crowns the land. Rejoice, ye souls awaiting your redemption, the work speeds on to set the captive free; thanks be to God for his eternal mercies, thanks be to God for endless liberty."

In each session of the Provo Temple's dedication, a special choir sang the "Hosanna Anthem." At a certain point, the choir director signaled the congregation to join in by singing "The Spirit of God." This great hymn reflects temple service with such phrases as "The visions and blessings of old are returning," "The Lord is extending the Saints' understanding," "The knowledge and power of God are expanding; the veil o'er the earth is beginning to burst," "We'll call in our solemn assemblies," and "That we through our faith may begin to inherit the visions and blessings and glories of God."[18]

In the Provo dedication, many were so overcome with emotion that they could hardly sing. Many did not feel like speaking until they were outside of the temple. The same spirit prevailed in the overflow locations. The huge Marriott Center—where over half of those participating in the dedication were in attendance—is normally the setting for such events as basketball games, which are typified by cheering fans. Therefore, witnessing throngs leaving this large facility in reverent silence at the conclusion of each dedicatory session was a most unusual experience.

Notes

1.   Lynn C. Callister, "Life of Harold Glen Clark: The Temple Years" (unpublished manuscript), 3, copy in possession of Richard Cowan.

2.   "Dates Set for Temple Dedications," *Church News*, November 13, 1971, 3, 8–9.

3.   "Provo Temple Open for Public Viewing," *Church News*, January 15, 1972, 5.

4.   "Provo Temple Open for Public Viewing," 5.

5. "Provo Temple Tours Set; Huge Crowds Visit Ogden," *Church News*, January 1, 1972, 3.

6. Lynn Callister, "Life of Harold Glen Clark," 5–6.

7. "Provo: Temple Dedication Feb. 9," *Church News*, February 5, 1972, 11.

8. "Inside a House of the Lord," *New Era*, April 1972, 25–27.

9. Truman G. Madsen and Ann N. Madsen, "House of Glory, House of Light, House of Love," in *The Temple: Where Heaven Meets Earth* (Salt Lake City: Deseret Book, 2008), 60–61.

10. "Truths of the Temple," *Daily Universe*, February 9, 1972, 1.

11. See chapter 2.

12. "Temple Dedicated at Provo," *Church News*, February 12, 1972, 3; see also "Details Outlined for Dedication of Provo Temple Wednesday," *Daily Herald*, February 7, 1972, 1; "Temple Dedication Services Today," *Daily Universe*, February 9, 1972, 1.

13. "Hyrum Smith Honored by Pres. Smith," *Church News*, February 12, 1972, 3–4; for the complete text, see appendix C.

14. "Dedicatory Sessions for Provo Temple are Heavily Attended," *Daily Herald*, February 10, 1972, 1–2.

15. "Sacred Day of Dedication in Canada," *Church News*, September 1, 1990, 6.

16. "Their Cries Heard, Their Tears Seen," *Church News*, December 23, 1984, 4.

17. "Dedication Prayer of Provo Temple," *Church News*, February 12, 1972, 5; for the complete text of the dedicatory prayer, see appendix D.

18. William W. Phelps, "The Spirit of God," *Hymns* (Salt Lake City: The Church of Jesus Christ of Latter-day Saints, 1985), no. 2.

Photo by Heidi Prigmore.

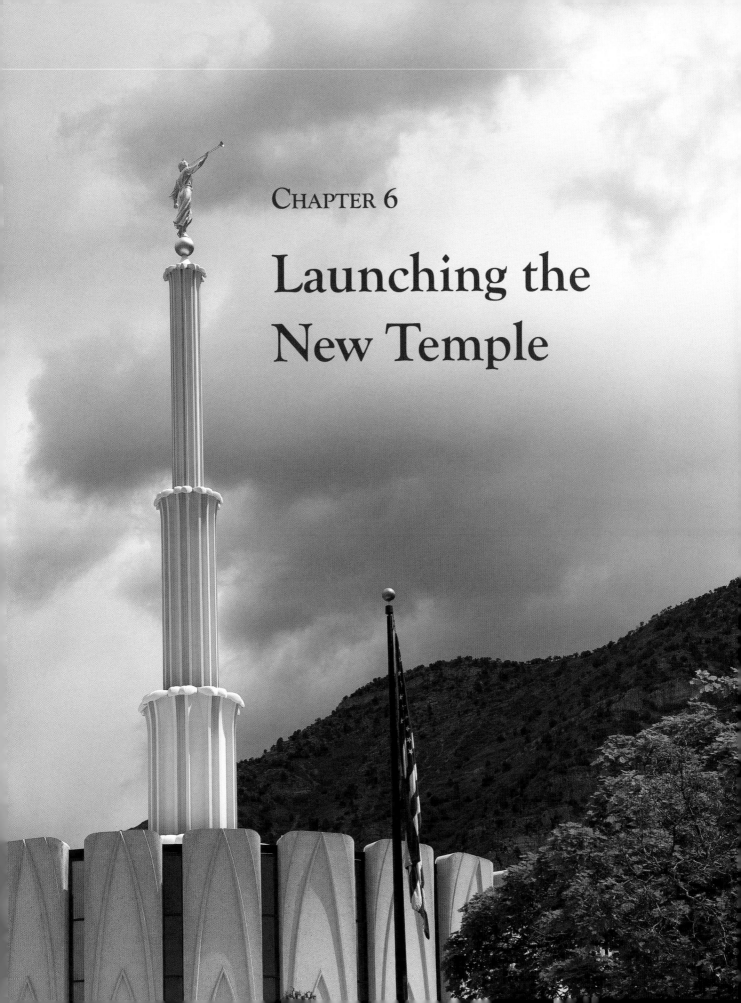

CHAPTER 6

Launching the
New Temple

1971   Temple presidency and recorder set apart (June 4)

1972   Temple dedicated (February 9)

First ordinances; baptisms for the dead done (February 23)

Endowments inaugurated (March 14)

1976   Record of 76,000 endowments performed in single month (January)

*N*ow that the beautiful Provo Temple was completed and dedicated, the next task was to call leaders and to put into place the surprisingly large number of workers needed to perform the sacred ordinances for which the temple had been built. This would involve a variety of steps.

New Leaders Called

Leaders for the new Provo Temple had been called nearly a year before its dedication. Harold Glen and Mary Deane Clark were invited to meet with President Harold B. Lee, First Counselor to Joseph Fielding Smith in the First Presidency. President Lee observed, "There are two callings in the Church that are the hardest to fill. One is patriarch and the other is temple president." Since Brother Clark was already a patriarch, it was easy for him to figure out what his new call would be. President Lee then called them to serve as president and matron of the Provo Temple. Brother Clark wrote the following about this experience:

> The silence that followed seemed like an eternity as he looked at us. I can't remember what I said, but my eyes, and Mary Deane's and President Lee's were glistening. "My husband is very worthy," Mary Deane said, "But I don't know about me." "We know all about both of you," President Lee replied. After a further exchange, President Lee said, "Think it over, pray about it, then come back and tell me how you feel about accepting the call." My reply was, "I can't think of what to pray about," and Mary Deane said exuberantly, "We accept." I am sure we gave the impression that we were eager to accept before President Lee could change his mind.[1]

Brother Clark's daughter and biographer recorded, "As the couple walked from the Church Office Building to their car, hand in hand, they were oblivious to the busy traffic, noticing only that the lumps in their throats caused them to walk in silence. They were sober and reflective on their way home, and thanked Father in Heaven for His faith in them, and the trust of a prophet in them as

"I am sure we gave the impression that we were eager to accept before President Lee could change his mind."

well." On March 16, 1971, President Joseph Fielding Smith—with his counselors Harold B. Lee and N. Eldon Tanner—set the Clarks apart in their new calling.[2]

Brother Clark regarded his call as a fulfillment of a promise made in his patriarchal blessing, which he received in 1924 from Hyrum G. Smith, Patriarch to the Church: "Thou shall . . . officiate in many of the sacred ordinances of the Gospel, and see the providence and power of the Lord made plain; thy testimony shall be increased and strengthened through a variety of important experiences."[3]

President and Sister Clark began receiving training immediately in the Salt Lake Temple from O. Leslie Stone, president of that temple. They also visited the temples in Logan, Manti, Oakland, and Los Angeles to gain perspective for their future service.

The complete temple presidency was announced at the Provo Temple's cornerstone ceremony: Joseph Y. Toronto (president of the Spanish Fork Stake), first counselor; O. Wendle Nielsen (who had served years earlier as President Clark's counselor in the bishopric), second counselor; and J. Wallace Boswell, recorder. The counselors and recorder were set apart June 4, 1971. The presidency had temporary offices in the nearby Sharon East Stake Center (then on 900 East) and began interviewing prospective temple workers. They were able to move into office space in the temple itself during December 1971.[4]

President Clark recalled:

> I can't forget the day when a special messenger from Salt Lake brought the *Book of Sacred Ordinances and Procedures of the Temple* and charged me, much like Moroni did the Prophet Joseph when he gave to his charge and safe keeping the golden plates. I imagine the Prophet Joseph Smith said as he handled these writings, "Could these really be from God? Did He really inspire men to write them? And who am I to be trusted with these things?" I read and prayed that I might know more and perform well. How thrilled we were as a presidency to read through these ordinances for the first time, compiled in printed form.

They were thrilled at the challenge of implementing in the Provo Temple the new method of presenting the endowment using film.

"We felt the hand of the Lord upon us as we worked to put His house in order."[5]

Following the temple's dedication, temple workers received more intense training in their specific responsibilities. Stake leaders

Provo Temple presidency. From back, left to right: Joseph Y. Toronto, first counselor; O. Wendle Nielson, second counselor; J. Wallace Boswell, recorder. Front: Harold Glen Clark, president. *Church News.*

Beginning Dates

Date	Work Done
February 14, 1972	First names received from the Genealogical Library
February 23, 1972	First baptisms for the dead performed
February 25, 1972	First living sealing performed
February 29, 1972	Initiatory work started
March 3, 1972	First sealing of living children to parents performed
March 8, 1972	First sealing for the dead performed
March 14, 1972	First endowment for the dead performed
March 17, 1972	First endowment for the living performed

"I shall never forget the moment I stood in the projection room and looked down on [the] beautiful women workers as they stood quietly ready to take the women through the veil for the first time. . . . I felt like I was looking into a little spot of Heaven. It was a glorious sight."

throughout the area met in the temple's chapel to receive instruction on how ordinance work would commence so that it could take place in an orderly manner. Baptisms for the dead were first, beginning exactly two weeks after the temple was dedicated. Initiatory ordinances commenced soon afterward so names could be ready for endowments. A few sealings were also performed during these opening weeks.

The endowment, which involves film presentation and larger companies of people, was the most complicated ordinance to present. Logically, it was the last to be launched—over a month following the temple's dedication. There was a series of "first endowment sessions" extending over several days. Leaders and their spouses from a given stake were assigned a specific time to be in the temple.

Sister Clark recalled her feelings about these early days: "I shall never forget the moment I stood in the projection room and looked down on [the] beautiful women workers as they stood quietly ready to take the women through the veil for the first time. I said a silent prayer of thanks to my Father in Heaven for His inspiration and guidance to me during the many days and weeks of preparation for this moment. I felt like I was looking into a little spot of heaven. It was a glorious sight."[6]

Harold Glen Clark also felt keenly his responsibility as temple president:

I never go into the groom's lecture room without praying that I might say what our leaders have asked us to say and what the Lord wants me to say. I try to visualize that in that groom's lecture room may be a prophet, or an apostle, or a great stake president or a bishop to be. Can I say the words in the right manner? May my words turn a boy in the direction of presiding over a great celestial family, from which leaders would come to build the kingdom of God. Reminding myself, through prayer, helps keep me in tune with what my mission is as a temple president.[7]

"I try to visualize that in that groom's lecture room may be a prophet, or an apostle, or a great stake president or a bishop to be."

President Clark also acknowledged the spiritual growth his temple service brought: "I bear witness that because of my temple participation, the scriptures have a deeper meaning. They fill me with more faith and hope and light and appreciation in God as my Father. I have asked many who work there if this has been true of them and they say, 'Yes.' Even our children say, 'Dad, you are different. You are more kind and act with greater patience and understanding. You look more at peace with yourself and others, and you have an untroubled mind.'"[8]

Promoting Temple Activity

In his dedicatory prayer, President Joseph Fielding Smith petitioned that the Provo Temple would be used to its fullest. Brother Clark felt strongly that the temple should be used to its capacity, so he "recommended that the temple presidency and their wives accept as many invitations as possible to speak about the temple." They thought of themselves as "temple messengers." They spoke in many sacrament meetings, firesides, stake conferences, and on other occasions—"sometimes several times each Sunday. It was challenging and time consuming but very enjoyable as well."[9]

As another means to raise temple consciousness, the temple presidency invited stake presidencies from the temple district and their wives to have dinner with them in the temple's dining room and then participate in an endowment session together. Ward bishoprics and priesthood leaders were also invited for special visits. In this way, "stakes, wards, and quorums were charged with the responsibility to promote temple work." [10]

The Provo Temple quickly became "the busiest temple in the Church in endowments and total ordinances performed." During the time of President Clark's presidency, the daily schedule expanded to include fifty endowment sessions, "beginning at 5:30 a.m. and closing the temple about 10:30 or 11 p.m." [11]

President Clark praised the temple's arrangement as "a very workable system" and believed that it would "likely influence the architecture of future temples." The Provo Temple became known as the "working temple." It averaged 3,300 endowments a day during 1975, and in January 1976 broke a record with 76,000 being completed in a single month. However, the numbers were not of primary concern to the temple president, who insisted, "The spirituality, kindness, and thoughtfulness of other people and the Spirit of the Lord in the temple is what we're really proud of, not the numbers. People came because they wanted to and everyone felt uplifted when they left." [12]

Personnel

The president is responsible for the total operation of the temple, specifically to foster the sacred spirit and to see that ordinances are performed correctly and efficiently. The temple's first fourteen presidents represented a variety of backgrounds. Seven of them had been administrators or professors at Brigham Young University, and two others had been educators in different settings; five had backgrounds in business, and one had been employed by the Church; four had served as General Authorities, four as regional representatives of the Twelve, one as an Area Authority Seventy, eight as mission presidents, and six as stake presidents. [13]

A temple presidency is quite different from the leadership in the mission field, where the president is constantly responsible for his missionaries and their work—his counselors perhaps helping with different matters such as relations with stakes or districts. A temple president's counselors are authorized to do virtually everything he does. "We really did work as a threesome," remarked later temple president

Jay Smith (2001–4). Their time is occupied with such activities as conducting shift prayer meetings for temple workers, answering questions, giving instructions to those receiving their own endowment, interviewing new temple workers, dealing with emergencies, and attending varied meetings. At least one member of the presidency should be present in the temple at all times. Over the years, schedules have been worked out, enabling each of them to get away about every third week for three or four days. "I was able to walk out of the temple knowing that a counselor was there to take care of any needs," President Smith acknowledged. "I felt very confident that everything could be done as we had planned together whether I was there or not."[14] The temple president's wife is officially designated as matron, and the wives of the counselors as assistant matrons. Their service is vital, and they function on a schedule like that of their husbands and have particular responsibility for the women who are temple workers.[15]

A surprisingly large group of workers is needed to operate the temple. In addition to the several hundred formally set-apart ordinance workers, other volunteers have helped in such areas as greeting and directing patrons, completing secretarial work, sorting clothing, and cleaning the temple. Many of the volunteers and ordinance

Temple Presidents

Dates	President
1972–76	Harold Glen Clark
1976–80	Orville C. Gunther
1980–82	A. Theodore Tuttle
1982–86	Leland F. Priday
1986–89	Arthur J. Sperry
1989–92	J. Elliot Cameron
1992–95	Arthur S. Anderson
1995–98	Robert J. Smith
1998–2001	Dean L. Larsen
2001–4	Jay M. Smith Jr.
2004–7	Carl W. Bacon
2007–10	Merrill J. Bateman
2010–13	Robert H. Daines
2013–	Alan C. Ashton

How Many Workers Does It Take to Staff the Temple?[20]

Many of these figures are only approximate because they are constantly shifting. In addition to these there have been approximately one hundred part-time or full-time workers.

Category	Dec. 31, 1973	Dec. 1990	2012
Presidency, Matrons, and Other Leaders	6	13	6
Sealers	30	80	90
Ordinance workers	375	1,250	3,100
Other volunteers	375	400	1,500
Total	786	1,743	4,696

"We didn't want anybody to leave the temple feeling that they were not loved. . . . [We] wanted them to enjoy their visit so much that they definitely would want to return."

workers are senior citizens. "Think of what that does to the lives of these elderly people," reflected temple president Carl W. Bacon. However, a truly unique feature of the Provo Temple is the large number of students, primarily from nearby Brigham Young University, who serve as ordinance workers—about one-fourth of the total. "That is a huge blessing," President Bacon pointed out. "After concluding their education, they leave this area with this unusual experience."[16] Of course this introduced a high rate of turnover, so training was an ongoing challenge. This orientation was the responsibility of temple leaders. In addition to the temple presidency there was a coordinator, an assistant coordinator, and an endowment coordinator. There were also coordinators for baptisms and sealings.

Provo Temple officials typically referred to their effort to make it a friendly temple. This was a priority in the training of temple workers. "We wanted the workers to feel positive about what they were doing, especially in their relationships with patrons," emphasized President Jay Smith. "We didn't want anybody to leave the temple feeling that they were not loved or that their interests had not been considered." President Smith's wife, JenaVee, the temple matron, added, "We didn't want to take the chance that they might be offended, but wanted them to enjoy their visit so much that they definitely would want to return. We knew that the workers could learn to do things just right. The main emphasis was to help patrons feel the peace of the temple and the love that we have there and to know that that was the place where they should be."[17]

In addition to the ordinance workers and other volunteers, there have typically been about one hundred full-time or part-time paid employees in such areas as building maintenance, security, secretarial work, laundry, and cafeteria. In addition, the temple has contracted with Brigham Young University to provide certain services—such as landscaping and grounds, including snow removal.

The temple recorder directly hires and supervises those who are employed to work in the temple. Thus he has two major responsibilities. As his title suggests, he certifies the accuracy and completeness of the records maintained in the temple and submitted to Church headquarters. He specifically supervises the brethren at the recommend desk, who, according to temple president Jay Smith, might be thought of as "the face to the temple."[18] He is also responsible for physical facilities; the engineers report directly to him.[19] "I call him the chief operating officer of the temple," explained temple president Robert Daines (2010–13). Because a recorder's tenure typically covers many years, he provides continuity between temple presidencies. One or more assistant recorders have been employed to help discharge these weighty responsibilities.

With these leaders and the hundreds of workers in place, the Provo Temple was ready for decades of service.

Notes

1. Lynn Callister, "Biography of Harold Glen Clark: The Temple Years" (unpublished manuscript), 82.

2. Callister, "Biography of Harold Glen Clark," 82.

3. Quoted in Callister, "Biography of Harold Glen Clark," 83.

4. "Counselors, Recorder Called in Provo Temple Presidency," *Church News*, May 22, 1971, 4; Callister, "Biography of Harold Glen Clark," 85.

5. Callister, "Biography of Harold Glen Clark," 86. The new method of presenting the ordinances referred to the use of film in presenting the endowment, which had been pioneered during the 1950s, and the efficient scheduling of sessions made possible by having six presentation rooms; see the discussion in chapter 3.

6. Callister, "Biography of Harold Glen Clark," 89.

7. Callister, "Biography of Harold Glen Clark," 90.

8. Callister, "Biography of Harold Glen Clark," 95.

9. Callister, "Biography of Harold Glen Clark," 91.

10. Callister, "Biography of Harold Glen Clark," 92.

11. Callister, "Biography of Harold Glen Clark," 92.

12. Phyllis Phillips, "Ex-Temple Leader Reminisces," *Daily Herald*, April 11, 1976, 46.

13. For brief biographical sketches of the temple presidents, see appendix F.

14. Jay Smith, interview by Richard O. Cowan, May 2, 2011, recording in possession of Richard Cowan.

15.   For a complete list of temple presidencies, matrons, and assistants, see appendix E.

16.   Carl W. Bacon, interview by Richard O. Cowan, May 31, 2012, recording in possession of Richard Cowan.

17.   Smith, interview.

18.   Smith, interview.

19.   Robert H. Daines, statement to Richard O. Cowan, February 2013.

20.   Statistics based on interviews and historical notes in possession of the authors.

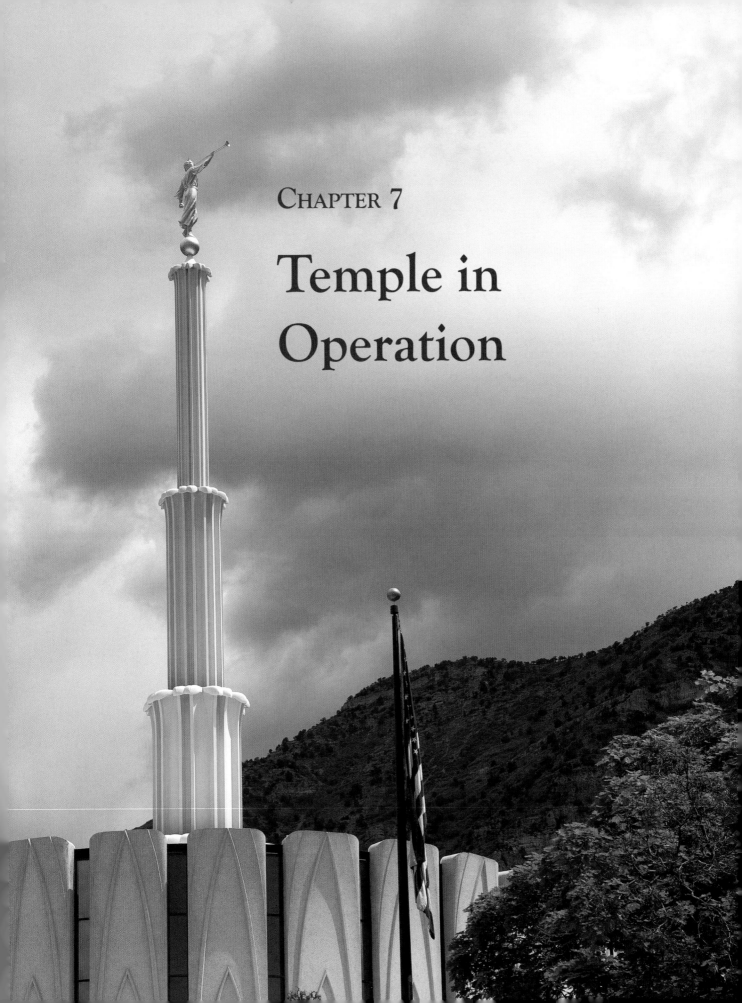

CHAPTER 7

Temple in Operation

1974   Waiting/meeting room created in basement

Special sessions offered in Spanish, for hearing impaired, and so forth

1976   Missionary training complex dedicated nearby (September 27)

1978   All missionaries being trained in Provo (beginning October 26)

1985   Expanded parking opens across the street from the temple

1997   With opening of Mount Timpanogos Utah Temple, Provo Temple no longer the most productive

2000   Escalators removed (May)

2003   Statue of angel Moroni added to temple tower (May 12)

2006   "Holiness to the Lord, The House of the Lord" sign placed next to entrance (July)

South entrance to parking lot added

2009   More ordinances done at Provo than in any other temple during a single year

ince its inception, the Provo Utah Temple has served a wide variety of groups. Over the years, it has undergone several physical upgrades to enable the temple to serve these groups more adequately.

Patrons

In addition to Utah Valley, the Provo Temple district included stakes in the Heber Valley of Wasatch County. Until the 1997 dedication of the Vernal Temple, even Saints in the Uintah Basin of northeastern Utah went to the Provo Temple. Thus at the time of its dedication, the Provo Temple drew from over a hundred thousand Church members. By the end of the twentieth century, Utah Valley's Latter-day Saint population had reached more than one-third of a million.

Over the years, missionaries in training have constituted an important and visible component of those using the Provo Temple. "They bring a special spirit to the temple" has been an oft-stated observation by temple leaders. At the time the Provo Temple was dedicated, all missionaries reported to the Missionary Home in Salt Lake City for a one-week orientation. Missionaries needing to learn a language then received an additional two months of instruction—at the Church College of Hawaii (now BYU–Hawaii) in Laie for the Pacific and Asia, at Ricks College (now BYU–Idaho) in Rexburg for Scandinavia and the Netherlands, and at the Language Training Mission in Provo for all other languages.

In December 1974, however, the First Presidency decided that all language training would be consolidated in Provo and announced that a new thirteen-building complex would be built just southwest of the Provo Temple. Languages formerly taught in Hawaii were offered in Provo beginning in the spring of 1975. The last language to be transferred from Idaho came to Provo in May of the following year. For a time there was severe overcrowding until the new complex was completed and dedicated on September 27, 1976. Two years later, Church leaders decided to close the Missionary Home in Salt Lake City and send all missionaries directly to Provo, where those not needing to learn a new language received a three-week orientation.

New Missionary Training Center near the temple. Courtesy of Richard O. Cowan.

Therefore, beginning October 26, 1978, all missionaries reported to what was renamed the Missionary Training Center (MTC). The resulting increase in missionaries nearly filled the 1,300-person capacity of the new complex, and of course directly impacted the Provo Temple.

Attending the temple was not only an important part of preparation for missionary service, but it was also significant to missionaries personally. Elder Glenn Griffin recalled, "As a new missionary I was quite nervous about the following two years. I will never forget

the peace that I felt whenever I walked the grounds of the Provo Temple."[1] A sister missionary, BreeAnna Barney, appreciated the power she felt as she walked toward the temple with a group of enthusiastic missionaries.[2]

Students at Brigham Young University have been another important group using the Provo Temple. For many students, the nearest temple was hours away from their hometown, so in Provo they were grateful to be only minutes from the temple. Clayton Schmoekel thought of the temple as "a place of refuge" while he was away from home. "Sometimes school can be very difficult, and trials and temptations build up. Every time I go to the Provo Temple I feel less heavy, and I feel that I can handle the situations I am dealing with. The temple always gives me hope," he acknowledged.[3]

When Rylie Jex left home, she encountered new faces and new challenges. "I was grateful for one steadfast thing in my life amidst all the changes," she reflected.[4] Gladys Ibarra, a

"As a new missionary I was quite nervous about the following two years. I will never forget the peace that I felt whenever I walked the grounds of the Provo Temple."

"One of the greatest blessings to me was having a temple nearby. It was the one place where every time I entered I knew where I was, who I was, and I felt peace and at home."

student from Florida, remembered, "When I came to BYU my whole world turned upside down—with its beautiful tall mountains, dry climate, snow, and members surrounding me everywhere I knew I was far away from the tropical paradise I called home. It was a huge and intimidating change in my life, but one of the greatest blessings to me was having a temple nearby. It was the one place where every time I entered I knew where I was, who I was, and I felt peace and at home."[5]

Briana Crook described how driving down University Parkway from Orem, she could "see the Provo Temple lit up in all its glory, welcoming me home."[6] Brooke Lefevor thought of the temple back home as "my temple," but acknowledged that after coming to BYU the Provo Temple had assumed that role. She was grateful that the temple workers became acquainted with her by name; one time when she came alone without her friend, one kindly worker said, "Oh, don't you worry. We will always be here for you; you are never alone." This simple assurance "brought immediate tears to my eyes," she gratefully reflected.[7]

When Kate Kimball was called to leadership in her campus ward Relief Society, she was overwhelmed. However, she acknowledged, "When I attended the Provo Temple as a willing servant of God, I received promptings which directed me how to best fulfill my calling. I was able to see the sisters in my ward as if through the eyes of God. My love for them grew with each thoughtful visit to the temple."[8]

Returned missionaries and married students constituted the ever-increasing number performing endowments in the temple. Many returned missionaries linked attending the temple with memories of their earlier experience at the MTC. Young married students looked upon attending the temple together as a powerful means to strengthen their eternal relationship. For many, Friday-evening temple trips became a favorite date night and included dinner in the temple cafeteria before the endowment session.

Another group of students found the temple to be a particular strength as they prepared for eternal marriage. Cory Hinds recalled that as he took his fiancée to the font to be baptized for the dead, "I felt the Spirit very strongly confirm to me that we were helping those who had gone before. I also, for the first time, came to recognize the priesthood responsibility I was about to assume." Later, when he was present as she received her endowment, he realized, "The joy I felt watching new converts on my mission enter into the waters of baptism did not come close to comparing to the joy I felt as my soon-to-be bride entered into temple covenants with the Lord."[9] Daniel Wahlgren, a new husband, affirmed, "I love the temple and want to share that with my wife. We've only been married a few weeks, but I want our marriage to be a temple, forever and eternal marriage."[10]

Sister JenaVee Smith reflected on these young people who flock to the temple as a response to frequent comments about the increasingly evil conditions in the world. Specifically, she thought of missionaries "who just flow through the temple all day long." She was impressed by the young couples who were going to school or working in the area who would take advantage of a holiday or day off "to make this a special time together by going to the temple. You know the world is in a good condition, because these are the leaders of tomorrow."[11] Still, BYU students and missionaries from the MTC represented only about 15 percent of the patrons using the Provo Temple.

The needs of other diverse groups of patrons have also been met at the Provo Temple. Special sessions for the hearing-impaired were held as early as 1974. Eventually specialized equipment enabled deaf patrons to view interpretation in American Sign Language on a television monitor.

Those who speak languages other than English have likewise been accommodated at the temple. Sessions in Spanish began in 1974. Sessions in Portuguese, German, Japanese, Mandarin, and other languages have also been conducted over the years. More recently, electronic equipment in the temple has enabled patrons to use earphones to receive ordinances in eighty-two languages.

Beginning in the 1980s, the Provo Temple has served the special requirements of yet another group—hundreds called as missionaries to serve in dozens of temples worldwide. They have received orientation at Provo for their temple responsibilities. In cooperation with the Church's Temple Department, a training program was developed for them.

Local Church leaders launched a new outreach program during the early 1980s. Stakes in the area set apart tour guides, particularly from among local seventies. During the summer these tour guides were stationed outside of the temple. They escorted interested visitors—often members of other faiths—around the beautiful grounds and answered their questions about the restored gospel, Latter-day Saint temples, or the Provo Temple in particular.

Youth and Baptisms for the Dead

During the closing decade of the twentieth century and the opening years of the twenty-first, there was a particular surge in the number of youth and young adults coming to the temple to perform baptisms. Mackenzie Mann reflected, "I love to think about the fact that in no other church are there so many college [and high school] age students sacrificing time, sleep, and other things to get up early in the morning to participate in church ordinances."[12] Many observers were convinced that it would be difficult to find a similar example of young people willingly and eagerly getting up early—often before dawn—to perform such a religious activity.

Thousands of unendowed students have found spiritual strength from participating in baptisms for the dead. Because many young men in this age bracket were serving missions, the majority of those who were coming to the temple for baptisms were young women. Going to the temple to do these baptisms sometimes resulted in a wait of up to three hours. "Annoyed about waiting, I spent the first twenty minutes silently complaining about coming," Alexis Bradshaw admitted. She said:

> I felt that I had no purpose there. Clearly, the temple had more than enough people to do the work and I was wasting my entire Saturday just sitting in line. As I watched the people before me participate in baptisms, however, I felt my heart begin to soften in response to the peace of the temple. Instead of worrying about what I needed to do when I got back, I spent the time waiting reading scriptures, praying, and pondering. I realized that the time I had there was a gift, not a

burden. The two hours I spent waiting were the most peaceful, reflective hours of my week. I now love to attend the Provo Temple, and am grateful that there are so many faithful members attending with me.[13]

Another student, Karina Osgood, cherished her experience in the Provo Temple. Those waiting to be baptized sat on typical Church pews facing the font. Temple workers quietly instructed those who were waiting to slide along the pews and then proceed to the font when it was their turn. "I was able to watch the process while taking in the serenity of the Lord's house," she concluded.[14] Even though one young lady, Maren Evans, had icicles in her hair when she returned to her apartment on a wintry morning, she still affirmed, "I wouldn't trade my experiences in the Provo Temple for anything."[15] Jacob Egan reflected, "I'm not sure why, but the scriptures always come so much more alive when I am studying in the temple. I better reflect on their words and find more ways to implement them into my life."[16]

Madison Thornburg leaving temple with wet hair. Photo by Lee R. Cowan.

Because so many young people flocked to the temple to do baptisms for the dead, temple leaders opened the baptistry additional hours in the evening. "On that first Thursday evening," temple president Carl W. Bacon (2004–7) recalled, "So many youth came to the temple that we couldn't handle it. The temple recorder and I went down to the baptistry and explained, 'Thank you for being here. We are grateful you want to be in the temple. But, because of the volume of people who are here, you will need to wait two hours and then be able to be baptized for just one person. You are welcome to leave; neither the Lord nor we will be offended or condemn you.' Nobody left."[17]

"There is a wonderful spirit in that baptistry as students come with reverence and a strong feeling of appreciation," President Bacon reflected.[18] When Dawn Cowan took some names she had researched to the baptistry, she was thrilled to see

"If we had another baptistry," President Bacon acknowledged, "it would probably be filled too."

the number of young people there. "Several benches were full of the youth waiting for their turn to enter the font. As soon as the front bench was empty, the other rows would move up. More were always coming in to take their places. As soon as they came from the dressing rooms they were quiet. All sat in reverent silence as they waited to perform their sacred service."[19] Temple leaders had even asked about the possibility of adding a second font to the Provo Temple. "If we had another baptistry," President Bacon acknowledged, "it would probably be filled too."[20] When plans were announced in 2010 for the Payson Temple, President Merrill J. Bateman (2007–10) quipped, "We're going to get our second font. It will be located in Payson."[21]

Physical Improvements

Each year the temple closes two times for a couple of weeks—once in the summer and again during the Christmas holidays. These breaks in the temple's usual busy schedule have allowed needed maintenance such as cleaning and painting. Carpets, curtains, and drapes have been replaced as needed. Mechanical equipment in the endowment presentation rooms has been serviced or replaced.

Payson Temple rendering. © Intellectual Reserve, Inc.

Other projects have enhanced the temple's facilities. A waiting room was created in the basement in 1974; a number of years later, a folding partition was added to divide it into two separate areas. A second recommend desk was added in 1988 to better accommodate the ever-increasing number of patrons coming to the temple.

For nearly thirty years, escalators on each side of the building were a unique feature of the Provo Temple.

Unfortunately, this custom-designed equipment proved difficult to maintain. Occasionally grease spots stained white temple clothing. Some workers and patrons regarded the escalators' constant rumble as a distraction from the temple's reverent silence. Therefore, during May 2000 the escalators were removed and replaced with ordinary stairways. Interestingly, this major and sometimes noisy construction project was carried on without closing the temple. First on the north side and then on the south, a temporary plywood wall isolated the construction area from adjoining parts of the temple, and the builders accessed the site from outside. As part of this project, newer high-speed elevators were also installed to help those who would find climbing the stairs to be difficult.

Still other projects have specifically added to the temple's beauty. These have included improving the ceilings and adding gold leaf trim to the endowment and sealing rooms. Beautiful chandeliers have replaced florescent lighting panels in several areas, including upstairs hallways. The celestial room was renovated in 2004. Marble flooring replaced carpeting, particularly in areas of heavy traffic on the main floor.

Meanwhile, improvements were also being made outside. In 1985 the area across the street west of the temple was paved to provide parking for 285 additional vehicles. Lighting in the parking lots was also improved. In 2006, a separate entrance from the south facilitated delivery of food to the cafeteria and other supplies to the temple. Attention was also given to improving the landscape on the east side of the temple, which actually is its official front.

The roadway adjacent to the temple's entrance was closed, as the need for greater security was one concern. For example, a car had crashed into and damaged one of the portico columns in 1989. Furthermore, because there was only a one-way flow

Temple's south entrance. Photo by Lee R. Cowan.

Temple entrance after the circular drive was removed. Photo by Lee R. Cowan.

along the temple's roadways, those parking in the south lot needed to drive around the circle past the temple's entrance on their way out. This traffic posed a safety hazard to wedding parties, many with children, as they emerged from the temple. Closing the road also enabled the front of the temple to be beautified. This included the installation of two beautiful fountains, several nicely arranged benches, and gardens that extended down to the road. This beautification enhanced the backdrop for wedding pictures following temple sealings.

At the time the Provo Temple was built, the familiar inscriptions "Holiness to the Lord" and "The House of the Lord" were placed on its east façade. The temple's entrance is on the west side, however, so most patrons never saw these phrases. To remedy this problem, temple leaders requested that these words be repeated in a more visible location. Consequently, in July 2006, raised gold letters proclaiming these sacred ideals were added to the wall at the right of the main entrance, where they could remind all coming to the temple whose house this is and suggest the spirit with which they should enter.

Perhaps the most noticeable change since the beginning of the twenty-first century was the placing of a statue of the angel Moroni on the temple's tower.

Statue of the Angel Moroni Added

Latter-day Saints often associate the statues of Moroni atop their temples with John's vision of "another angel flying in the midst of heaven, having the everlasting gospel to preach unto them that dwell on the earth" (Revelation 14:6). Thus architect Emil Fetzer explained that these statues "symbolize the Savior's charge to take the gospel throughout the world."[22] Elder Thomas S. Monson had earlier taught

Inscriptions added to west entrance in 2007. Photo by Lee R. Cowan.

that "the Moroni statue which appears on the top of several of our temples is a reminder to us all that God is concerned for all His people throughout the world, and communicates with them wherever they may be."[23] Furthermore, because Moroni is specifically associated with the Book of Mormon—whose announced mission is to convince all that Jesus is the Christ—these herald statues remind us of the Savior and the need to prepare for His Second Coming.

Fifteen temples (including Kirtland and Nauvoo) had been built before those at Ogden and Provo. Only the largest two—Salt Lake and Los Angeles—were adorned with the familiar statue of the herald angel. Two years after the dedication of the Ogden and Provo Temples, the Church's third-largest temple, at Washington, DC, would also be fitted with the angel. Because most people were acquainted primarily with these three larger temples, they assumed that statues of the angel Moroni were standard features of Mormon temples—even though the vast majority had been built without them.

Los Angeles Temple's angel Moroni sculpted by Millard F. Malin. Photos by Paul Garnes.

In 1980, the Church announced plans to construct additional smaller temples. The First Presidency emphasized that they would be of "temple quality," and yet could be constructed "at a cost that [would] not be burdensome for members to bear."[24] As a means to achieve the desired economy, towers were omitted. As these smaller temples were still in the planning stages, however, their designs were modified to include a spire, and it would be surmounted by a statue of the angel Moroni. Hereafter, the figure of Moroni would adorn virtually all new temples regardless of their size.

Since the decision to incorporate the angel Moroni into the design of most temples, the familiar statue has been added to several temples that had been built without it. Officials of the Idaho Falls Temple district believed that their temple's tower, which was not surmounted by the angel, was ideal for the statue. The First Presidency concurred, and in 1983 a helicopter was brought in to place the ten-foot figure atop the temple.[25] In subsequent years, several other temples added the angel to their towers. Seven- or ten-foot figures of the angel for the new temples were made of fiberglass, which was stronger yet much lighter in weight, more weather-resistant, and less expensive than steel or bronze. Two Latter-day Saints, Karl Quilter and LaVar E.

Wallgren, had just developed the difficult technique of shaping fiberglass into works of art. Fiberglass copies of Quilter's sculptured angel would adorn over one hundred temples worldwide, including Provo's.[26]

During the fall of 2002, a statue of Moroni was placed atop the Ogden Temple's tower, but there was no announcement about whether the twin temple in Provo would receive the angel as well. This became a prime topic for speculation. Earlier statues of Moroni weighed several tons, which the Provo Temple was not designed to support, but the development of fiberglass made addition of the iconic figures feasible. On Saturday, May 10, 2003, Provo's *Daily Herald* quoted a Church spokesman confirming that the decision had been made to place

Temples Built without Statues of Moroni

Temples	Statues Added
Kirtland, Ohio, 1836	-
Nauvoo, Illinois, 1846	September 21, 2001
St. George, Utah, 1877	-
Logan, Utah, 1884	-
Manti, Uah, 1888	-
Laie, Hawaii, 1919	-
Cardston, Alberta, 1923	-
Mesa, Arizona, 1927	-
Idaho Falls, Idaho, 1945	September 1, 1983
Bern, Switzerland, 1955	September 7, 2005
Hamilton, New Zealand, 1958	-
London, England, 1958	December 15, 2008
Oakland, California, 1964	-
Ogden, Utah, 1972	Fall 2002
Provo, Utah, 1972	May 12, 2003
São Paulo, Brazil, 1978	August 20, 2003
Tokyo, Japan, 1980	December 10, 2004
Sydney, Australia, 1984	September 3, 1985
Freiberg, Germany, 1985	December 20, 2001
Boston, Massachusetts, 2000	September 21, 2001

the statue of Moroni on the Provo Temple, but no exact time was announced. "Keep your eye on the temple, that is all we can say," he wisely counseled.[27] Just two days later, on the warm afternoon of Monday, May 12, two tall cranes were set up on the south side of the Provo Temple. One crane lifted the roughly two-hundred-pound, thirteen-and-a-half-foot golden figure of the angel while a workman in a basket that was suspended from the other crane guided it into place and secured it to the tower.

The approximate 250 onlookers did not know until the last minute which direction Moroni would face.[28] Would he face west toward the temple's entrance, or to the east? Most (but not all)

Opposite:Top left: Angel Moroni up-righted. *Top right:* Angel Moroni flying to the tower. *Bottom left:* Moroni reaches the tower. Note the lightning rod being inserted into the top of the tower. *Bottom right:* Moroni in place. Photos courtesy of Ephraim Hatch.

Temple president Jay M. Smith and his wife, JenaVee, with statue of Moroni. Courtesy of Ephraim Hatch.

Latter-day Saint temples face east, so ideally statues of Moroni should face that direction. Because the Second Coming of Jesus Christ has been likened to the dawning of a new day (see Joseph Smith–Matthew 1:26), orienting the herald angel toward the east suggests a call to prepare for the Savior's advent. The Provo statue was placed facing east. However, because of the shape of the site, the temple itself is rotated slightly from the cardinal points of the compass. Hence people approaching the temple's west entrance saw not only the angel's back, but a portion of his side as well. While the cranes were still present, the golden tower on the temple was painted white, increasing the contrast between it and the gold-leafed figure.

The Provo Temple has been a source of inspiration even to those who view it from outside. A young man, Adam Bryant,

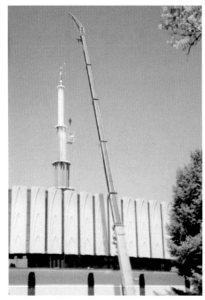

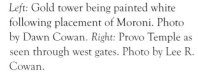

Left: Gold tower being painted white following placement of Moroni. Photo by Dawn Cowan. *Right:* Provo Temple as seen through west gates. Photo by Lee R. Cowan.

reflected, "Entering the temple wasn't necessary for me to feel the calming effects that came with being in close proximity to it. I could park alongside the temple and face the valley, pondering and praying about anything imaginable that could be stressing me."[29] Michelle Gessel had similar feelings: "I will usually drive up there late at night, park my car in the far west lot and gaze up at the glowing spire mirrored by Squaw Peak in the background. There, feeling the peace of the temple's presence, I talk to God the way I would talk to someone face to face. I tell him my fears, my heartaches, my disappointments and my questions."[30]

The Temple's Legacy

The Provo Temple maintained the distinction of being the most productive temple throughout its first quarter century. Several factors contributed to this record. In addition to having its efficient design, the Provo Temple drew from a rich pool of faithful patrons. Over 90 percent of Utah Valley's inhabitants are Latter-day Saints, the highest ratio of any major metropolitan area. Furthermore, it has one of the highest levels of Church activity of Saints anywhere—even excluding the students at BYU. When the Mount Timpanogos Utah Temple was dedicated in 1997, the temple activity of Utah Valley was divided between these two temples. This allowed the Salt Lake Valley's Jordan River Utah Temple—fourth largest in the Church—to take over as first place. Still, the combined activity of the two Utah Valley temples was far greater than had been Provo's alone.

Over the years, the Provo Temple gradually increased its activity, once again becoming the leader during the early twenty-first century. President Merrill J. Bateman believed that "Provo Temple patrons may have performed more total ordinances during 2009 than any other temple had ever experienced during a single year."[31]

The Provo Temple had regained first place, even before the new Draper and Oquirrh Mountain Utah Temples divided the activity of the large body of Church members in the southern part of the Salt

Next page: Photo by Reinhard Franz.

© Kurt J. Jensen.

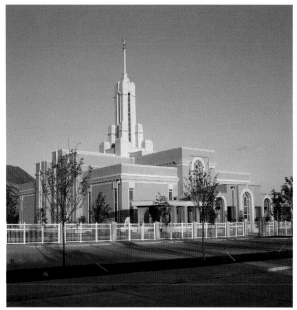

Top: Mount Timpanogos Utah Temple. Courtesy of Jed A. Clark. *Bottom*: Ogden Utah Temple. Photo by Scott Sumner, © Intellectual Reserve, Inc.

Lake Valley. One could only speculate on what impact new temples would have on the future patterns of temple activity in the Utah Valley in general and the Provo Temple in particular.

In February 2010, the First Presidency announced plans to completely reconstruct the Ogden Temple. Immediately the question arose about the future of the almost identical Provo Temple. On February 18, however, Church officials emphasized that there were no plans for a similar makeover in Provo. Elder William R. Walker, a member of the Seventy and executive director of the Church's Temple Department, explained that needed upgrades would be accomplished during the Provo Temple's regular closings each year, which might be extended beyond the usual two weeks to accommodate the work.[32]

Furthermore, substantial improvements have been made in Provo that would not occur if there were plans in the works to completely reconstruct the building. For example, in 2012, a beautiful mural of the Savior teaching people in the Holy Land was added to the front curved wall of the Provo Temple's chapel. Additionally, during the extended closings in 2013, improvements were made to strengthen the temple seismically. These included sinking additional footing piles and then tying the temple's structure more firmly to this enhanced foundation. It appears that the Provo Temple will remain a unique spiritual beacon to residents of Utah Valley as well as to the thousands passing through every day on the interstate.

Notes

1.   Glenn Griffin, statement to Richard O. Cowan, September 14, 2012.

2.   BreeAnna Barney, statement to Richard O. Cowan, September 13, 2012.

Aerial view of the temple. Photo by Mark Philbrick and Jaren Wilkey, courtesy of BYU Photo.

3. Clayton Schmoekel, statement to Richard O. Cowan, September 13, 2012.

4. Rylie Jex, statement to Richard O. Cowan, September 8, 2012.

5. Gladys Ibarra, statement to Richard O. Cowan, September 6, 2012.

6. Briana Crook, statement to Richard O. Cowan, September 13, 2012.

7. Brooke Lefevor, statement to Richard O. Cowan, September 12, 2012.

8. Kate Kimball, statement to Richard O. Cowan, September 12, 2012.

9. Cory Hinds, statement to Richard O. Cowan, September 6, 2012.

10. Daniel Wahlgren, statement to Richard O. Cowan, September 13, 2012.

11. Remarks by JenaVee Smith in Smith interview, May 2, 2011.

12. Mackenzie Mann, statement to Richard O. Cowan, September 12, 2012.

13. Alexis Bradshaw, statement to Richard O. Cowan, September 10, 2012.

14. Karina Osgood, statement to Richard O. Cowan, September 12, 2012.

Opposite: Photo by Lee R. Cowan. *Section start:* Courtesy of Brent Nordgren. *Following:* Photo by Kazumasa Aoyama.

15. Maren Evans, statement to Richard O. Cowan, September 10, 2012.

16. Jacob Egan, statement to Richard O. Cowan, September 12, 2012.

17. Carl W. Bacon, interview.

18. Carl W. Bacon, interview.

19. Dawn H. Cowan, statement, September 2012.

20. Carl W. Bacon, interview.

21. Merrill J. Bateman, remarks to Richard O. Cowan, 2010.

22. "38 Years After Dedication: Statue Will Top Idaho Temple," *Church News,* July 24, 1983, 12.

23. Elmer W. Lammi, "Moroni Statue Tops D.C. Spire," *Church News,* May 19, 1973, 3.

24. "Smaller in Size: 7 New Temples to be Erected," *Church News,* April 5, 1980, 3.

25. "Statue of Angel Is Placed atop Idaho Falls Temple," *Church News,* September 11, 1983, 3.

26. *Church News,* September 4, 1983, 8–9, 13; "Sculptor's Works Top Temple Towers Worldwide," *Ensign,* April 2006, 78.

27. Caleb Warnock, "Provo Temple Will Hold Moroni Statue," *Daily Herald,* May 10, 2003, A1. The *Church News* of the same date does not report this statement. So it may have been given Friday afternoon after the *Church News* had been printed but in time to be included in the *Herald* the following morning; the Church's report the following week—"Statue Finds Home atop Provo Utah Temple," May 17, 2013, 14—did not give any information about when the announcement was made.

28. "Moroni Statue," *Daily Herald,* May 13, 2003, A1.

29. Adam Bryant, statement to Richard O. Cowan, September 10, 2012.

30. Michelle Gessel, statement to Richard O. Cowan, September 17, 2012.

31. Merrill J. Bateman, e-mail to Richard O. Cowan, August 29, 2012.

32. Scott Taylor, "LDS Church Isn't Planning to Renovate Provo Temple," *Deseret News,* February 18, 2010.

PART 2

A Temple in the Center of the City

HOLINESS
TO THE LORD
THE HOUSE
OF THE LORD

CHAPTER 8

The Provo Tabernacle

1849   Fort Utah founded

1867   Meetinghouse or "Old Tabernacle" dedicated (August 24)

1883   Cornerstone laid for larger Provo Tabernacle (April)

1886   April general conference convenes in the uncompleted Provo Tabernacle

1898   Provo Tabernacle dedicated by President George Q. Cannon (April 16)

1909   US President William Howard Taft speaks in Provo Tabernacle (September 24)

1917   Central tower removed from tabernacle, stained glass added to tabernacle

1919   Old Tabernacle torn down

1960s   Seventies quorum in Provo inaugurates tabernacle tours

*T*he building that would become Provo's second temple has a long and significant history. It was a "tabernacle," and it played a different function than that of an ordinary meetinghouse.

Members of The Church of Jesus Christ of Latter-day Saints began building tabernacles upon entering the Salt Lake Valley in the 1840s. They were intended to serve larger groups than would typically be accommodated by ward meetinghouses. These sacred structures were built throughout Utah Territory and other parts of the Intermountain Region primarily for religious devotion, but they also became venues for cultural as well as civic gatherings.

The "Old" Provo Tabernacle

Fort Utah, the original settlement of Provo, was founded in 1849. Two years later it became overcrowded, and the Saints decided to expand southward, relocating their families to undeveloped city lots across the Provo River. This short distance gave members of the Church a chance to peacefully build their town away from the tension sometimes experienced with the Native Americans at the old fort.

Without a dedicated structure for Sunday services, however, Latter-day Saints gathered either in members' homes, outdoors, or in the local schoolhouse. All three locations were uncomfortable and proved to be inadequate. After about a year of meeting inconveniently, Elder George A. Smith, member of the Quorum of the Twelve Apostles and president of the Utah Stake, was appointed to "superintend the building of a chapel for the Saints to meet in for worship."[1]

Soon construction began on a one-room meetinghouse, which was to be completed in 1855. However, due to insufficient funds and an Indian war, the project was discontinued almost immediately. Four years later, in 1856, building resumed, but at a different location—at the present-day corner of Center Street and University Avenue. Construction of this building, later known as the Old Provo Tabernacle, was finally finished in 1867—twelve years overdue.

Despite the lengthy delay, the Old Provo Tabernacle was built with love and pride by faithful Latter-day Saints, and after completion it was considered the "finest house of worship in the territory." Apparently the chapel was "a reproduction of a church attended by President Brigham Young in the east."[2] A pulpit made by Thomas Allman and a gallery of detailed paintings by James Gledhill beautified the interior of the adobe brick building, which measured eighty-one by forty-seven feet. This adornment made the structure "worthy of preservation for that reason alone." Atop the single tower on the front of the meetinghouse was a bell, which over the years "summoned thousands to worship."[3]

The dedication of this original adobe meetinghouse was held on Saturday, August 24, 1867, at the beginning of a two-day conference. A brass band greeted President Brigham Young and his large company. Several members of the Quorum of the Twelve Apostles made the trip southward from Salt Lake City—including Orson Pratt, Orson Hyde, Wilford Woodruff, John Taylor, and of course George A. Smith, who was former president of the Utah Stake. Joseph Young of the First Council of Seventy and Presiding Bishop Edward Hunter also attended. John Taylor offered the dedicatory prayer:

O Lord, we pray Thee to let Thy blessing rest upon this house; upon

Thy people who are assembled here; and upon all who shall assemble

in this house to worship Thee. Let the peace and blessing of God abide

Old meetinghouse or first tabernacle as
it appeared on Center Street after about
1890. Courtesy of Curtis Cropper.

in this place; and when Thy servants the Holy Priesthood shall arise, in this stand, to declare Thy word, let them be full of the Holy Ghost and the power of God; and administer the words of life. And when the people shall assemble in this house to hear Thy word, to pray, or call upon Thy name, let Thy blessing, our Father, rest upon them, and Thy spirit enlighten their minds; and show unto them the beauties of Thy law, and the blessings of the everlasting gospel. And when thine elders shall gather together to call upon Thy name, in the order that Thou hast appointed, then hear Thou, O Lord, their prayers, according to Thy mercy and loving kindness, and answer their petitions.[4]

At this same session, Brigham Young—already somewhat aggrieved by the Old Provo Tabernacle's delayed construction—deemed the building "entirely too small" and held the afternoon session outdoors so that all attendees could hear the dedicatory services. In this later meeting, Brigham announced plans for a new, larger meetinghouse to be built adjacent to the property of the Old Tabernacle. This pronouncement surprised the crowd, since they had literally just completed their first chapel. Plans for the new Provo Tabernacle developed over time, and construction did not commence until fifteen years later.[5]

William H. Folsom.

Plans for the New Provo Tabernacle

On August 30, 1882, local leaders met in the basement of the original adobe building in Provo and appointed a three-man building committee to oversee appropriation and material matters for the new tabernacle. Two days later, the committee—consisting of Harvey Harris Cluff, John Peter Rasmus Johnson, and James Clark Snyder—approved initial floor plans for the building. This project would move forward during years when the Latter-day Saints faced intense persecution arising from the practice of plural marriage.

The tabernacle was designed by William Harrison Folsom, an assistant to Church architect Truman O. Angell. Folsom had been an architect and construction superintendent on a number of important projects throughout the territory—including the Salt Lake

Theater, Provo Theater, St. George Temple, and Manti Temple. Some called Folsom "the most sophisticated architect working for the Mormons," and he was asked to "pattern the tabernacle after the Salt Lake Assembly Hall," which he did.[6] After drawing up plans for the new Utah Stake Tabernacle, construction was to begin in the fall of 1882. But the "lateness of the season" stalled the project. Instead, local leaders stockpiled the brick and lumber until the following spring.[7]

By January 1883, however, some members of the Church in other parts of Utah County became sensitive about having the new tabernacle in Provo. The tabernacle was to be "a stake house for all the people of the county," but many members apparently felt that the new edifice was only "for the purpose of building up Provo." As the project moved forward, many local members "were not as interested as they should be" in fund-raising for the new building, and many "traveling agents" designated to collect money for the tabernacle fund had difficulty in certain parts of the valley, such as Salem, Springville, and American Fork. Eventually, Abraham O. Smoot, president of the Utah Stake, and a number of local bishops traveled throughout Utah County making "spirited speeches" and convinced members that Provo was the "grand center" of the valley and the ideal location "on which to build the Tabernacle."[8]

On April 3, 1883, Harvey Cluff—chairman of the building committee—announced cornerstone-laying ceremonies for the new tabernacle. However, no report of such ceremonies appeared in the newspapers before construction officially commenced in early May, when Samuel Liddiard—a leading brick mason and contractor—was hired to take on the massive project of building the walls.[9] Born in England in 1841, he came to Utah in 1863 after becoming a Latter-day Saint. He lived many years in Provo, where he was responsible for the construction of several business blocks, as well as numerous private residences. James Snyder became foreman of the carpenters who constructed the roof structure as well as the beautiful interior woodwork. Born in Pennsylvania in 1820, he joined the Church in 1857 and came to Provo four years later. A master carpenter, he was in charge of finishing the old meetinghouse, or first tabernacle, and

Abraham Smoot. Courtesy of John Livingstone.

like Liddiard, was involved in building many other important structures around Provo.

The new tabernacle was to be the largest house of worship in Utah Valley at the time. It measured 152 by 86 feet, with the main assembly hall being 126 by 64 feet. The ceiling was 44 feet and 6 inches high, and the central tower reached 147 feet above ground level. The octagonal towers on each of the building's four corners were 88 feet high.[10]

The main hall was entered by large doorways on the east, north, and south. The stand was at the west end of the hall; a gallery or balcony ran around the other three sides. Each corner tower contained a spiral stairway connecting the balcony to an outside exit. A Salt Lake newspaper commented on the unique arrangement of the building's entrances: "The peculiarity is that the gallery and main entrances are separate and distinct, each being entirely free from contact with any other and have a perfect communication with the outside." It also stated that Folsom "claims that this portion of the plan was revealed to him in a vision." The newspaper concluded that "as the arrangement is altogether novel and a great improvement over similar edifices throughout the Territory there is no reason for discrediting his somewhat startling assertion."[11]

Early Use of the Unfinished Tabernacle

In anticipation of the tabernacle's approaching dedication, local leaders began thinking about what functions could be held at the building. The first major meeting in the yet unfinished tabernacle was on August 8, 1885—a memorial service for the late Ulysses S. Grant, eighteenth president of the United States, who had passed away two weeks earlier on July 23. Despite the hall being under construction, two thousand people gathered to honor the former Civil War general; they sat in temporary seats, as the unfurnished building did not have permanent floors, pews, doors, or windows. The building continued to be completed and used in various stages.[12]

Because of the antipolygamy "raid" of the 1880s, many Latter-day Saint men—including some Church leaders—needed to go into hiding in order to avoid arrest. For this same reason, five general conferences convened at locations away from Salt Lake City: both the April and October conferences of 1885 met in Logan,[13] and it was rumored that the upcoming April 1886 conference was going to be held at the new tabernacle at Provo. While the building would still not be completed, construction accelerated to accommodate as best as possible the large crowds sure to gather at the spring conference. The Utah Valley Saints, headed by Utah Stake president Abraham O. Smoot, showed their "enthusiastic desire" to host the annual meeting, knowing that it would result in "a great deal of good" for Utah County.[14]

After a "race against time" and the appointment of several committees, the fifty-sixth annual general conference was held in the nearly completed tabernacle on April 4, 1886. Large crowds gathered to the point that the tabernacle overflowed and "hundreds of persons surrounded the building." Despite the unfinished condition of the tabernacle and the absence of several General Authorities, including the entire First Presidency, those in attendance were "well-satisfied with the treatment received."[15] The October conference that year convened in Coalville, Summit County, Utah. The April conference of 1887 met once again in the Provo Tabernacle.[16]

While these conferences in Provo were a success, the tabernacle suffered serious financial setbacks, causing the building to remain unfinished for several ensuing years. During this time, there was a "continual cry" from local leaders to raise funds through the Utah Valley ward units. Little by little members organized events to raise the necessary funds, including a "Grand May Day Festival" in May 1889 as a benefit to purchase an organ for the building. Still, even after a new building committee was appointed in March 1892, progress on the tabernacle remained slow.[17]

On March 6, 1895, Abraham O. Smoot—perhaps the most vocal champion for the tabernacle—passed away. Smoot had "hoped to live to see the tabernacle completed and ornamented with an organ and beautified as a house of worship," but his dream went unfulfilled. The funeral was held in the still-unfinished tabernacle and was attended by over five thousand people. Edward Partridge Jr., Smoot's first counselor in the stake presidency and successor as president of

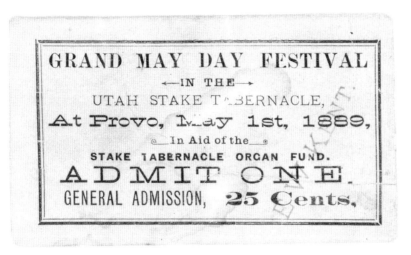

Grand May Day Festival ticket at the Provo Tabernacle. Courtesy of Curtis Cropper.

the Utah Stake, believed the anxiety of fund-raising and completing the tabernacle may have hastened Smoot's death. Smoot's son and future member of the Quorum of the Twelve Apostles, Reed Smoot, became the second counselor in the Utah Stake presidency; together with Partridge, he completed the fifteen-year struggle to raise funds for the tabernacle.[18]

Dedication

After years of struggle and setbacks and at a cost of $100,000 (about $2.8 million in today's money), members of the Utah Stake finally witnessed the dedication of their highly anticipated tabernacle. On April 16, 1898, over four thousand men and women gathered for the two-day event, some even calling it "the largest and most interesting conference ever held in Provo." Poor health prevented President Wilford Woodruff from attending the dedication (he would die just a few months later in San Francisco), but his counselors, George Q. Cannon and Joseph F. Smith, represented the First Presidency. Music was provided by a special choir; a young girl present later recalled how she was so impressed at seeing all the ladies in the choir dressed in white.[19]

By the time President Cannon stood to deliver his remarks and subsequent dedicatory prayer, "every entrance to the building was crowded, and crowds thronged the corridors." After giving a "descriptive account of the work of completing the tabernacle, and speaking in the highest terms," President Cannon thanked everyone—"regardless of creed"—who helped with the building's extensive construction, either by monetary contributions or physical labor.[20] Unfortunately, the text of President Cannon's dedicatory prayer has not been preserved.

Those who worked on the tabernacle—"some of whom were not members of the Church"—could finally "behold with gladdened eyes the change from the former comparatively barren place of worship." Those who contributed to the building's ornate interior—particularly the heavy ingrain wallpaper, ceiling panels, and grained oak woodwork—were especially proud of the final product. According to a writer for the *Salt Lake Tribune*, the most "attractive" features in the hall were the three chandeliers, each holding twenty-four incandescent bulbs, contributed by the Provo Woollen Mills employees. Upholstered opera chairs for the choir and two eight-by-ten-foot paintings, *The Ascension of Christ* and *Joseph Smith's First Vision*, also beautified the internal structure of the tabernacle,[21] which immediately ranked it as one of the very finest ecclesiastical houses of the state.

Perhaps the most attractive feature of the Provo Tabernacle was its nearly one-hundred-foot-high central tower promenade, which drew large sightseeing crowds. The tower afforded "a grand view of

Next page: View of new tabernacle from southwest. Note the open windows on upper level. Old meetinghouse seen to the left. Courtesy of Curtis Cropper.

Turn-of-the-century photo of the tabernacle seen from southeast. Courtesy of Curtis Cropper.

Utah Lake and the surrounding country." Some even called the panorama "the finest that can be obtained from this locality." One BYU student noted that from the top of the tower, "the dwelling houses far below you look as though they might be the habitations of the Dwarfs in Central Africa." Furthermore, it was not uncommon to find visitors sitting and meditating, "thus suspended between heaven and earth" and "enraptured with the awe and grandeur of the scene from the Provo Tabernacle."[22]

Due to structural deficiencies and winters of heavy snow, eventually the central tower began to cause the roof to sag. As a result, the tower was removed in 1917—a difficult project for the period. Because this did not completely solve the problem, the remaining base of the

The Provo Tabernacle depicted as it would have appeared in the late nineteenth century. Painting by Al Rounds, 1992. Courtesy of Intellectual Reserve, Inc.

tower with its promenade walk was removed and the central part of
the roof rebuilt in 1917. In this latter year, stained glass replaced the
semifrosted glass in the windows, perhaps to help compensate for
the loss of the tower. These changes significantly altered the exterior
design as well as the interior ambient lighting.

The Tabernacles in Operation

The old and new tabernacles stood side by side for three decades.
The older building continued to be used for conferences of the
Mutual Improvement Association, Primary, priesthood, and other
auxiliary organizations. It also accommodated overflow for meetings

Old and new tabernacles seen from the
southwest. © Intellectual Reserve, Inc.

Opposite: The "Y Bell" formerly hung in the tower of Provo's first tabernacle. Photo by Lee R. Cowan.

Pipes from earlier organ in tabernacle preserved at Pioneer Museum in Provo's North Park. Courtesy of Curtis Cropper.

in the new tabernacle. The Provo Sixth Ward met there from its inception in 1902 until its own chapel was completed a few years later. The building also served as the site for art and county fair exhibits, athletic events, and other activities such as banquets and dances. The building was finally torn down during the winter and spring of 1918 and 1919.[23] In the tower had been a nickel bell that was cast at the McShane Bell Foundry at Baltimore, Maryland, in 1887. This bell was presented to Brigham Young University, and for many years it rang out from the education building on the corner of Fifth North and University Avenue (now the Provo Public Library). It was later removed from the Education Building and eventually placed in a permanent tower at the southwest corner of the Marriot Center. Known as the "Y Bell," it is customarily rung following athletic victories and on other special occasions, such as graduations.[24]

Space for a pipe organ had been provided in the new tabernacle's design, but none was installed until 1907. The new pipe organ was built by the Austin Organ Company of Hartford, Connecticut. The $9,450 cost (nearly $250,000 in twenty-first-century dollars) was financed by numerous donations, large and small, and by fund-raising events which had extended over several years. Twenty years later it was "vastly enlarged" by the Austin Company, including the installation of a new console. A further enlargement in 1962 made the organ an instrument "to match the revered building in which it is located." Its pipes "form an impressive backdrop for the stand and choir section."[25]

Over the years, stake conferences have been the most common meetings held in the tabernacle. As the original Utah Stake was divided and then repeatedly subdivided, an increasing number of stakes held their conferences there. Until 1978, stake conferences included two sessions—at

Stake conference seen from east balcony.
Photo by Ephraim Hatch.

10:00 a.m. and 2:00 p.m. Later, when the time came that two stakes needed to hold their conferences on the same weekend, afternoon meetings were held once again. But this time, one stake held its session in the morning and a different stake in the afternoon.

Graduation ceremonies for Brigham Young University also took place in the tabernacle through 1940. Traditionally, graduates walked in a procession from the Education Building six blocks away. In later decades, convocations of individual BYU colleges continued to take place in the tabernacle.[26]

The Provo Tabernacle has also provided the setting for various civic meetings. Probably the most notable political figure to speak there was William Howard Taft, the twenty-seventh president of the United States. Interestingly, when President Taft arrived in Provo on September 24, 1909, he was immediately escorted to various points of interest around town, including a walk up the old Temple Hill. He then addressed a capacity crowd in the tabernacle. In addition to the customary red, white, and blue bunting, there was a large banner with the inscription "God Bless Our President."[27] After his speech, President Taft shook hands with nearly two thousand onlookers, or "friends," as he called them.[28]

The tabernacle also hosted a variety of cultural activities, including lyceums and concerts. Hundreds of these events were organized by Herald R. Clark, a dean at BYU.[29] Well-known performers included violinist Fritz Kreisler, baritone Paul Robeson, the Minneapolis Symphony, vocalist Emma Lucy Gates, the Chicago Symphony Orchestra, and the Bach Festival.[30] For several decades, it was the home of the Utah Valley Symphony Orchestra. One particular event stands out in the memory of many Provo citizens. The concert of the famed pianist Sergei Rachmaninoff was briefly interrupted by the passing of a Salt Lake and Utah interurban electric train, whose tracks passed just behind the tabernacle. "Playing one of his own concertos with much gusto before an enraptured audience, the great one suddenly heard the rumble of the approaching electric

Provo Tabernacle as seen from the east.
Photo by John Livingstone.

US president William Howard Taft at Provo Tabernacle. Photo by T. C. "Chris" Larson, courtesy of Curtis Cropper.

train. He ceased playing at a 'rest,' held both hands in midair in a long pause until the noisy car had passed, then crashed down on the next note and continued his performance."[31]

From time to time, the tabernacle has undergone needed renovations. In 1951–52, for example, the roof was reshingled, plumbing and electrical systems were upgraded, and a motorized lift was installed for the stage. Then in 1965–67, exterior illumination was installed, cement steps at the east entrance were improved, a shelter was added over the rear entrance, and an old cottage behind the

Provo Tabernacle Rededication

September 21, 1986

Rededication program cover.

tabernacle was removed to provide space for parking. A major renovation beginning in 1982 included a restoration of the interior to its original appearance, including replacing the pale green paint with antique white. Woodwork was treated to bring out its natural grain.

Following this latest upgrade, the tabernacle was rededicated on September 21, 1986, with a capacity crowd present. President Ezra Taft Benson presided and spoke at the meeting. "Husbands and wives must love and cherish one another. Selfish attitudes must be overcome. Faults must be overlooked. Contention must cease. Husbands and wives must be true and loyal to each other and to the sacred covenant of marriage." President Benson asked his second counselor, President Thomas S. Monson, to offer the dedicatory prayer. In his prayer, President Monson acknowledged: "We feel the spiritual influence of those who have preceded us in standing at this pulpit. Their lives become a living witness and testimony of thy work and we want to dedicate our lives that we might be true to the pioneer tradition of this building."[32]

Over the years, many interested people visited the tabernacle. Many came as a result of leaflets distributed in motels or restaurants, while others came to the tabernacle simply because they were "attracted by its character and charm." As the number of people stopping at the tabernacle increased, local seventies quorums—beginning in the 1960s—conducted tours of the building. They answered questions about the Church as well as the history of the tabernacle. They distributed brochures and copies of the Book of Mormon. When visitors expressed a desire to learn more about the Church, they were referred to the missionaries. "Reports of baptisms stemming from the overall Utah experience, including the tabernacle visit, often filter back."[33]

Thus, for nearly a century and a quarter, the Provo Tabernacle continued to occupy a key place in the life of the Latter-day Saints and others in Utah Valley. An event in 2010, however, would alter the building's future forever.

Notes

1.   Journal History of the Church of Jesus Christ of Latter-day Saints, August 21, 1852, CR 100 137, vol. 31, reel 11, Church History Library; microfilm copy available in L. Tom Perry Special Collections, Harold B. Lee Library, Brigham Young University, Provo, UT.

2.   "Old Meeting House to Be Torn Down," *Deseret Evening News*, July 3, 1917, 10.

3.   "Old Meeting House to Be Torn Down," 10.

4.   N. LaVerl Christensen, *Provo's Two Tabernacles and the People Who Built Them* (Provo Utah East Stake, 1983), 66–67.

5.   As cited in C. Mark Hamilton, *Nineteenth-Century Mormon Architecture and City Planning* (New York: Oxford University Press, 1995), 162.

6.   Laurel B. Andrew, *The Early Temples of the Mormons: The Architecture of the Millennial Kingdom in the American West* (New York: State University of New York Press, 1978), 177; Hamilton, *Nineteenth-Century Mormon Architecture*, 72.

7.   Christensen, *Provo's Two Tabernacles*, 107.

8.   *Territorial Enquirer*, January 6, 1883, quoted in Christensen, *Provo's Two Tabernacles*, 108–110.

9.   Christensen, *Provo's Two Tabernacles*, 108.

10.   Christensen, *Provo's Two Tabernacles*, 113.

11.   *Salt Lake Herald* as quoted in *The Territorial Enquirer*, April 6, 1886, quoted in Christensen, *Provo's Two Tabernacles*, 126.

12.   Christensen, *Provo's Two Tabernacles*, 120, 123.

13.   Andrew Jenson, *Church Chronology: A Record of Important Events Pertaining to the History of the Church of Jesus Christ of Latter-day Saints* (Salt Lake City: Deseret News Press, 1899), 119, 124.

14.   Christensen, *Provo's Two Tabernacles*, 124.

15.   Christensen, *Provo's Two Tabernacles*, 130.

16.   Jenson, *Church Chronology*, 131, 138, 146.

17.   Christensen, *Provo's Two Tabernacles*, 139.

18.   Christensen, *Provo's Two Tabernacles*, 143–44.

19.   Christensen, *Provo's Two Tabernacles*, 144–45.

20.   "The New Tabernacle Dedicated," *Salt Lake Tribune*, April 18, 1898.

21.   "The New Tabernacle Dedicated," *Salt Lake Tribune*, 7; see also "Dedication of Tabernacle Brings Out Many," *Deseret News*, April 18, 1898, 2.

22. *Daily Inquirer*, April 6, 1886, 10, 28; see also *Daily Inquirer*, March 21, 1890, 14, 24.

23. Christensen, *Provo's Two Tabernacles*, 86–87.

24. Christensen, *Provo's Two Tabernacles*, 87–90.

25. Christensen, *Provo's Two Tabernacles*, 155.

26. Christensen, *Provo's Two Tabernacles*, 147.

27. Christensen, *Provo's Two Tabernacles*, 148.

28. "U.S. President Speaks in Provo Tabernacle," *Salt Lake Herald*, September 25, 1909.

29. Ernest L. Wilkinson and W. Cleon Skousen, *Brigham Young University: A School of Destiny* (Provo, UT: BYU Press, 1976), 337, 634. David and Donna Dalton compiled a list of 334 performances between 1921 and 1971 arranged by Herald R. Clark, the majority taking place in the tabernacle. E-mail to Richard O. Cowan, December 17, 2014.

30. Christensen, *Provo's Two Tabernacles*, 147.

31. Christensen, *Provo's Two Tabernacles*, 147.

32. "Provo Tabernacle Rededicated," *Ensign*, December 1986, 70; "Members Admonished to 'Refurbish' Their Lives," *Church News*, September 28, 1986, 3, 7

33. Christensen, *Provo's Two Tabernacles*, 151.

CHAPTER 9

Refiner's Fire

2010   Stake Christmas fireside, last event in the Provo
Tabernacle (December 12)

Dress rehearsal for *Gloria* (December 16)

Tabernacle destroyed by fire (December 17)

Gloria performed at Utah Valley University (December 19)

Stabilizing tabernacle walls commences (December 20)

2011   Final report sets loss at $15 million (March 31)

*S*ince its inception in 1947, the Provo East Stake—like
other stakes in the area—has held its regular conferences
in the Provo Tabernacle. Most other stake-sponsored
activities took place in the stake center or one of the ward chapels.
Such an event was the annual stake Christmas music fireside, usually
held in the stake center on the second Sunday evening in December.
It featured an orchestra made up of stake members and a few invited
guests, a stake choir, and selected soloists. The program presented
honored classics and beloved hymns of the season. For many years,
the stake center was able to accommodate this event, but it attracted
ever-growing audiences. In 2008, therefore, this popular event was
moved to the Provo Tabernacle, where there was plenty of room.
Thus, on Sunday evening, December 12, 2010, stake members gathered in and almost filled the tabernacle for the annual Christmas
fireside. As was the custom, members of the stake presidency shared

Last event in tabernacle, five days before
the fire. Photo by Ephraim Hatch.

brief thoughts about the meaning of Christmas and the Savior's earthly ministry, and members of the orchestra and choir—together with organists and soloists—presented a meaningful and impressive evening long to be remembered. This fireside would be the last regularly scheduled event to take place in the century-and-a-quarter history of the Provo Tabernacle.

"I'm writing, and it's just like it's just coming straight from heaven, it's so wonderful! I couldn't do this on my own!"

Gloria

The next event scheduled for the tabernacle was another holiday season special event. On Thursday evening, December 16, 2010, a large cast assembled in the Provo Tabernacle for the dress rehearsal of *Gloria*, which was scheduled to be presented there the following two evenings. The group included an orchestra, the Millennium Choir, additional singers from the institutes at the University of Utah in Salt Lake City and Utah Valley University in nearby Orem, and outstanding soloists recruited from various parts of the country for this production.

Gloria was part of a projected trilogy by a noted Latter-day Saint composer, Lex de Azevedo, treating the life and ministry of the Savior. *Gloria* presents the circumstances surrounding his birth, while *Hosanna* treats the last week of Christ's life on earth—culminating with the Atonement, Crucifixion, and triumphal Resurrection. The third part of the trilogy, *Alleluia*, presents other aspects of His earthly ministry. The text is drawn completely from the scriptures, and de Azevedo felt that he was being divinely guided as he composed the music. When his producer, Kim Egginton, visited him, she recalled him exclaiming, "Oh my goodness, I'm so excited! I'm writing, and it's just like it's just coming straight from heaven, it's so wonderful! I couldn't do this on my own!"[1]

As producer, Egginton coordinated everything, including "the costumes and the musicians, and the sheet music, and the contracts, and the decorations, and the sets, and the time." A number of people from Brigham Young University were present because BYU Television was going to broadcast the production over its worldwide facilities. "The people there are just wonderful and very talented, just great to work with," Kim Egginton remembered with appreciation.

The usual "church" configuration of the stage was modified
only slightly to provide space for the production. Large, lightweight
arches had the appearance of stone to give the feel of biblical
Jerusalem, and "it was a very nice effect," Kim reflected. There were
also flowers, wreaths, and evergreen trees with twinkling lights.[2] Tom
Ashby, a member of the choir, described the building's decorations
as "phenomenal." He noted that on each side of the pipe organ
"there were three levels of lighted Christmas trees. There were gar-
lands strung along the bottom of the pipes at the base of the organ.
There were numerous lights rigged in the ceiling that projected red
and green splashes along the walls."[3] Kim Egginton remembered, "It
had the feel of old Jerusalem, with the modern-day Christmas. Just
gorgeous. It really felt celestial." BYU Broadcasting even backlit the
tabernacle's stained-glass windows, "so we had this wonderful light
coming into the building." Summing up her feelings, Kim affirmed,
"I can't imagine that the . . . Provo Tabernacle could ever have looked
more beautiful. . . . Everything just shone."[4]

Gloria rehearsal. Courtesy of Kim
Egginton.

The tabernacle "just glowed, just shone, and the Spirit was so strong. I hated to leave."

In the past, *Gloria* had been staged in beautiful Protestant churches, but they were small and not really adequate venues. Reflecting on the privilege to use the Provo Tabernacle and to have the help being provided by BYU Broadcasting, Lex de Azevedo gratefully expressed, "Thank you Lord, thank you, thank you. I felt all along that this was important, and now you're giving me this wonderful venue and all this support." He felt the production had finally come home. Kim Egginton was one of the last to leave at about 11:00 p.m. She reflected that the tabernacle "just glowed, just shone, and the Spirit was so strong. I hated to leave."[5] But the eagerly anticipated presentations of *Gloria* in this remarkable setting the next two evenings were not to be.

The Tabernacle Destroyed by Fire

Different individuals later remembered having smelled things during the dress rehearsal for *Gloria* on Thursday night—things that in hindsight they regarded as suspicious. Most assumed at the time that they were odors typically associated with hot lights or other equipment. Kim Egginton reported, however, that in carrying out her responsibilities as director throughout the evening, she had been in and out of the building, "up and down the stairwells, up in the balcony," and she had "never smelled anything out of the ordinary."[6]

A night watchman was hired to keep an eye on BYUtv's equipment located outside just behind the tabernacle. He was also instructed to enter the building at least once every three hours to be sure everything was all right and that the temperature was favorable for the musical instruments and other items that had been left inside overnight.

At about 1:00 in the morning, a delivery driver passed the tabernacle on University Avenue. He later described seeing what he thought might be thin smoke or fog surrounding the lights just east of the building. A few minutes later, at 1:10 a.m., the watchman entered the tabernacle to make his routine check. He heard an alarm horn sounding and saw a flashing yellow light on the panel. He did

not know what kind of alarm it was, but thought it might be report-
ing a break-in. Making his rounds inside the building, he found no
intruders but reported hearing a creaking sound as he walked along
the northeast part of the balcony. He neither saw nor smelled any
smoke. Upon inquiry, he learned that the alarm had repeatedly given
false signals in the recent past, so he was instructed to disregard it.

Just after 2:30, a security guard at the neighboring Nu Skin
facility reported to the tabernacle's watchman that he saw what
appeared to be steam or smoke coming from the building's roof. The
tabernacle guard immediately entered the building to investigate.
He saw fire burning in two places—one in a ten-foot-wide area on the
center of the stage near the piano, and the other around the edges of
a ten-by-twenty-foot east-west hole that had burned through the ceiling. At 2:43 he called the Provo City Fire Department. Because the
firemen were returning from a call in the area, they arrived at the tabernacle just over one minute later. When they entered the building,
they could see that the fire had progressed further up into the choir
area. When they observed burning debris falling from the ceiling, the
decision was made to "use a defensive strategy, and all personnel were
ordered to operate from the exterior of the structure."[7]

"The fire department initially hoped to salvage the building,"
stated deputy chief Gary Jolly, but "it posed a unique challenge
because of its size and the large wooden timbers used to support its
roof."[8] Its narrow aisles and numerous pillars supporting the balcony
would also complicate fighting the flames.[9]

LeGrand "Buddy" Richards—president of the Provo South
Stake, within whose boundaries the tabernacle was located—received
a phone call notifying him that "smoke had been reported coming
out of the attic of the Provo Tabernacle." He recalled:

> When I arrived at the scene my worst fears were confirmed; smoke
> was pouring out of every opening. No flames were yet visible, but
> apparently the fire department had already decided that the building
> and its contents could not be saved. I watched as the water cannon
> broke through the stained-glass windows to pour water on the precious
> contents in the building in hopes of keeping the fire from spreading to

other parts of the city. I stood in horror as the flames broke through the roof, and when I saw flames appearing over the precious organ I decided I could not watch any longer and returned to my home, devastated by what I had witnessed.[10]

Flames first broke through the roof at about 3:20 a.m. Just over an hour later, a section of the roof at the west end collapsed. At about 6:00 a.m., the entire roof came down with a thundering roar,

pulling the tops of the north, east, and south brick gables with it into the structure. At this point, fire filled the entire interior of the building. Its total loss seemed increasingly inevitable.[11]

Most residents of the area first learned about the fire as they turned on their radios or televisions for the morning news. As they heard a traffic report noting that University Avenue was closed because of the Provo Tabernacle fire, they wouldn't have known how bad the fire was, and may have hoped that most of the building could

Left: West end of tabernacle burned first.
Right: Fire separates roof from west gable.
Photos courtesy of Laura Rowley.

Above: Extending a ladder into the smoke. Courtesy of A4gpa. Photo edited. *Below: Top:* Hectic activity just before dawn. Courtesy of Doug Fallon. *Bottom:* Donna Coleman was one of many who came to photograph the tabernacle as it was destroyed by fire. She took many of the following images. Courtesy of *Daily Herald.*

be saved. Full news reports, however, quickly revealed the extent of the damage.

Only the exterior brick walls remained standing. Normally such walls are demolished quickly so as not to be a safety hazard. Still, when one of the firemen aimed his water cannon at the wall evidently to topple it, fire chief Blair Camp quickly instructed him to back off. "We need to cool these walls rather than knock them down." The supervisor immediately thought, "Why did I just say that? It is contrary to all our training." Likewise, when another fireman suggested that a bulldozer would come to level the walls, he was surprised to be told that they were to remain standing.[12]

Firefighters poured water directly into the building from their extended ladder. Temperature extremes posed a major challenge; while the fire burned at 1,200 or 1,500 degrees, temperatures outside were as low as 17 degrees. As a result, water from the hoses coated equipment with ice and weighted down the trees as spray froze on their branches. Icicles even hung from parts of the burning building. These temperatures and the added weight of ice on their equipment

made work difficult for the firemen. "It beats you down," one of them commented.[13]

In addition to the building itself, other losses were substantial. They included one of the finest pipe organs in the western United States, hundreds of thousands of dollars' worth of video production equipment brought in for the *Gloria* production, choir uniforms and costumes, the Fazioli grand piano (worth over one hundred thousand dollars), a harp, and other musical instruments.[14] For example, Rob Brough was bereft at the loss of his timpani and mallets, which he had collected from all over the world.[15] "It's a total loss for so many people," choir president Dixon lamented, "for businesses, for the BYU production company."[16] Another treasure that was lost was an original painting by Minerva Teichert depicting Peter, James, and John bestowing the Melchizedek Priesthood on Joseph Smith and Oliver Cowdery.

Above: Left: View from Nu Skin balcony. Note tent and trailers brought in for *Gloria* performance. Photo by Laura Rowley. *Right*: Firefighters spray the interior. Courtesy of Tai Gray. *Below*: View through the south entrance. Note the condition of the trees under the weight of the ice buildup. Courtesy of Donna Coleman.

Just before noon on Friday, water continues to be pumped into smoldering structure. Courtesy of Donna Coleman.

As smoke continued to pour from the beloved building, onlookers stood by amid feelings of shock, disbelief, sadness, and questioning. Kathy Kenison recalled playing Christmas carols on the organ in

an earlier year with the doors open so the music poured out into the street. "But on Friday," as one news article reported, "Kenison stood solemnly on University Avenue with other residents, many of whom

Fire continues to burn well into the afternoon. Courtesy of Donna Coleman.

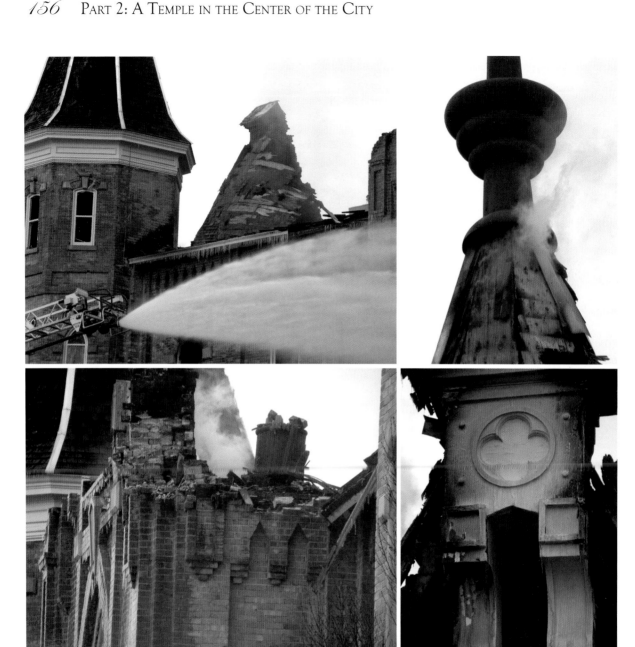

Top left: Water continues to be poured on the tabernacle. Note the west gable still stands. *Top right:* Smoke seen escaping under finial of southwest tower. *Bottom left:* Central support column for stairway leading to attic still visible above the south wall. *Bottom right:* Gablet still adorns the west gable. Images courtesy of Donna Coleman.

had tears in their eyes, watching the street fill not with music but with smoke and soot."[17] The fire continued to burn for a day and a half. Ugly gray smoke could be seen from most parts of the city.

Not until Saturday afternoon could the firemen suspend their efforts to put out hot spots. Provo mayor John Curtis was then taken up the spiral stairway in the northwest tower. Where the stairs would have emerged onto the balcony there was an abrupt drop-off, as all had been burned away. Charred rubble about nine feet deep filled what once was the main auditorium of the tabernacle and blocked entrance through the ground-level doors. "It looked like World War II," he remarked. "It was exactly like what you see in the movies."[18] Even two weeks later, smoldering areas were found as the rubble was removed.

View from Nu Skin balcony. Note the north gable collapsed at the attic vent. Courtesy of Fallon.

On Saturday afternoon, an event unfolded that some observers regarded as miraculous. President Richards was among those taken by fire officials to visit the still-smoldering building. As he looked through one of the front windows, he could see a reprint of Harry Anderson's painting *The Second Coming*. He recalled that he could "clearly see the image of the Savior among the charred rubble. The wall that had supported the picture was even destroyed. Nearly

Glimpses of former beauty remain after the fire. Courtesy of Donna Coleman.

Left: Rubble fills doorway. Courtesy of Fallon. *Right*: Firefighters observe the damage after the fire has been put out. Courtesy of Tai Gray.

Copy of painting which survived the fire. Note how figure of Christ was undamaged. Courtesy of A. LeGrand "Buddy" Richards.

all of the material goods, some of significant cost, were destroyed, but that image stood as a clear reminder that we should remember the Savior. It didn't make it through the ordeal without damage—but left us with a perfect reminder of whose house this was," Richards reflected, "and why there remains great reason to hope, even in the midst of smoking rubble."[19] Firefighters then carefully removed this painting from the tabernacle's front foyer. Although the frame remained intact, it and the painting itself were charred—"except for the exact outline of the figure of Jesus Christ himself." Provo councilwoman Cynthia Dayton, who happened to be present at the time the painting was removed, remarked, "I was so awestruck that I don't have words for it." She expressed appreciation for firefighters who were willing to risk their lives for us and felt that it was "fitting" that they should be the ones to rescue this meaningful piece of art at Christmastime. The painting was turned over to representatives of the Church, who immediately took it to Salt Lake City for "emergency conservation and stabilization."[20]

A Keenly Felt Loss

As Provo area residents were stunned by the fire, they questioned how this disaster had come to be, wondered what the future held—but had no answers. Many reflected back on fond memories of participating in or attending events in that historic building. Longtime residents Monroe and Shirley Paxman remembered being in the tabernacle at sunset when "the sun coming through those beautiful stained-glass windows was really heavenly." Shirley remembered how perfect the tabernacle was when a group of interested listeners filled the building for a speech given by Tasha Tudor, a children's writer.

Brent Ashworth, a downtown businessman who had served as chairman of Provo's Landmarks Commission, regarded the tabernacle as "the spiritual center of the community," whose "size and location made the building perfect for concerts, meetings and other gatherings." He added that its artwork "made it a historical artifact."[21]

Carma de Jong Anderson, daughter of Gerrit de Jong (who pioneered the College of Fine

Fire Timeline

11:00 p.m.	Last of *Gloria* cast exits building
11:15 p.m.–1:10 a.m.	Fire alarm activates sometime during this period
1:00 a.m.	Delivery driver sees mist or smoke near the tabernacle
1:10 a.m.	Watchman enters the building, hears alarm and crackling sound
2:39 a.m.	Nu Skin watchman reports seeing smoke or steam coming from tabernacle roof
2:43 a.m.	After seeing the fire, tabernacle security guard calls in alarm
2:44 a.m.	First fire truck arrives at tabernacle
3:02 a.m.	Decision to fight the fire strictly defensively, from the outside
3:28 a.m.	First flames visible on roof
4:46 a.m.	Portion of roof near west end collapses
6:00 a.m.	Remainder of roof collapses
	Fire continues burning for a day and a half

One of many expressions concerning loss. Courtesy of Donna Coleman.

Painting by Abigail Christiansen Palmer. The color of the sky was chosen mostly for artistic reasons but also as a symbol of the destructive fire.

"I've buried many friends and relations this past year. To have the tabernacle die is too much for me to bear."

Arts at BYU and served as its dean for thirty-nine years), reminisced, "I've lived in that tabernacle. I remember as a four-year-old girl sitting on the benches watching my parents perform." She continued, "I walked around this morning sobbing to see the window fallen in because of heat. To see the smoke billowing, it tore my heart out. I've buried many friends and relations this past year. To have the tabernacle die is too much for me to bear. To see those skeleton windows where religion and art fused in beauty, it tears my heart. It's a landmark of my highest aspirations." Jenny Lund, manager of Church historic sites for the LDS Church History Department, pointed out, "It's not only on the national Historical Registry but is also on the Church's landmarks list. That means it is very significantly historical."[22]

Several shared their feelings on Facebook. Pauline Riley wrote, "Oh, heartbreaking news. . . . My ancestor who was a stonemason helped build this beautiful building. Makes me want to weep seeing these pictures." Likewise, Mariah Inanna Jonas lamented, "This brings tears to my eyes. What a tragedy. I did so many

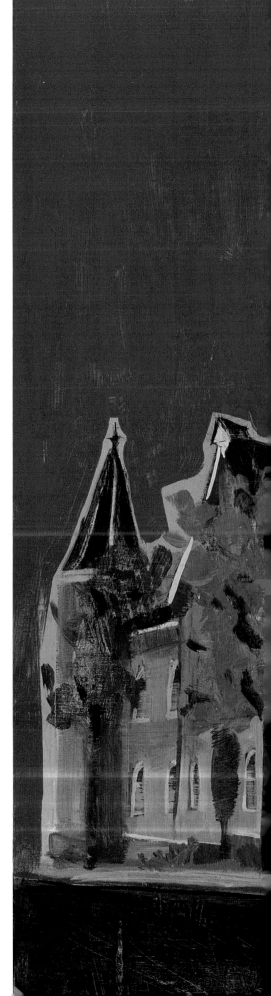

wonderful things in that building growing up and with my husband and children. I now live out of state, but it will be deeply missed."[23]

The Message of *Gloria* Not Silenced

While the devastating flames were still consuming the tabernacle's interior, another drama was unfolding. After leaving the tabernacle late, Kim Egginton did not reach her home in Layton until after midnight. Anticipating that she might have another late evening, Kim chose to sleep in on Friday morning. Finally, her daughter came in and said, "Mom, your phone just keeps ringing and ringing, and you're getting texts, would you please come and see what's going on? I can't sleep." Just then her phone rang; one of the baritones was on the line. "'What are we going to do now?' he exclaimed in his big booming voice. I said, 'What are you talking about?' He said, 'Woman, don't you watch the news? The tabernacle burned down!'" Kim reflected, "I couldn't absorb it. I turned on the news and was

View of the tabernacle from the north. Photo by Lee R. Cowan.

just horrified." On her phone she could see there was call after call and text after text. She called Lex de Azevedo, who was also devastated: "There is no alternate plan. We don't perform. We're done; I'm finished. I give up."[24] After reviewing more of the messages, Kim called Lex back and reported, "Everyone still wants to perform. . . . We can't let the Lord's message be defeated." Lex instructed her to call George Dyer, one of the key guest vocalists in Missouri, to tell him not to get on the plane. But he responded, "No, I'm coming anyway. I'm about to board; we'll figure something out."[25]

Kim's task was to find another place where they could perform. Everything at BYU was booked. She found that the Alpine Stake Tabernacle in American Fork was surprisingly available. Normally, the annual *Messiah* sing-along was scheduled there on that evening, but it had been moved to another week; arrangements were made to perform there Friday night. "So then we started to see miracle after miracle,"[26] Kim gratefully testified. President Matthew Holland of Utah Valley University offered the McKay Special Events Center free of charge, as well as a crew to operate sound and lights, for a Sunday evening performance. The Hale Center Theater offered costumes to replace those which had been burned. Therefore, Kim began preparing for two performances, each in a distinctly different venue.

The performance in the Alpine Stake Tabernacle, which took place on Friday evening while the tabernacle was still burning, was like a funeral. Many dignitaries attended the UVU presentation on Sunday night—including Utah's governor, Gary Herbert. These performances not only celebrated Christ's birth, but in a very real sense became solemn memorials to the lost tabernacle.

Almost immediately, there was a groundswell of interest in rebuilding the tabernacle. A day after the fire, Provo's *Daily Herald* announced that the Provo Foundation—an organization of volunteers promoting progress in the city—had set up a special bank account which could receive donations toward the reconstruction of the tabernacle. The article also indicated that many civic and business leaders in the community were "leading the charge to rebuild and heal."[27] At the two *Gloria* performances, many people wanted to make substantial donations for the restoration of the Provo Tabernacle. They

"We started to see miracle after miracle."

wanted to help right then, but no decision had yet been made concerning the future of the building. Some of the funds donated at the two performances helped compensate individual musicians for the instruments they had lost.[28]

Investigating the Causes

Provo fire marshal Lynn Schofield arrived on the scene at 3:08 a.m. on the morning of the fire—less than a half hour after the first fire trucks. He immediately walked around the building, paying attention to where smoke could be seen and what its color was—darker smoke indicating a less complete combustion of materials. He carefully noted where the fire was first seen and how it progressed.[29] He issued a warning that anyone attempting to enter the site to collect mementos, or for any other purpose, was subject to being prosecuted, because—at least for the time being—it was being treated like a crime scene.[30]

Under Schofield's direction and with the cooperation of David Peterson, of the Church's Risk Management Department, a task force made up of representatives from The Church of Jesus Christ of Latter-day Saints (which owned the building), the State of Utah, and the Provo Fire Department interviewed dozens of individuals during the next several days. "It's standard procedure to interview the last people in the building. In this case, there were a couple hundred of them," he stated. These eyewitnesses included the night watchman, broadcast and lighting technicians, *Gloria* cast members, and those with responsibility for the tabernacle, as well as anyone in the general public who might have seen anything that awful night. Schofield expected to spend every hour of every working day at the tabernacle for the next few weeks in an attempt "to identify exactly what destroyed the iconic building."[31]

John Emery, a project manager employed by Jacobsen Construction of Salt Lake City for a dozen years, had received an order to head to Provo Friday morning while the building was still engulfed in flames. His assignment was to cooperate with the firefighters and to give attention to possibly preserving any parts of the building.

Once the fire was put out, an immediate goal was to stabilize the brick walls of the tabernacle, making it safe for investigators to go inside to look for clues. On Saturday, Emery met with Schofield to confirm plans. On Monday, December 20, Jacobsen Construction began what the fire department described as "hazard mitigation and structural stabilization."[32] Emery invited Roger Jackson and David Brenchley to examine the brick walls with him because he "valued their knowledge of old masonry."[33] Both men would play a significant role in subsequent months. "After preliminary analysis," the group concluded only four days after the fire, "the masonry system is in very good condition. We feel very strongly that this building can be renovated to its original granduer."[34] The original plan was to demolish the remains of the west gable—the only one remaining after the fire. A selective demolition of other areas was contemplated as well. This plan was changed, however, in favor of installing steel bracing to preserve the brick walls as completely as possible. Work started on the western wall and then moved to the south before eventually encircling the entire structure.[35] The reinforced steel buttresses were set on concrete footings, providing additional stability. Remaining pieces of the roof were removed using chain saws and cranes.

On December 29—nearly two weeks after the fire—the fire marshal escorted members of the press around the tabernacle, even climbing up the circular stairs in the southeast turret. In the stairwell, the green walls were streaked with smoke, but the carpet was still surprisingly soft underfoot.[36] "It really appears the investigation is going really slowly," Schofield admitted, "but the reality is we've been 10, 12, 14 hours a day interviewing people, reviewing building plans, watching videotapes. Actually, the investigation is progressing very nicely.

Top: Steel construction of the support buttresses to stabilize the walls. *Bottom:* Bars used to strengthen the window openings. Photos by Lee R. Cowan.

Top: Concrete blocks poured to create firm foundation for buttress supports on the east. *Bottom:* Reinforced south window. Note leading and stained-glass remnants. *Opposite:* Northwest tower seen through east window. Photos by Lee R. Cowan.

. . . We've just got to get inside." They couldn't do this, however, until the brick walls were completely stabilized.[37] The object was to search for clues concerning the origin and spread of the fire. "This is a great big jigsaw puzzle," Schofield remarked, "and it's got 25,000 pieces. What we're trying to do right now is take all of those 25,000 pieces, whether it's physical evidence or witness statements or a three-second clip off of a videotape, and put those pieces of the puzzle together." Scott Trotter, spokesman for the Church, acknowledged, "We anticipate that it will be several weeks before we are able to determine next steps regarding the Provo Tabernacle."[38]

Based on photographs taken from a Utah Highway Patrol helicopter, a grid pattern was established inside the building. Reinforced plastic sheeting was placed on the grass to the north of the building, and a grid identical to the one inside was laid out so items brought from the building could be placed in their relative locations. "Every item from the burned-out interior will be documented, photographed, and cataloged, its location marked using a GPS unit, and then moved to a huge plastic sheet to the north of the building. There, fire investigators and historic preservation teams will be able to sort through the debris for clues to a cause and to potential future restoration." The process of removing rubble from the building would last from January 3 to 21. "There's a lot of heavy lifting, though for workers it's a labor of love," Dylan Curtis, part of the fire cleanup crew, remarked. "It feels kind of cool to be part of it."[39]

On January 19, about one month after the fire, the investigators released a preliminary report. Provo's fire chief Blair Camp disclosed that investigators were convinced that the fire did not result from arson. "We've studied the burn patterns in the building. We have

also brought in an accelerant-sniffing K-9. We found no accelerant in the building. We're confident the fire was accidental."[40] He also reported that seventy-five tons of debris had been removed from the building and investigators had spent over eight hundred man hours in their review of evidence so far.[41] Chief Camp acknowledged that he had fought fires with more flames, but because of the building's prominence and historical significance, "the tabernacle fire was the most significant he has seen."[42]

On March 31, 2011, Schofield issued his 135-page final report. The report set the loss at fifteen million dollars.[43] Investigators determined that the fire started in the tabernacle's attic because of the watchman's description, and sometime between 11:15 p.m. Thursday and 1:10 a.m. Friday the alarm system detected a problem in the attic.

Debris being removed from tabernacle. Photo by Donna Coleman.

"The Task Force has concluded that . . . the most probable cause of the fire at the Provo Tabernacle was a heat source" such as one of the 300-watt lights removed from the ceiling "placed too close to combustible materials."[44]

The investigators identified several factors that likely contributed to the devastating damage caused by the fire: the fire alarm sensors were located too low in the attic, so they would not likely detect a fire until it had become quite extensive; the alarm was not monitored off-site; and the alarm would not likely be heard unless someone was inside or very close to the building. In addition to its frequent false alarms, the fire alarm system had other problems: one of the smoke sensors had failed a routine test just two weeks earlier. There were other factors besides the faulty alarm system that contributed to the disaster: the building lacked an automatic sprinkler system,[45] and the lightweight construction of the arches set up for the *Gloria* production allowed the fire to spread rapidly from the stage into the choir loft. Finally, the report concluded that human error was a factor.

While there were many significant losses, surprisingly, this baby-changing table survived the fire. Photo by Lee R. Cowan.

Observers wondered if the building could have been saved had the fire been discovered at 1:00 a.m., when the alarm was first heard. However, the report concluded that even if firemen had been called at this time, it would have been difficult for them to fight the fire and save the building. By that time, the fire in the attic was probably "large and well developed." Furthermore, the only access to the attic was a narrow spiral staircase that would allow only a single firefighter to ascend at one time. There would not have been enough room for the number of hoses required to fight a fire of this size. Finally, "once they arrived at the attic, firefighters would have found medium to heavy smoke conditions in a space that was unfamiliar and elevated nearly 45 feet above the floor level. It is unlikely that a fire command officer would place crews into this type of danger."[46]

After the fire department had released its lengthy report, Church spokesman Scott Trotter issued the following statement: "The Provo Tabernacle was a meaningful part of Church history and the Provo community. . . . The recent fire is a tragedy for all who loved the building and its link to our pioneer past."[47]

Opposite: Top left: West gable in traction. *Top right:* Looking from the west through the second floor windows. Note the county courthouse scene. *Bottom:* Detail of surviving leading and stained glass. Photos by Lee R. Cowan.

Notes

1. Kim Egginton, interview by Richard O. Cowan, December 17, 2011; recording and transcript in Cowan's possession.

2. Egginton, interview.

3. Genelle Pugmire, "Birth and Life of a Community Icon," *Daily Herald,* December 18, 2010, A6.

4. Egginton, interview.

5. Quoted in Egginton interview.

6. Egginton, interview.

7. "The Provo Tabernacle Fire: Origin, Cause, and Circumstances," official report submitted March 31, 2011, by the fire marshal (online at http://www.provo .org/img/File/tabernacle_final_report.pdf), 3; hereafter cited as official report.

8. Jim Dalrymple, "Heritage Lost," *Daily Herald,* December 18, 2010.

9. Joe Pyrah, "Building's Charm Made Fire Hard to Fight," *Daily Herald,* December 18, 2010.

10. A. LeGrand Richards, "For the Temple of God Is Holy, Which Temple Ye Are," remarks written December 8, 2011, to be given at stake conference December 11, 2011, 1–2; typescript in possession of Richard Cowan.

11. Official report, 7–9; see also Dalrymple, "Heritage Lost," A4.

12. Conversation with Lynn Schofield, May 19, 2015; John Emery to Richard Cowan, May 18, 2015; story related by Sylvia Newitt, February 15, 2015; notes in possession of Richard Cowan.

13. Pyrah, "Building's Charm," A5.

14. Dalrymple, "Heritage Lost," A4.

15. Egginton, interview.

16. Dalrymple, "Heritage Lost," A4.

17. Dalrymple, "Heritage Lost," A4.

18. Caleb Warnock, "Provo Mayor: 'It Looked Like World War II,'" *Daily Herald*, December 19, 2010, A2.

19. Richards, "Reflections on the Provo Tabernacle," 2; typescript in possession of Richard Cowan.

20. Caleb Warnock, "Scorched Portrait of Christ Salvaged from Building," *Daily Herald*, December 19, 2010, A1–A2.

21. Heidi Toth, "Community Reflects on Loss of Provo Landmark," *Daily Herald*, December 18, 2010, A5.

22. Pugmire, "Birth and Life of Icon," A6.

23. "Shared on Facebook," *Daily Herald*, December 18, 2010, A5.

24. Quoted in Egginton interview.

25. Quoted in Egginton interview.

26. Quoted in Egginton interview.

27. "Fundraising for a Rebuild," *Daily Herald*, December 18, 2010, A4.

28. Egginton, interview.

29. Official report, i, 9–10.

30. Warnock, "World War II," A1–A2.

31. Jim Dalrymple, "Weather Hinders Tabernacle Fire Probe," *Daily Herald*, December 21, 2010, A5.

32. Official report, 39.

33. John Emery, statement to Richard Cowan, May 12, 2015.

34. David Brenchley, statement to John Emery, December 21, 2010, copy in possession of the authors.

35. Jim Dalrymple, "Crews Work to Remove Debris and Stabilize Sections of Building," *Daily Herald*, December 29, 2010, A1–A2.

36. Dalrymple, "Crews Work to Remove Debris," A2.

37. John Daley and Marc Giauque, "Journalists Tour Provo Tabernacle," *Deseret News*, December 29, 2010, B2.

38. Dalrymple, "Crews Work to Remove Debris," 1; see also Daley and Giauque, "Journalists Tour Provo Tabernacle," B2.

39. Daley and Giauque, "Journalists Tour Provo Tabernacle," B2.

40. Jared Page, "Alarm in Provo Tabernacle Sounded Long Before Alert," *Deseret News*, January 20, 2011, A1.

41. Page, "Alarm in Provo Tabernacle," A5.

42. Jim Dalrymple, "Investigators Rule Out Arson: Building Alarm Ignored Before Fire," *Daily Herald*, January 20, 2011, A5.

43. Jim Dalrymple, "Officials Put Final Damage to Landmark at $15 Million," *Daily Herald*, April 1, 2011, A1.

44. Official report, ii.

45. Official report, 84.

46. Official report, 84.

47. Dalrymple, "Landmark at $15 Million," A5.

Next page: Photo by Brent Nordgren.

CHAPTER 10

From Tabernacle
to Temple

2010   Tabernacle destroyed by fire (December 17)

Stabilizing tabernacle walls commences (December 20)

2011   Church buys property on block to the south of the tabernacle (August)

Plans announced to rebuild the tabernacle as a temple (October 1)

Foundation of first tabernacle located by ground-penetrating radar (November)

2012   Student archaeologists excavate first tabernacle (winter)

Name selected for Provo City Center Temple (spring)

ven before the Provo City Fire Department issued its final report, important behind-the-scenes developments were moving forward to save what remained of the tabernacle. Within hours of the devastating fire, individuals who would play a key role became intimately involved.

The Architect

Like so many others, Roger Jackson was shocked by news of the Provo Tabernacle fire. During that weekend, at the urging of an architectural historian friend, he contacted Church officials with whom he had been working and urged them not to allow the building to be torn down. Although the flames had gutted the wooden interior, the brick walls had likely remained sound. He reminded them that "we had done the same thing to the Uintah Stake Tabernacle except that we didn't use fire but tore everything out on our own." He was able to display a photo of the future Vernal Temple when there were only gutted brick walls and point out that enough remained in Provo to allow the structure to be rebuilt. Within days following the Provo fire, Church officials were eager to consider Jackson's ideas and commissioned him to be the architect of this project.

Roger P. Jackson inherited his love of architecture from his father, Richard W. Jackson, who had a long career as an architect and had designed dozens of Latter-day Saint meetinghouses.[1] Immediately after Roger received his master of architecture degree from the University of Utah in 1984, he went to work with the firm of FFKR Architects. Important projects included the remodeling of various school buildings and the expansion of the Utah State Capitol.

Over the years, Robert Fowler, one of FFKR's founders, had been the architect for remodelings and upgradings at the Hotel Utah. In 1987 when the Church announced that it would close the hotel and convert it into an office building, Fowler's firm received the contract. This included a thorough seismic upgrade, rebuilding the tenth floor, and putting in the motion picture theater. By the time this work was completed in 1993, Roger Jackson had become the architect in charge of this project.

Because of this expertise with work on older buildings, FFKR received the contract the following year to rebuild the Uintah Stake Tabernacle into the Vernal Utah Temple and Jackson became the project architect. In 1999 he received the same role in rebuilding the historic Nauvoo Temple. Roger Jackson was also the architect for the 2005–7 renovation of the iconic Salt Lake Tabernacle. He remarked that these latter projects were "not once-in-a-lifetime but once-in-ten-thousand-lifetimes' experiences," and marveled that he had two of them. FFKR and Jackson even became the architects for other temple construction projects including Draper, Kansas City, and Brigham City. Hence his assignment in Provo became one more in this series of "once-in-ten-thousand-lifetimes' experiences."

FFKR named David Brenchley to work under Jackson's direction as the firm's manager for the Provo project. He would carry a heavy responsibility as director of FFKR's large architectural team and as the firm's direct contact with contractors. Mark Wightman

Architect Roger P. Jackson. Photo by John Sturr.

became the member of the architectural team directly responsible for interior design. All these individuals worked closely with the Special Projects Department of the Church.

Other Key Team Members

Two others became involved almost from the beginning. In January 2011, the Church hired Andy Kirby to be "the site project manager to oversee the activities for support, fire and insurance investigations and cleanup of the Provo Tabernacle."[2] He was born in Provo, grew up in nearby Mapleton, and could remember attending stake conferences and other events in the Provo Tabernacle. He earned his degree in civil engineering at Brigham Young University. Kirby was impressed with the pioneers' craftsmanship and concluded that the tabernacle had been "built by hand with love."[3] He felt that their efforts to erect such a beautiful building "represented their dedication to God." He therefore regarded the privilege of helping to preserve this structure as a great honor.[4]

Emily Utt, a curator in the Historic Sites Division of the Church History Department, worked very closely with Kirby. She had received a bachelor of arts in both history and religious studies, with a minor in sociology, from Case Western Reserve University in Cleveland, Ohio. At the Church History Department she had conducted preservation work on the Gadfield Elm Chapel in England, historic sites in Southern Utah, and buildings on Temple Square. At the time of her work in Provo, she was pursuing a master of arts degree in historic preservation from Goucher College in Baltimore, Maryland.

Church officials needed to know what had survived the fire so they could determine whether or not it would be physically possible to save the building. A variety of tests were performed on the brick walls to discover the impact the fire might have had on their stability. Kirby and Utt spent endless hours sifting through the tabernacle's remains. "We wanted to look through every inch of debris," Utt recalled. Andy remembered seeing Emily covered with soot as she sifted through buckets of material. This work was done during the

Top: Bricks salvaged for possible future use. *Bottom:* Decorative stones reflect building's architecture. Photos by Donna Coleman.

winter. "It was really cold," she reflected. Even though they found hot spots as long as four or five months after the fire had been extinguished, they also uncovered items encased in ice which had formed from the water used in fighting the flames.

As pieces of debris, both large and small, were laid out on the grid formed on the grass north of the building, a wide variety of items were found. This included newel posts, pieces of railing or wooden molding, hardware from doors, hundreds of nails, and much more. In some cases, the fire had actually uncovered features that had been hidden for decades. It burned away layers of later paint or remodeling to reveal original colors of paint or designs of wallpaper. The goal was to re-create a basic floor plan as well as detailed plans for specific features. "My favorite discovery," Emily Utt concluded, was some original stenciling that had been hidden behind two temporary walls, some mechanical equipment, and four layers of wallpaper—all burned away by the fire. The investigators took photographs and had architects prepare careful drawings of these items that would provide keys to an understanding of the building's original architecture and character.

Andy Kirby and Emily Utt prepared a thick volume to document all they had discovered. "We know this building better than any other tabernacle in the Church," Emily believed. They spent an interesting six months meeting with the architect and others, exploring possible options for what could be done with the Provo Tabernacle.

John Emery, who also had been on-site since the morning of the tabernacle fire, would carry an important responsibility as Jacobsen Construction's project manager. He was an experienced builder and contractor. He had been with Jacobsen for twelve years and had directed a number of large projects for them. He had worked on remodeling the Idaho State Capitol and the Salt Lake Tabernacle. He affirmed that he loved his work and enjoyed coming to the site each morning.[5]

Questions about the Tabernacle's Future

While the walls were being stabilized, they were cleaned so that most of the brick work looked brighter than it had in years. The fire department had completed enough of its investigation by the end of January that custody of the structure was returned to the Church.[6] This enabled Andy Kirby, Emily Utt, and their associates to push their work even faster.

As winter turned into spring, interest in the tabernacle's destiny mounted. "Rebuild Provo Tabernacle" was a Facebook group formed by interested people who were "dedicated to helping Provo raise money to rebuild the tabernacle or at least help and encourage the Church of Jesus Christ of Latter-day Saints to do so." Ingrid M. Asplund, a member of the group, asserted, "This building is priceless. . . . Let's rebuild it for ourselves, for our community and for our posterity."

Kirk Huffaker, executive director of Utah Heritage Foundation, believed the tabernacle's destruction had "removed a piece of historic fabric from the city. It has taken away an important piece of the story of the city's rise to modern prominence, and eliminated opportunities for economic development downtown from regular use, special events and tourism." He emphasized that his statewide organization was standing by to lend its resources and expertise to discussions of the tabernacle's future.

Opposite: Map created by Reginald Beales.

Many went through a grieving process for some time. Helen Anderson—Provo City community relations and public information officer—acknowledged, "The fire was devastating, not just for the city but also the wider community. Many went through something of a grieving process for days and weeks after. But I think most people trust that the LDS Church will make a good decision about what to do next." Meanwhile, the Church and other organizations sorely missed the tabernacle as a venue for conferences, concerts, graduations, and a multitude of other events.

The fact that the walls had been cleaned and stabilized augured well for the tabernacle's future. After such care had been taken, it was not likely that the building would be torn down. Other developments during coming weeks gave further reason to believe that an important future was being planned for the Provo Tabernacle.[7]

For weeks, a group had been meeting at Church headquarters to review what had been found at the tabernacle site and to consider confidentially how these findings might give direction to plans for restoring the building. In June 2011, without any explanation, these meetings were suspended. Participants were left to speculate what the reason might be.

Other developments were known more widely. On Wednesday, August 31, a Facebook post announced that the LDS Church had bought the Travelodge Motel, located across the street to the south of the tabernacle, and the Los 3 Amigos restaurant next door. The motel had been in operation in that location since 1959. Its owner acknowledged that his property had been sold: "But I am under contract to not say who I have sold to." However, the restaurant owner stated that he "signed papers on the sale to the LDS Church on Wednesday." Responding to these reports, Church spokesman Scott Trotter reiterated that the Church was "still evaluating plans for the Provo Tabernacle and surrounding area" and acknowledged that "to provide options moving forward we have acquired the hotel and restaurant immediately south of the Tabernacle."[8]

In September, the Provo City Council agreed to sell a portion of 100 South Street and additional property in the block south of the tabernacle to the Church's Corporation of the Presiding

Surroundings of the Provo Tabernacle

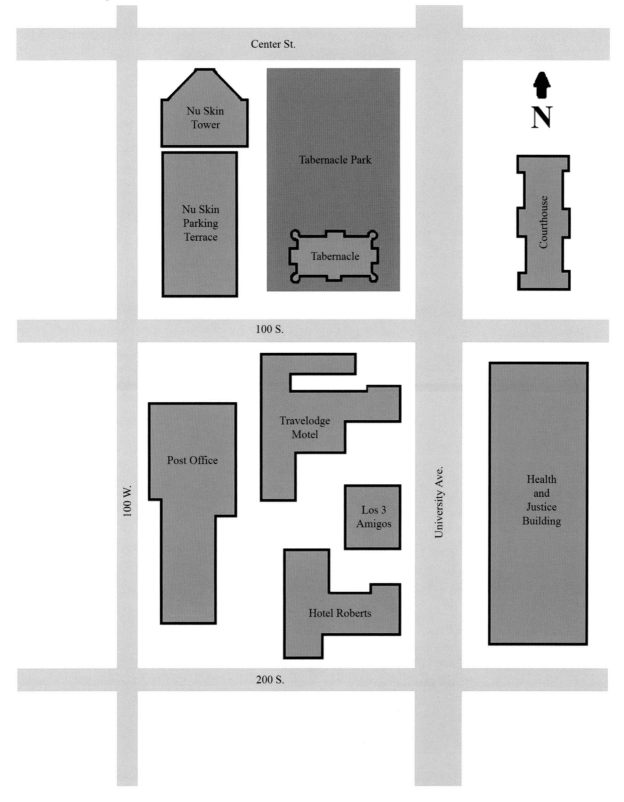

Bishopric. This was a vacant lot on the southeast corner of the block where the old Hotel Roberts had stood; interestingly, this was where missionaries first stayed when they came to Provo for language training beginning in 1961. The hotel was demolished in 2004, and the property was purchased by the city in 2010. "The LDS Church will purchase the property for $500,000. With that sale nearly the entire block of 100 to 200 South and University Avenue to 100 West will be owned by the LDS Church. Only the post office remains."[9] Since the postal service had announced that it was downsizing its operation, and therefore closing many local post offices, the Church hoped to buy this property as well.[10] A few months later, the Church bought the multilevel Nu Skin parking terrace just across the street from the post office.[11]

With all these purchases, rumors continued to run rampant concerning the tabernacle's future. They included the possibility of the Church creating a walking garden or shopping center, speculation on what country would provide a new organ for the reconstructed tabernacle, and the possibility of restoring the tall central tower that originally graced the tabernacle's roof. Provo mayor John Curtis confided that he was constantly being asked about what would happen to the Provo Tabernacle. "I have been asked in meetings, at the grocery

Hotel Roberts. Courtesy of Cowan MTC Archives.

store, and I was even asked when I was visiting in Des Moines, Iowa, what the church would do. This shows how important it is to our community." Paul Glauser, Provo Redevelopment Agency director, indicated that he had heard about the Church's negotiating to purchase the properties south of the tabernacle and added, "What I'm hearing is pretty exciting if it's true. Whatever the Church does it will be first class."[12]

As the fall 2011 general conference approached, many in Provo hoped the Church might announce something "at least about the tabernacle itself." People in the city administration and others close to the situation, however, sounded a voice of caution: "Wisdom dictates the LDS Church will announce when ready."[13]

President Monson's Announcement

As had become the custom in recent years, in his opening remarks in general conference President Thomas S. Monson announced plans for several new temples. These plans included such locations as Barranquilla, Colombia; Durban, South Africa; Kinshasa in the Democratic Republic of the Congo; Star Valley, Wyoming; and Paris, France. "First, may I mention that no Church-built facility is more important than a temple," the prophet emphasized.

President Thomas S. Monson.
© Intellectual Reserve, Inc.

> Temples are places where relationships are sealed together to last through the eternities. We are grateful for all the many temples across the world and for the blessing they are in the lives of our members." Then he continued, "Late last year the Provo Tabernacle in Utah County was seriously damaged by a terrible fire. This wonderful building, much beloved by generations of Latter-day Saints, was left with only the exterior walls standing. After careful study, we have decided to rebuild it with full preservation and restoration of the exterior, to become the second temple of the Church in the city of Provo. The existing Provo Temple is one of the busiest in the Church, and a second temple there will accommodate the increasing numbers of faithful Church members who are attending the temple from Provo and the surrounding communities.[14]

The *Deseret News* reported that when President Monson made this announcement, "an audible gasp reverberated throughout the Conference Center in downtown Salt Lake City. And, evidently, about 40 miles to the south." Denis McGuire said, "My favorite part of conference is waiting for President Monson to announce the temples. I was not prepared for this one. I did not have my box of Kleenex ready."[15]

Rendering of Provo City Center Temple.
© Intellectual Reserve, Inc.

President Monson's announcement sparked a sudden rush of online comments. A person with a definite sense of humor posted this comment: "Provo Tabernacle gets a promotion after getting fired." In a more serious vein, one Provo resident wrote, "The Lord is amazing in His way of preparing as well. There is no way they could've gutted a historical Provo building for a temple, . . . but the fire was such a sad thing, which prepared Provo for an *amazing* blessing! This sad thing has now become one of Provo's greatest joys! God is so good."[16]

Bishop Randall Stokes of a young single adult ward in Provo reflected, "I think that it shows that out of any supposed tragedies, the Lord can make something ever better. You can never assume that a tragedy is really a tragedy until you see where it's going."[17] Lex de Azevedo, who had felt so dejected when *Gloria* was thwarted by the fire, now commented, "I feel a lot better about the Provo Tabernacle now." He even referred to the event as "a divine fire. All part of a greater plan."[18] Later, Linda S. Reeves, second counselor in the Church's Relief Society general presidency, expressed a similar thought as she spoke in the annual Relief Society meeting about the gospel's power to change lives: "A devastating fire gutted the interior of the beloved, historic tabernacle in Provo, Utah. Its loss was deemed a great tragedy by both the community

"The fire was such a sad thing, which prepared Provo for an amazing blessing! This sad thing has now become one of Provo's greatest joys!"

and Church members. Many wondered, 'Why did the Lord let this happen? Surely He could have prevented the fire or stopped its destruction.'" Sister Reeves then noted that ten months after the fire, President Monson announced plans to rebuild the tabernacle as "a holy temple—a house of the Lord! Suddenly we could see what the Lord had always known! He didn't cause the fire, but He allowed the fire to strip away the interior. He saw the tabernacle as a magnificent temple—a permanent home for making sacred, eternal covenants."[19]

Others expressed the thought that they would miss the tabernacle because it was such an elegantly beautiful venue and just the right size for events such as stake conferences, concerts, or public lectures. Kena Jo Matthews, chair for the Utah Valley Ministerial Association, reflected, "It has been such a wonderful community building for so long. It's amazing what they are doing with it. I'm glad they are keeping the building. Communities are made up of their history. I am glad they're going to restore it to its original look. It's a very positive thing for the community." She continued, "Change isn't always bad. We'll miss it. We appreciate the LDS Church's hospitality in letting the community use it over the years." Linda Walton, chaplain of UVU and chair of the National Day of Prayer, admitted that she would miss the tabernacle as the venue for her annual event, but she looked forward to the temple drawing many people to downtown Provo. "I think it's going to be huge. . . . The malls have won for a while. It's a different kind of good."[20]

Planning the New Temple

A great deal of planning had preceded President Thomas S. Monson's momentous announcement. At the time he announced plans to rebuild the Provo Tabernacle as a temple, a Church press release indicated, "Church leaders have worked with architects, engineers and historical experts to determine the future of the building." The new structure will include "a complete restoration of the original exterior," including even the tall central spire that had been gone for nearly a century.[21]

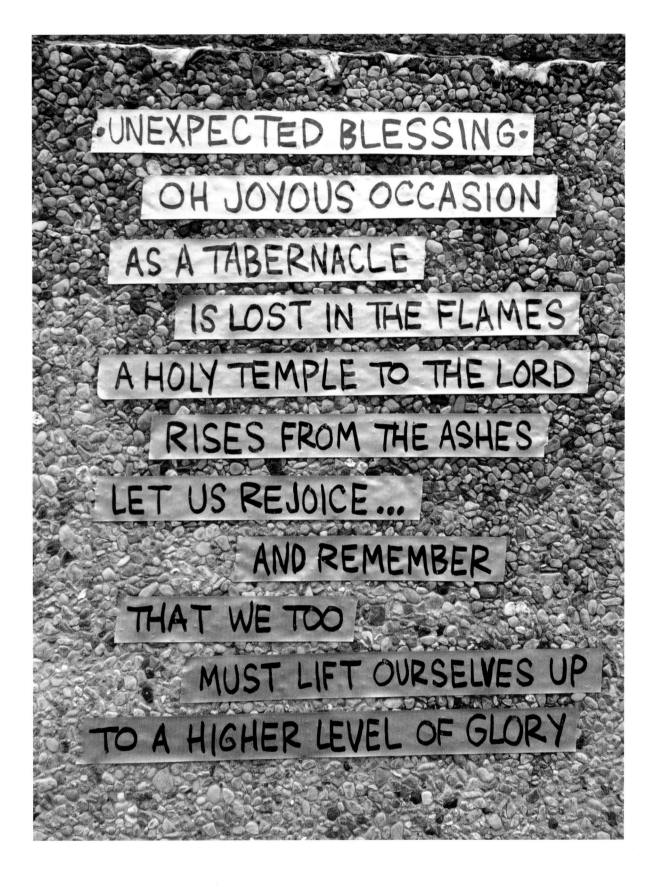

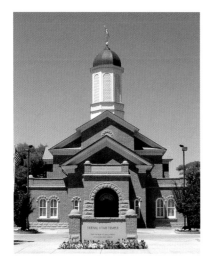

Vernal Utah Temple. Photo by Kenneth R. Mays.

This was not the first time a temple would be built from an existing older building. In 1994 the Church had announced the construction of an unusual temple. The exterior of the old stake tabernacle at Vernal in northeastern Utah would be restored to its original appearance, and temple facilities would be constructed inside. Roger Jackson was the architect for this building. The Vernal Temple was dedicated in 1997. A similar project transformed a historic chapel in Copenhagen, Denmark, into a temple, which was dedicated in 2004.

Initial discussions during the winter and spring of 2011 had focused on restoring the Provo structure as a tabernacle, but during June of that year these plans changed. Presiding Bishop H. David Burton and President Thomas S. Monson discussed the possibility of rebuilding the tabernacle as a temple. Architect Roger Jackson noted that its size was similar to the other temples he had designed, so he felt confident that this concept would work and would be "lovely." He had envisioned a temple having a capacity similar to his earlier temples, but learned that Church officials were thinking of endowment rooms with twice as many seats. With careful planning, Jackson was able to fit these larger facilities into the historic building, clearing the way for President Monson's startling announcement at the October general conference.

Because plans called for restoring the tabernacle's exterior to its familiar appearance (of course with the addition of the original tall central spire), there were to be no above-the-ground additions to the building. Therefore some of the space needed for a temple would have to be below the surface. While all actual ordinance functions were to be within the tabernacle's original footprint, dressing rooms would be on a lower level to the north, and underground parking was planned on the south and west. The baptistry would be on two lower levels directly below the east end of the tabernacle.

Within the original building, there were to be two stories above ground level. Offices for the temple presidency and others would occupy the west end of the ground floor. The temple's chapel would be located on this same level in the area where the building juts out to the north. Two endowment instruction rooms having 116 seats each would be at the east end of this floor. Temple patrons would begin their endowment experience in one or the other of these rooms before ascending the spiral stairs in one of the temple's corner towers to the second floor. They would then complete the endowment in the single large instruction room at the east end of that floor. A new session could begin approximately once every hour. The celestial room was to be at the temple's center directly under the tall tower. It would receive natural light through windows in the tower and art glass in the ceiling, as well as through stained-glass windows between the celestial room and adjoining sealing rooms to the north and south. There would be three additional sealing rooms in the west part of the second story, surrounding a grand staircase. There would also be five elevators. The temple's two entrances would both be on the south side, one at ground level and the other from underground parking on the first lower level.

The First Presidency instructed that the temple's interior should reflect elements of the tabernacle's original architecture—Eastlake Victorian on the main floor and pioneer Gothic on the second. The architect therefore examined objects which had survived the tabernacle fire and studied the interior of the Manti Temple, another building designed by William H. Folsom. The goal was to imagine how Folsom might have designed the Provo Tabernacle as a temple in the 1880s and then design the new structure accordingly. The architect also incorporated many specific features of the former tabernacle into the new temple. Newel posts and railings from the tabernacle's rostrum and details of the balcony are seen in the temple's grand staircase. The tabernacle's original elliptical ceiling is reproduced in the upper endowment room. The intricate Victorian stenciling, discovered following the fire, is reproduced in the bride's room. The tabernacle's pulpit had been removed from the podium and placed in storage prior to the production of *Gloria*; it therefore escaped destruction during the fire and will be used in the temple chapel.

When Jacobsen Construction won the contract to do the work, Andy Kirby was grateful that John Emery and the team with which he had been working remained in place. In December 2011 James Bruce Hansen was appointed to assist Kirby (who had been reassigned as the senior project manager over the temple) as site project

The First Presidency instructed that the temple's interior should reflect elements of the tabernacle's original architecture—Eastlake Victorian on the main floor and pioneer Gothic on the second.

manager, and he thus became a new key member of the leadership team. He would be the Church's representative to work directly with contractors and others at the site on a daily basis. Jim brought many years of experience to this assignment. Since 1973 he had been a carpenter, foreman, superintendent, project manager and, for many years, vice president of construction for a development company. In his work with the Church, he was site project manager for the new Bishops' Central Storehouse on Welfare Square in Salt Lake City from 2010 to 2011. Even after his Provo appointment, he spent five weeks early in 2012 helping out with the completion of the Kansas City Temple.[22]

From left to right: Andy Kirby and Jim Hansen visit with author Richard O. Cowan and his son Lee R. Cowan, who took most of the photographs for this book.

Soon afterwards, two full-time "construction service mission-aries," David and Bobbie Arnson, were also called to help in Provo. They were to minister to the spiritual needs of all the workers on this project, such as by organizing devotionals. Elder Arnson, a regis-tered architect, was to help ensure that the project met all plans and specifications. He and his wife were also to keep a detailed photo-graphic and written record of the construction. About a year later, the Arnsons were released, and in April 2013 were replaced by Jay and Sylvia Newitt. Elder Newitt had recently retired after teaching construction management for thirty-seven years at Brigham Young University, and he had written a widely used textbook on that subject.

Archaeologists on the Temple Site

Before construction on the new temple could begin, archaeologi-cal research was conducted to learn everything possible about the original meetinghouse that had stood on the site just north of the tabernacle. Destruction of the tabernacle and plans to build the new temple provided a window of opportunity to "remember and care for some of the Church's cultural heritage."[23] Beginning in November 2011, with the help of Brigham Young University's Department of Geology, ground-penetrating radar was used to map the precise location of the earlier building, sometimes called Provo's first taber-nacle. Radio waves beamed into the ground produced echoes, which were picked up by a special antenna. A computer analysis of these echoes allowed researchers to identify even specific features of the buried structure.[24] With the cooperation of the Church's Temple Department and Church History Department, Brigham Young University's Department of Public Archaeology, directed by Richard Talbot, received the contract to carry out the investigation. Beginning in January 2012, this project offered dozens of BYU archaeology and anthropology students "the chance of a lifetime"[25]—actual experience at a significant archaeological site "in their own backyard"[26] rather than at distant locations around the world. Because part of this site would be where construction would go forward with the new temple, and because groundbreaking ceremonies would be conducted in this

Next page: Student archaeologists excavate foundation of old meeting house north of tabernacle. Courtesy of Richard Talbot.

same area, there was some urgency to complete the archaeological investigation.

The entire stone foundation of the earlier structure was uncovered as the excavations reached several feet beneath the existing ground level. The foundation consisted of "limestone walls four feet thick and up to five feet deep." As the student archaeologists sifted the soil they removed, they found adobe bricks, nails, coins, buttons, clothing, brooches, toys, bottles, horseshoes, a piece of a lace bobbin, a gold ring, slate, comb, horseshoes, and even a fountain pen. Archaeologist Debra Harris remarked, "It was exciting to see all the little pieces fit together and give us a glimpse into what life was like for the people who used the original Provo Tabernacle." Talbot was particularly interested in the thousands of visitors who stopped by the site to observe what was going on and to inspect the items that had been discovered. The project was completed by the end of March 2012, so the site could be prepared for the temple's groundbreaking.

Richard Talbot points out to Richard Cowan discoveries of archaeological excavation. Courtesy of Richard Talbot.

A few months later, in the fall, the Church History Department invited Public Archaeology at BYU back to perform another study. This time Richard Talbot and his team of about a dozen student archaeologists excavated the site of the 1875 baptistry which had stood just northwest of the tabernacle. A portion of the original font floor survived. Talbot remarked that it was "very exciting and a rare opportunity" to see an early baptismal font in its original setting. He affirmed that this was "hallowed ground" for the early Utah Valley Saints because it was the first place they could be "baptized in a real font rather than in a cold river or lake." Ben Pykles, a curator for the Church History Department, described the excavation of the baptistry as "a significant discovery."[27] This, together with excavation of the caretaker's house, would be completed before excavation for the new temple's lower levels could begin.

Naming the New Temple

President Monson's announcement to rebuild the tabernacle into a temple did not specify a name. Several names emerged such as the "Provo Tabernacle Temple." Following the pattern of naming multiple stakes and wards, it might be called the Provo Second Temple. Fanciful suggestions included the "Templenacle."

Late in the spring, Church leaders disclosed that the name would be "Provo City Center Temple." Speaking at the temple's groundbreaking a few weeks later, Elder William R. Walker, executive director of the Church's Temple Department, commented that the chosen name "will identify clearly where the temple is and make sure there is no confusion with the existing Provo Temple [only three miles away], and it would not require the renaming of the original Provo Temple."[28] Furthermore, for over a century, the tabernacle truly had been at the center of activities in the city of Provo and the surrounding area. With the name having been announced, everything was now in readiness for construction to begin. This would commence with the traditional groundbreaking ceremony.

*"If you had not been
so faithful in going to
the temple and filling
the Provo Temple,
this would not have
happened."*

Groundbreaking

Three General Authorities came from Church headquarters to conduct groundbreaking ceremonies for the new Provo City Center Temple—Elder Jeffrey R. Holland of the Quorum of the Twelve, Elder L. Whitney Clayton, member of the Presidency of the Seventy with specific responsibility for Utah, and Elder William R. Walker, also of the Seventy and executive director of the Temple Department. Saturday morning, May 12, 2012, dawned bright and clear, "a picture-perfect day in Utah County," as Elder Holland put it. He described seeing an estimated 5,600 faithful Saints crowding the grounds as a "stunning sight." He believed that there had never been, nor would there ever be again, so many people gathered on this property at once, truly making history. This is a "remarkable moment," he concluded.[29]

Even a hot-air balloon hovered just overhead. The balloon's pilot, Doug Cannon, had hoped to attend the groundbreaking, but on the ground rather than in the air. When a flight planned for the day before had to be postponed, he found himself in the air during this event. Hot-air balloons can be navigated only by ascending or descending to find air currents going in the desired direction. Being concerned that the presence of his balloon might detract, Doug attempted to find currents to take him from the groundbreaking site, but currents would repeatedly start to take him away but then reverse and bring him back again.

The services opened with the congregation singing the appropriate hymn, "High on the Mountain Top." At this moment, Cannon was just above the tabernacle wall in his hot-air balloon; hearing the throng singing this beloved hymn was a special experience for him. A selected choir from the temple district presented two other numbers. Two of the speakers cited Old Testament scriptures that seemed particularly relevant and meaningful on this occasion. Sister Patricia Holland cited Isaiah's description of Jerusalem as "a tabernacle that shall not be taken down; not one of the stakes thereof shall ever be removed, neither shall any of the cords thereof be broken" (Isaiah 33:20). Elder Whitney Clayton quoted the Psalmist's encouraging words, "Weeping may endure for a night, but joy cometh in the morning" (Psalm 30:5).

Elder Walker believed that the historic significance of the tabernacle was a factor in the First Presidency's decision to restore it. He was also convinced that the Utah Valley Saints' faithfulness was another factor: "If you had not been so faithful in going to the temple and filling the Provo Temple, this would not have happened." He insisted that the temple would not only bless the faithful Saints who attend it, but "will be a great blessing to the entire community." To illustrate this, he referred to a letter President Thomas S. Monson had received from a woman in Provo. She had grown up as a member of another faith, but had "loved the tabernacle" and had "found peace and serenity on [its grounds] . . . as a young woman growing up. . . . Later, she joined the Church. When the tabernacle burned, she cried and cried and cried. Then, when President Monson announced the tabernacle would be restored as a temple, she cried and cried and cried again."[30]

Elder Cecil O. Samuelson, president of Brigham Young University and an emeritus Seventy, rejoiced in "the rebirth of the iconic Provo Tabernacle, literally rising from the ashes of a horrible fire to become a temple of the Lord."[31] He quoted the 1972 Provo Temple dedicatory prayer petitioning: "Let that great temple of learning—the Brigham Young University . . . be prospered to the full," and he insisted that a "BYU education is really not complete nor has it reached its heaven-intended potential unless it is joined with a consistent pattern of temple worship and service." Therefore, he continued, "it is a remarkable thrill to be bracketed on the northeast and southwest by houses of the Lord." He was convinced that serving in the House of the Lord would provide additional learning that could be gained in no other place. "In that sense, BYU is, and increasingly will be, the most complete university in the world."[32]

Elder Holland explained that groundbreakings are an act of faith. He recalled how after the first four groundbreakings, the Kirtland and Nauvoo Temples were lost, and those at Independence and Far West were never built. He then explained how Brigham Young responded when people questioned his plan to break ground

Top: Elder Jeffrey R. Holland at groundbreaking. *Bottom:* Large crowd at groundbreaking. Photos courtesy of *Deseret News.*

Opposite: Top: Elder Holland breaking ground. Courtesy of *Deseret News. Bottom:* Richard Cowan and Justin Bray participating in groundbreaking. Courtesy of Richard Cowan and Justin Bray.

for yet another temple in Salt Lake: "Some have wondered and some have asked if we should try to build another temple. They have asked if we would still be here to enjoy the effort we've expended. . . . I do not know the answer to such questions. I do not know where we will be tomorrow. I do not know whether we yet again will be able to enjoy the fruits of our labors in building a house unto the Lord. But this I do know. We are a temple-building people. This I do know. We should build a temple here and everywhere we go, and by the hand of the Lord, and the power of Almighty God we'll live to see the fruits of our labors."

On behalf of the leaders of the Church, Elder Holland acknowledged "how faithful and devoted you always have been to all matters of faith and service in the kingdom including temple attendance." Speaking of the tabernacle, he asserted, "No other public space in Provo has ever had such valued and varied use, and no other structure in this county has been such an integral part of the religious and civic life here." Therefore, he was grateful that the Brethren made their "inspired decision truly, to build this temple out of the ashes of this beloved tabernacle."

Elder Holland then offered the prayer, dedicating "already sacred ground for an even more sacred purpose—the construction of the Provo Utah City Center Temple . . . within the shadow of Y Mountain and against the shores of Utah Lake." He expressed gratitude that the First Presidency had decided "to not only save this space but sanctify it further by building a house unto thee, a house of the Lord." He also asked for divine protection for the site, building, and all those who would be working there. "May no unhallowed hand nor force of nature mar this project nor bring grief to these holy purposes." He then prayed: "May the workmanship of this house of the Lord be worthy of Thy Beloved Son, the best that mortal labor can provide. May the beauty resemble in its own way the original beauty of Solomon's Temple of old, with the added benefit today of a pioneer facade that will forever recall for us those faithful early Saints who made this day possible." He acknowledged that it is "only through the faithful tithes and offerings of thy Saints, the widow, the student, the economically distressed, as well as the financially prosperous, that this and every other temple goes forward."[33]

Following his prayer, Elder Holland and the other General Authorities present took shovels from a rack built from timbers salvaged from the tabernacle fire and turned the first soil symbolizing commencement of construction. Other Church and civic leaders were then invited to do the same. Finally, any of the Saints who wished to participate were invited to come forward and have their turn with the gold-colored shovels.

Many just wanted to linger and prolong the spirit of the occasion. Jennifer King and her mother-in-law, Laura King, of the nearby Provo First Ward, remarked, "I don't want to go home. . . . I want to sit here for a while."[34]

On this occasion, Church leaders announced that the district for the future temple would consist of the eight stakes in Springville, and the eight Provo stakes. With this announcement, all eagerly anticipated the time when the new temple would be in service to bless their lives.

Notes

1. See Richard W. Jackson, *Places of Worship: 150 Years of Latter-day Saint Architecture* (Provo, UT: Religious Studies Center, 2003).

2. Andy Kirby, e-mail to Richard Cowan, November 14, 2014.

3. Kirby, remarks at Provo South Stake fireside, July 21, 2013, notes in possession of Richard O. Cowan.

4. Kirby, remarks at the Provo City Library, June 13, 2014, notes in possession of Richard O. Cowan.

5. John Emery, statement to Richard Cowan, April 30, 2012.

6. Jim Dalrymple, "Fire Chief: Final Report Coming Soon," *Daily Herald*, February 22, 2011, A3.

7. Gustavo Ramos, "Future of Fire-Stricken Tabernacle Still Unknown," *Daily Universe*, August 1, 2011, 1, 3.

8. Genelle Pugmire, "Church Buys Property near Provo Tabernacle," *Daily Herald*, September 1, 2011, A1–A2.

9. Genelle Pugmire, "Hotel Roberts Property Going to LDS Church," *Daily Herald*, September 28, 2011, A1, A3.

10. Pugmire, "Church Buys Property," A1–A2.

11. Donald W. Meyers, "LDS Church Aims to Buy Street by Provo Tabernacle," *Salt Lake Tribune*, February 17, 2012, B2.

12. Pugmire, "Church Buys Property," A1–A2.

13. Pugmire, "Hotel Roberts," A1.

14. Thomas S. Monson, "As We Meet Again," *Ensign*, November 2011, 4–5.

15. Joseph Walker, "Temple to Rise from Ashes of Tabernacle," *Deseret News*, October 2, 2011, B1, B4.

16. Amy Smith, Facebook, https://www.facebook.com/LDS/posts /279255988760659.

17. Walker, "Temple to Rise from Ashes," B1, B4.

18. Lex de Azevedo, text message to Kim Egginton, October 1, 2011, 11:30 a.m. (immediately after President Monson's announcement).

19. Linda S. Reeves, "Claim the Blessings of Your Covenants," *Ensign*, November 2013, 119.

20. Genelle Pugmire, "Provo Tabernacle Plan Raises Mixed Emotions," *Daily Herald*, October 4, 2011, A1, A2.

21. Joseph Walker, "Temple to Rise from Ashes of Tabernacle," *Deseret News*, Oct. 2, 2011, B1, B4.

22. James Bruce Hansen, e-mail to Richard Cowan, February 18, 2015.

23. Jeff Finley, "Tabernacle Excavation Gives BYU Students Real-World Experience with Archaeology," *Daily Universe*, January 12, 2012, 1.

24. John H. McBride, Benjamin C. Pykles, Emily Utt, R. William Keach II, "Rediscovering Provo's First Tabernacle with Ground-Penetrating Radar," *BYU Studies* 51, no. 2 (2012): 61–77.

25. Ryan Morgenegg, "Work Completed! Interesting Discoveries Made and Many Pioneer Artifacts Found," *Church News*, April 29, 2012, 6; see also Genelle Pugmire, "Learning from the Past: Excavation, Demolition Happening Around the Provo Tabernacle," *Daily Herald*, January 10, 2012, 1, 2.

26. Finley, "Tabernacle Excavation," 1.

27. Genelle Pugmire, "1875 Baptistry Unearthed at Site," *Daily Herald*, November 15, 2012, A1, A4.

28. "Provo City Center Temple Groundbreaking," Provo Channel 17, May 21, 2012; hereafter cited as groundbreaking video. See also Sarah Jane Weaver, "'Out of Ashes': Ground Broken for Provo City Center Temple," *Church News*, May 20, 2012, 4; for the complete text, see appendix G.

29. Weaver, "Out of Ashes," 3–4.

30. Groundbreaking video; see also Weaver, "Out of Ashes," 4.

31. Weaver, "Out of Ashes," 4.

32. Groundbreaking video.

33. Groundbreaking video; see also Weaver, "Out of Ashes," 4.

34. Weaver, "Out of Ashes," 4.

Next page: Photo by Kazumasa Aoyama.

CHAPTER 11

Constructing the New Temple

2012   Ground broken for Provo City Center Temple (May 12)

Octagonal turret roofs removed and placed on ground to the north (August)

Reinforced concrete applied to inside of brick walls (September and October)

Support piles driven ninety feet into the ground (November and December)

2013   Excavation for lower floors to depth of about forty-five feet (January and February)

Foundation, five feet thick, put into place (spring)

Basement walls engage with brick walls above; support piles are removed (summer)

First steel beam placed in temple's interior structure (August 20)

Central spire lifted into place, completing steel structure (December 5)

2014   Final turret roof put back into place (January 20)

Statue of angel Moroni placed atop central spire (March 31)

"Holiness to the Lord" stone placed on east gable (August)

Stained-glass windows installed in temple's exterior (November and December)

2015   Three-tiered bronze Victorian fountain set in place (April 21)

First trees planted (December)

ollowing the ceremonial breaking of ground on May 12, 2012, Utah Valley Saints eagerly anticipated the time when the Jacobsen Construction team would begin their work. Preliminary preparations had begun even before the groundbreaking. One of the first steps was to clear the block south of the tabernacle, which the Church had purchased in August 2011. This was accomplished during January of the following year, and Jacobsen Construction's office trailer was set up there temporarily. The block would also become an important staging area when actual construction started. In June, the month following the groundbreaking, the portion of 100 South which the Church had purchased was closed to traffic. This allowed the merging of the two adjacent blocks into a single construction site.

Church leaders had instructed that as much as possible of the original tabernacle's remaining structure should be saved.[1] Steps had

Top left: Demolition of building south of the tabernacle. *Top right:* Jacobsen's trailer on cleared south lot. *Bottom left:* 100 South closed to traffic. *Bottom right:* Two blocks combined into single construction zone. Photos by Janetta Price.

already been taken to preserve the brick walls. The fire and crashing of the roof caused considerable damage to the brick. Soon after the fire, the walls were thoroughly braced and cleaned. Then, during the summer of 2012, some bricks were removed from the tops of the walls, including the remnants of the north, east, and south gables to allow for a reinforced concrete "bond beam" that eventually would support the roof. The west gable, which had survived the fire largely intact, was carefully braced so it could be preserved.

In August 2012, the octagonal conical roofs of the corner turrets were removed and stored off to one side for possible use in the coming reconstruction. There was some concern that removing them might damage the brick walls to which they were attached, but to everyone's surprise, they had been held in place largely by gravity with the help of only a few nails (note the skewed turret following the fire, page 152). Therefore, they came off relatively easily and cleanly.

Top left: As of August 4, 2012, two towers caps down, two to go. *Bottom left and right*: Removal of the northwest tower cap, August 8, 2012. Photos by Lee R. Cowan.

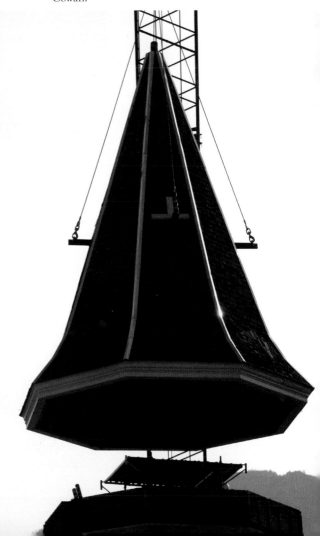

A Temple on Stilts

Plans called for some temple facilities to occupy two levels beneath the historic tabernacle. Determining how to excavate for this basement while preserving the original brick walls posed "a significant challenge." The original thought was to do this for one half of the building at a time. Conversations among the Church's project manager, architect, Jacobsen Construction, and others developed ideas of how to accomplish this. The plan was finalized with the help of structural experts at Reaveley Engineering.[2] It would be possible to do the excavation for the whole building at once. "You normally don't want to modify a design after you have a contractor because it tends to cost you more," Andy Kirby reflected. "But, with their help, we improved the design, so they were able to provide a better foundation in less time and for less money." Kirby described this collaboration and following the promptings they received as a "great process" which resulted in "an engineering construction marvel."[3] This plan would unfold dramatically during the latter half of 2012 and first half of the following year.

The first major step was to reinforce the walls, which were five bricks thick. The original lime mortar was soft, so these masonry walls were brittle and lacked horizontal strength. They would likely have crumbled easily in an earthquake. Frames were built around window and door openings to provide added stability. The inner two layers of brick were removed from the walls, leaving the exterior intact. Fourteen- to sixteen-inch-long spiral steel anchors or "helical ties" were then drilled several inches into the bricks from inside to hold the remaining three layers together. A sufficient length of the anchors was left exposed so it could become firmly connected to a reinforced concrete inner lining. Thousands of these slender spike-like anchors were placed in a grid pattern about a foot and a half apart from each other throughout the entire inner surface of the building's walls. Two layers of steel reinforcing bars were also put into place to be covered by the "shotcrete," which would be applied to the inside

Opposite: *Top left*: Turret caps awaiting repair. Note the central pole that supported finials and the reinforced holes halfway where beams were inserted for removal. *Top right*: Southwest tower cap, the most severely damaged, was the last to be removed. Note new timber used as splints to reinforce cap for lift. *Bottom:* Two tower caps in north staging area awaiting reconstruction. Photos by Lee R. Cowan.

Jacobsen Construction Leadership Team

Senior project manager: John Emery

Project manager/project engineer:
    Mark Robins

Cost engineer: Bruce Motogawa

Project engineers: Jon Bryan,
    Shawn Thomas, and Paul Lin

Superintendents: Dan Tullis
    (*over concrete and structural*),
    Dennis Pack (*over finish work*),
    and Amador Gomez

Steel anchor used to fasten exterior bricks to shotcrete. Rod seen on salvaged brick from tabernacle. Photo by Lee R. Cowan.

Top left: Rebar around window frames. Photo by Lee R. Cowan. *Top middle:* The west gable had implied windows to match the other three gables but had no actual openings because of the organ piping inside. Photo by Lee R. Cowan. *Top right:* Rebar in place for shotcrete. Note the outline of the future windows that match the façade. Bricks to be later removed for new windows, part of the reconstruction. Photo by Lee R. Cowan. *Bottom left:* Openings created for west gable windows in June. Note removed bricks stacked for possible future use. Photo by Lee R. Cowan. *Bottom right:* Applying shotcrete. Courtesy of Doug Fallon.

surface of the brick walls. This was a special drier form of high-strength concrete that could be pumped under high pressure and sprayed on the walls. However, before any was actually applied, trials were conducted during September with mock-up panels to thoroughly test the strength of the shotcrete in various types of situations and to give the nozzlemen ample experience in applying the mixture evenly and consistently on the walls and around the steel anchors and rebar. This concrete lining was from six to ten inches thick, depending on the location. Rebar connectors and beam pockets were provided to tie these walls to the future basement walls, which would be built up from below and to the floors that would be constructed within them.

By the end of October 2012, the shotcrete was completed. The result was a steel-reinforced concrete structure with a brick veneer. From outside the building, thicker reinforced concrete could be seen extending about three feet above the brick walls. This was the beam that would support the roof; it would eventually be covered with bricks matching the rest of the temple's exterior. Now that the walls were more permanently stable, the external bracing was removed. At this point, the archaeologists from BYU were invited back to examine the pioneer baptistry just northwest of the tabernacle (as discussed in the previous chapter).

The next task was to provide the support for the tabernacle's reinforced brick walls while ground was excavated and two levels of basement were constructed beneath them. During November and December, Nicholson Construction drilled hollow steel casings,

Top left: Shotcreting partially complete, October 2012. *Top right:* Window opening showing layers of brick on the exterior, and reinforced shotcrete interior. *Bottom left:* Concrete seen above brick wall would later support the roof, October 13, 2012. *Bottom right:* Concrete extending above the pioneer brick wall. Photos by Lee R. Cowan.

Needle beams through foundation under east wall. Photo by Julie Cannon Markham.

nine inches in diameter, into the ground to a depth of sixty feet for 146 shoring piles at predetermined locations just inside and outside of the walls. These holes were then drilled an additional thirty feet into clay layer below. Concrete was then injected into the entire ninety-foot-deep hole. Enough dirt was then removed to expose the tabernacle's original stone and lime mortar foundation. At fifty-six locations, holes were punched through this stone foundation so a temporary steel "needle beam" could connect the top of a pile outside of the wall with the corresponding one just inside. Steel shims and a "pancake jack" on top of these beams were adjusted to carry the weight of the wall above. Thus the weight of the structure, an estimated 6.8 million pounds, was shifted from the historic foundation to the system of steel and concrete piles. This process was completed just before Christmas of 2012.

Top left: Pressure to support walls regulated by hydraulic jacks system. Courtesy of Doug Fallon. *Top right:* Early stage of excavation, January 15, 2013. Photo by Lee R. Cowan. *Bottom:* Complex support system under the southwest turret. Photo by Lee R. Cowan.

Top: Excavation deep enough on January 15 to drive equipment under the foundation. Safety netting installed to catch falling bricks and debris. *Bottom left:* Excavation for dressing area north of temple. Four tower caps preserved for future use. *Bottom right:* Excavation approaching first lower level, January 23, 2013. Photos by Lee R. Cowan.

Excavation for the temple's basement took place during the opening weeks of 2013. As the earth was carefully removed from around the piles, the tabernacle walls appeared to be gradually lifted up in the air, standing on tall stilts. Actually the building had remained in its exact original position. An area was excavated to a depth of twenty-five feet for the temple's first lower level, extending beyond the original tabernacle's footprint, especially in the north where the dressing rooms would be located. This floor was already below the level of the surrounding water table. Therefore in late

January, before the excavation went deeper, a large machine simultaneously dug a wide trench and filled it with a mixture of sand, cement, and Bentonite—a special clay that expands when coming into contact with water to form a tight seal. This waterproof cut-off or barrier wall completely surrounded the temple area to below the depth of the future basement. Only then would a further excavation to a depth of forty-five feet, mostly directly beneath the original building, accommodate the temple's second lower level. As this excavation proceeded, diagonal bracing was applied to the piles at various levels

Top left: Constructing water barrier wall around temple, January 23, 2013. Photo by Lee R. Cowan. *Top right:* Barrier wall equipment surrounded by concrete slurry. Photo by Lee R. Cowan. *Bottom left:* Support piles cross-braced after reaching first lower level. Photo by Lee R. Cowan. *Bottom right:* Series of cross bracing being welded. Photo by Julie Cannon Markham.

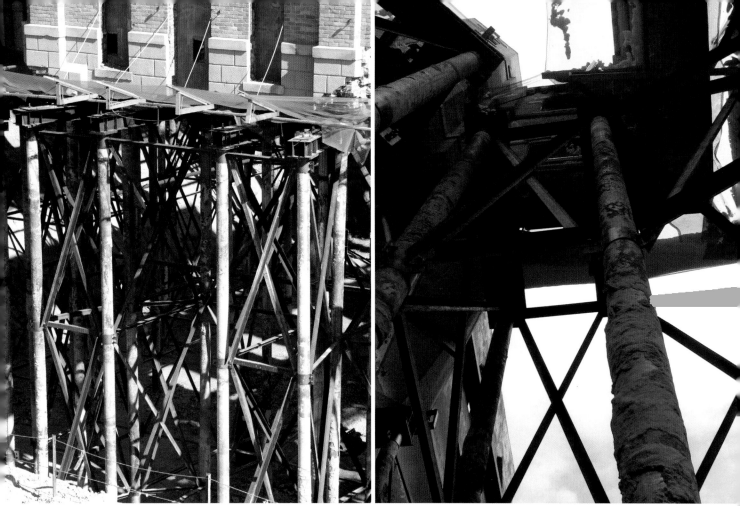

Top left: Excavation to second lower level. Photo by Lee R. Cowan. *Top right:* A unique perspective. Courtesy of Doug Fallon. *Bottom:* Laser target mounted on wall for detecting any movements. Photo by Julie Cannon Markham.

Opposite: Looking east along north wall. Excavation to second lower level under temple. Note retaining wall holding back ground near University Avenue. Photo by Lee R. Cowan.

to keep them from buckling and to maintain the rigidity of the supporting structure.

Each pair of piles had a monitor to measure the weight it was bearing. By means of laser beams aimed at small targets on the walls, even the slightest movement could be detected, such as that caused by the slight shift in heating in different parts of the structure from morning to afternoon. The system was designed to be flexible. It

functioned perfectly, maintaining the integrity of the brick walls even though they now were forty-five feet above the ground. Still, Andy Kirby conceded that he did not sleep well; he worried about the walls especially when there was a strong wind blowing.

None of the tabernacle's workmen had ever done such a thing before. This unique process had been done as far as they knew only two other times in all the world—once in France and once in Italy on much smaller buildings—and had gone down only one rather than two stories.[4] Consequently, this project attracted worldwide attention. The decision to accomplish this challenging and costly feat was evidence of how the Church honored the pioneer builders and its commitment to preserve their work as much as possible. The next step was to prepare the site for the construction phase.

Temple on "stilts" as seen from the Nu Skin balcony, March 5, 2013. Photo by Lee R. Cowan.

Construction Begins

Water was an ongoing concern. It was continually pumped from the excavation inside of the water-barrier walls, which had been constructed in January so work could proceed. A major concern was the upward pressure that would result when the water table was allowed to return to its normal level. Over 900 "micropiles" were drilled throughout the area, 411 within the former tabernacle's footprint. They did not just support the building but also anchored it from "floating" as the water level came back up. A thin concrete "mud slab" had been laid down at the bottom of the excavation to facilitate moving equipment around and precisely locating where the micropiles should be sunk.

The temple's footing or foundation, over five feet thick from top to bottom, was put into place during the early spring of 2013. It started with a six-inch layer of clean sand over the mud slab. Next came a twelve-inch layer of gravel, enclosing an elaborate system of

Left: Barrier wall successfully keeping water from temple construction. *Right*: Micropiles in various stages, March 30, 2013. Photos by Julie Cannon Markham.

Diagram of Foundation Layers

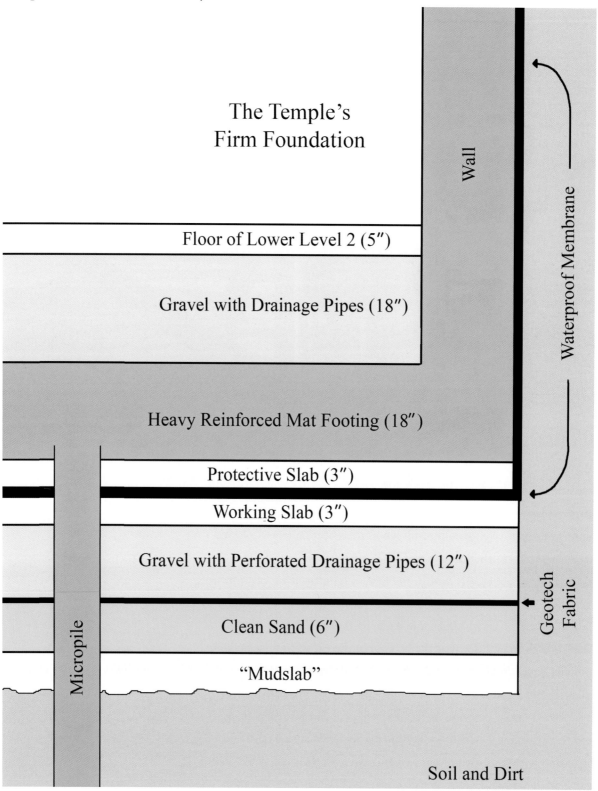

The Temple's Firm Foundation

Floor of Lower Level 2 (5″)

Gravel with Drainage Pipes (18″)

Wall

Waterproof Membrane

Heavy Reinforced Mat Footing (18″)

Protective Slab (3″)

Working Slab (3″)

Gravel with Perforated Drainage Pipes (12″)

Geotech Fabric

Clean Sand (6″)

Micropile

"Mudslab"

Soil and Dirt

perforated pipes covered with a special fabric to prevent sand from entering and clogging them; this layer was intended to drain water out from under the temple. A three-inch concrete working slab was poured on top. A waterproof membrane made of tar and rubber then covered the top of this slab. Using electronic sensors, workers criss-

Top: Preparation for water drainage. Note the perforated pipes. Courtesy of Doug Fallon. *Bottom*: Base for the overhead crane set up during March 2013. Photo by Julie Cannon Markham. *Opposite*: Diagram of foundation layers by Reginald Beales.

crossed the membrane looking for even the smallest potential leak; they knew they had to be thorough and make any needed repairs quickly because only a few days later it would be covered and protected by another three-inch slab of concrete. The top of each micropile was coated with Bentonite and fitted with a rubber boot to prevent leaks.

On May 24, 2013, all these preparations were completed and the temple's main foundation was poured. It was called a "mat footing" because it covered the temple's entire footprint rather than being just under the walls as is the case with most foundations. This eighteen-inch-thick slab was laced with a network of heavy reinforcing steel rebar, an inch and three-eighths in diameter, linked with the tops of steel bars at the center of each micropile. This was just one of several pours of more than a thousand cubic yards each during the course of construction. (Ultimately, nearly forty thousand yards would be

Top left: Forms in place for mat footing. Courtesy of Doug Fallon. *Top right*: Pouring the mat footing began early in the morning May 24, 2013. Photo by Lee R. Cowan. *Bottom left*: Mat footing being poured as seen through the maze of piles and supports. Photo by Lee R. Cowan. *Bottom right*: Pouring of mat footing progresses. Photo by Lee R. Cowan.

used during construction.) It started at about 1:00 a.m. when there was less competition for the output of local cement suppliers. A steady stream of cement trucks dumped their load into the hopper of a pumper truck situated just outside of the south brick wall. The wet concrete was pumped through a large tube that extended up over the top of the brick walls and then down inside. Several men wrestled a heavy hose, about six inches in diameter, to where the concrete was needed.

On top of the mat footing was another layer of gravel, eighteen inches deep. This was a second line of defense in case there should be any unexpected and certainly unwanted leaks through the waterproof membrane. If so, water would drain into sumps along the center of the building, where pumps would automatically turn on to remove it. Finally, the five-inch thick concrete floor of the temple's second lower level was laid directly on this gravel.

Top: Inside forms to top of second lower level in place. Photo by Julie Cannon Markham. *Bottom left:* Beginning to build forms for the lowest temple walls, the day after the mat footing poured, May 25, 2013. Photo by Lee R. Cowan. *Bottom right:* "First lift" completed, inside forms in place for "second lift." Photo by Julie Cannon Markham.

Second lift complete. Only a gap
separates the temple from its new
foundation, June 27, 2013. Photo by
Lee R. Cowan.

As soon as the mat footing had dried, the process of erecting
the future temple's basement walls started. These heavily reinforced
concrete foundation walls were about thirty inches thick. They were
built between the inside and outside piles, directly under the tabernacle's brick walls. The more efficient practice of using prefabricated
forms for pouring cement could not be used here, because the forms
had to be fitted around the cross-bracing members between the piles.
This tedious process must have tested the rule against swearing on
the worksite. The walls were poured in two major "lifts," roughly corresponding to the two future basement levels. This brought them up
to within about six feet of the existing brick walls with their shotcrete
inner lining.

As soon as all moisture had dried from the concrete, the exterior of these basement walls was carefully and completely covered
with the rubber and tar waterproofing mixture. Applied in several
layers at 450 degrees, this was a rather uncomfortable job in the
summer heat. Still, as the mixture was applied at this temperature, it
melted and became thoroughly welded to adjoining areas or layers.
The outer layer was designed to wick water downward, where it could

pass under the temple rather than remaining to exert pressure on the walls higher up. When completed, the waterproofing membrane incorporated a layer of mesh and was from one-quarter to three-eighths of an inch thick.

Left: Concrete port for final pour. *Middle*: Connecting the hose from the pump truck. *Right*: Inserting vibrator into concrete to work out all air pockets. Photos by Lee R. Cowan.

When the shotcrete had been applied to the inside of the brick walls nearly a year earlier, the bottom of each vertical steel rod incorporated a threaded "form saver" sockets. Extension rods were now screwed into these sockets and became an integral part of the network of rebar being assembled in the gap between the original wall above and the new one rising from below. Finally, after extra-sturdy wooden forms had been carefully constructed on the inside and outside of the wall, nonshrinking concrete was pumped under high pressure to completely fill the space between the walls above and below. Workmen used industrial vibrators to remove any unwanted air pockets from the concrete. This process of "engaging" the original walls to their new foundation began in mid-July. As this was completed with the last pour on August 9, the tabernacle's reinforced brick walls once again rested on a firm foundation. Building supervisors reported, only somewhat facetiously, that they once again could sleep at night.

With the foundation walls in place, the piles or "stilts" that had so spectacularly held up the tabernacle's walls some forty feet in

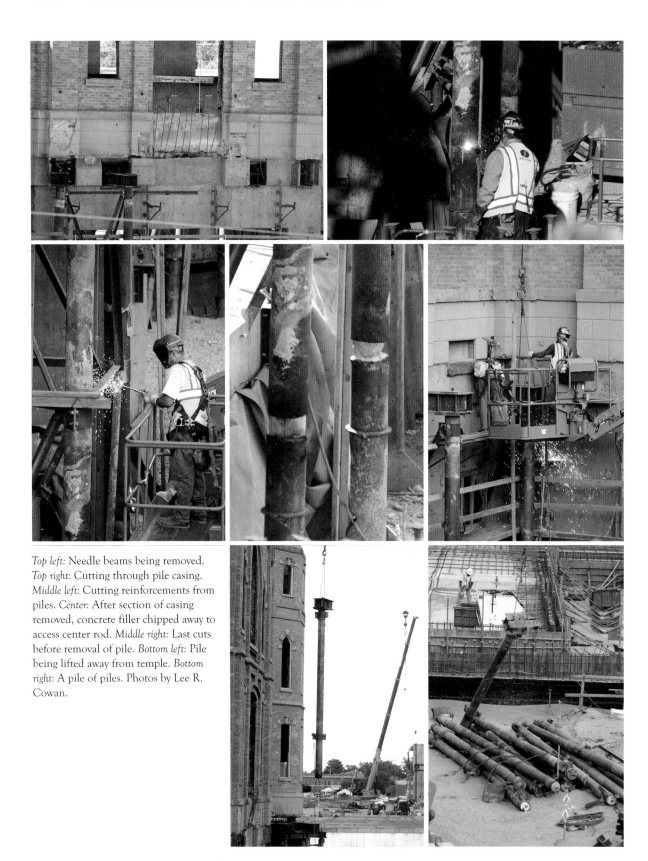

Top left: Needle beams being removed. *Top right:* Cutting through pile casing. *Middle left:* Cutting reinforcements from piles. *Center:* After section of casing removed, concrete filler chipped away to access center rod. *Middle right:* Last cuts before removal of pile. *Bottom left:* Pile being lifted away from temple. *Bottom right:* A pile of piles. Photos by Lee R. Cowan.

Left: Filling hole in foundation after needle beam removal. *Right:* A variety of other constructions going on at the time of the final pour. Photos by Lee R. Cowan.

the air could be removed. Beginning in August, they and the needle beams which had been punched through the temple's original stone foundation were cut by torches and lifted out of the way. With most of the piles removed, a new phase of construction could begin.

The Steel Structure

Most of the weight of the temple's floors and interior walls would be supported by a network of steel beams constructed inside the existing brick shell. On the morning of August 20, 2013, SME Steel of West Jordan, Utah, put the first of these beams into place. A vertical beam over forty feet in length and other similar vertical members were fastened with heavy nuts to bolts embedded in and projecting up from the concrete mat foundation. Other beams were bolted to them, such as would be done with a child's construction kit, but on a massive scale. As the framework

Bird's-eye view of temple shell just before steel work. Courtesy of Doug Fallon.

Top left: Main vertical beam being uprighted for transfer, August 20, 2013. *Top right:* Beam being lowered into position. *Bottom left:* Main beam (white coded) being guided into place. *Bottom right:* Beam being fitted onto bolts embedded in the foundation. Photos by Lee R. Cowan.

Opposite: Top left: Steel reinforcement being stockpiled to the south of temple. Photo by Lee R. Cowan. *Top right:* Main beams supporting corrugated metal of first lower level floor, August 26, 2013. Note pockets in cement wall into which beams will be inserted. Courtesy of Doug Fallon. *Second row, left:* Corrugated steel sheath being carried to where it will be used. Photo by Lee R. Cowan. *Second row, middle:* Steel framework of grand staircase being built. Photo by Lee R. Cowan. *Second row, right:* Rebar mesh for dressing room annex floor, August 28, 2014. Photo by Lee R. Cowan. *Third row, left:* Support columns being built for annex roof. Photo by Lee R. Cowan. *Third row, right:* Annex roof partially completed, October 16, 2013. Photo by Lee R. Cowan. *Bottom left:* Only few beams visible above brick wall, October 22, 2013. Photo by Lee R. Cowan. *Bottom right:* Center tower steel work completed only two days later. Photo by Lee R. Cowan.

reached the level of each floor, corrugated steel plates were put into place and the concrete floor was then poured on top of them. While this work was going on inside the temple, work was progressing to the north. This is where the dressing rooms would be located on the first lower level.

By October 22, a few beams could be seen extending up from behind the brick walls. Amazingly, only two days later, the basic steel framework for the square base and first octagonal section of the central spire were in place. The next step was to add more supports and to tighten the joints as these components were added. Soon the roof structure began to take shape. The first of several trusses was lifted into place on November 12. By Thanksgiving Day, most of the roof's structure was completed. Peaks of the north, east, and south gables, which had been lost during the fire, were reconstructed using cinderblocks. When the roof was covered over with metal decking,

temporary plastic sheeting was put in the window openings to enclose the building. This enabled it to be heated so work could continue inside even during the coldest winter weather.

The metal components of the thirty-five-foot central spire had been assembled on the ground north of the tabernacle. Its octagonal base was designed to be attached to the framework already in place above the building's roof. Long slender steel I-beams formed the tall octagonal pyramid. They were then covered with corrugated steel

Top left: Roofs structure seen from the east. *Top right:* Roof structure seen from Nu Skin balcony, November 27, 2013. *Bottom left:* Framework for central spire being constructed November 27, 2013. *Bottom middle:* Richard Cowan examines central spire before it is lifted to the temple roof, December 5, 2013. *Bottom right:* Signatures on beam in temple spire. Many key individuals are included. Photos by Lee R. Cowan.

Opposite: Top left: Work moving quickly—three beams being transferred at once. *Top middle:* Workmen preparing to receive steel beams. *Top right:* Wagon wheel–shaped framework seen from post office parking lot. Will be part of celestial room ceiling. *Middle left:* Ridge line beam reaches out to engage the west gable. *Middle right:* Beginning reconstruction of north gable. *Bottom left:* Maze of beams in the process of fastening. *Bottom right:* Workmen connecting steel beams. Photos by Lee R. Cowan.

Left: Crowd witnesses temple spire being lifted into place–the "topping off" of the steel structure. *Middle:* Spire in the air. *Right:* Workers guiding the spire into place. Photos by Lee R. Cowan.

Opposite: Top left: Dawn and Richard Cowan watching from the Nu Skin balcony as their son Lee photographs the spire being put into place. Photo by Julie Cannon Markham. *Top right:* Original timbers seen on northeast turret roof. Courtesy of Doug Fallon. *Middle left:* Reconstruction of the most severely damaged southwest turret roof. Photo by Lee R. Cowan. *Center:* Northwest turret roof being lifted into place. Note the interior construction with original and new timber. Photo by Lee R. Cowan. *Middle right:* Roof being lowered onto northwest turret. Photo by Lee R. Cowan. *Bottom left:* Guiding the roof to a final fit. Photo by Lee R. Cowan. *Bottom right:* Turret roofs in place, January 20, 2014. Photo by Lee R. Cowan.

sheeting similar to that used elsewhere in the building. The large overhead crane lifted this whole assembly into place on December 5, 2013, a cold but sunny winter day. This represented the "topping out" of the steel framework, so the occasion was celebrated with a barbecue for the builders. Residents on Provo's east bench were then treated to a rare spectacle. The tower's shiny metal skin was at just the right angle to reflect the rays of the early morning sun to these viewers several miles away. Eventually the tower would be covered with slate shingles, however, so this glorious sight was not permanent.

Since the summer of 2012, the conical roofs of the corner turrets had stood in a row on the ground north of the tabernacle. At the time they were removed from the building, builders thought that only one of them was in good enough condition to be reused. However, one general objective had been to preserve as much as possible of the original structure. A careful inspection of the turret roofs revealed that they were in better condition than believed, so all four were refurbished. Amazingly, the main timbers giving the tower its basic shape, including the outward flare at the bottom, had been hewn by hand using only a broad chisel or hatchet. Timbers forming the ridges of the octagonal roof had been attached at the top to a central vertical log about six to eight inches in diameter. Damaged timbers, particularly on the more badly burned southwest turret, were spliced or replaced where necessary. In December 2013, the first of these corner roofs was lifted back to its location on the same

Ever since statues of the angel Moroni became familiar standard features of Mormon temples, placing the herald figure atop the tallest tower has been a milestone event in the construction of a temple.

southwestern turret. Careful measurements of the tabernacle's walls revealed that the pioneer builders were not able to be precise in their work, so similar parts of the building were not identically the same. Therefore each turret roof was lifted into place temporarily, careful measurements were made, and it was then returned to the ground for adjustments or refinements before it could be fitted into place permanently. While the tower roofs originally were held in place by gravity and only a few handmade nails, they now were welded to the walls below. The last of the four roofs, on the northwest turret, was finally put into place on January 20, 2014. With the major components of the roof in place, the building now had the basic form of the future Provo City Center Temple.

Another Angel in Provo

Ever since statues of the angel Moroni became familiar standard features of Mormon temples, placing the herald figure atop the tallest tower has been a milestone event in the construction of a temple. Hence Latter-day Saints in the Provo area eagerly looked forward to this key step in the building of their new temple. The angel could not be set in place until the slate shingles covered the octagonal pyramid of the central spire, because the base of the statue would fit over them. When an unprecedented cold wave in the eastern United States halted work at the slate quarry in Vermont, Provo builders feared that there would be a delay. Despite the icy weather, the slate shingles arrived in a timely manner, and by the last weekend in March, the temple's tower appeared to be ready. Church officials had determined to place the angel as a low-key event in the normal course of construction rather than scheduling any public celebration. Perhaps this was due to the temple's location on a major thoroughfare.

Builders had planned to place the angel early in the morning on the first day of April, but made a last-minute decision to accomplish this task one day earlier because of forecasts of unfavorable weather. Word of this decision leaked out, and early in the afternoon on Monday, March 31, interested spectators began to gather around

Top: Figure of Moroni delivered to temple site March 31, 2014. Photo by Lee R. Cowan. *Middle left:* Moroni's horn came as separate piece. Photo by Lee R. Cowan. *Center:* Horn bolted into place. Photo by Lee R. Cowan. *Middle right:* Camera taped to crane hook. Photo by Lee R. Cowan. *Bottom:* Small loop intended for lifting the figure of Moroni. Courtesy of Doug Fallon.

the construction site. At about 1:30, the gilded figure arrived on the back of a flatbed truck. The horn was then slipped through an opening in the angel's hand, attached to his mouth with a special strong adhesive, and then bolted into place. The large overhead crane that had been working at the northeast corner of the construction site for several months then carefully lifted the angel into a vertical position. Workmen on the scaffolding high above the temple prepared the tip

Left: Moroni rising. *Right top:* Moroni ready to be lifted. *Right bottom:* Detail of head. Photos by Lee R. Cowan.

of the tower to receive the statue. A pole extending down from the statue's base needed to be inserted into the top of the hollow tower; a large electric cable from inside the statue would become the top of the building's lightning rod. Promptly at the appointed time of 2:30, the angel was lifted through the air to the top of the tower. As the statue was lowered into place, applause erupted from the crowd of about one thousand eager onlookers who had gathered by this time.

Left top: Detail of feet. Photo by Lee R. Cowan. *Left middle:* Artist signature seen when statue was lifted. Photo by Doug Fallon. *Left bottom:* Receptor at top of tower for lightning rod and statue's base. Photo by Lee R. Cowan. *Right:* "I Saw a Mighty Angel Fly." Photo by Lee R. Cowan.

Top left: Final fitting. *Top right:* Richard and Dawn Cowan witness this momentous milestone. *Bottom:* Birds finding a new roost would pose a problem. Photos by Lee R. Cowan.

Some sang "An Angel from on High" or "I Love to See the Temple." With the angel in place, the former tabernacle now truly looked like a temple.

Opposite: Lightning rod being inserted into tower. Photo by Lee R. Cowan.

A Further Restoration of the Building's Exterior

While placing the figure of Moroni atop the temple's tower was undoubtedly the most visible achievement, many other projects also beautified the temple's exterior. "Repointing" the brick was a significant step. The old mortar was dug out to a depth of about an inch. Masons discovered that the texture of the handmade bricks of fired clay was still of a high quality. If any bricks were damaged, however, they were replaced with similar bricks that were carefully selected and stockpiled ahead of time. The new mortar matched the lime, sand, and water composition of the original because it had to be softer than the bricks and breathe the same as the existing structure. Experts in historic masonry provided valuable information and advice. Workmen applied the new mortar with trowels, just as had been done by their pioneer counterparts.

Left: Repointing the bricks. Photo by Julie Cannon Markham. *Right:* Brick corbels reconstructed to mimic details of the original Victorian design. Photo by Lee R. Cowan.

Victorian attention to detail certainly characterized the building's restoration. Skilled bricklayers reconstructed such intricate features as arches over windows and doors as well as corbelled dentils along the roofline. Finally, after the bricks were washed, they were sprayed with a solution to solidify them but not to change their appearance. Still, the temple shone. This could not be appreciated fully right away because an elaborate system of scaffolding surrounded the temple during this phase of the work.

Left top: Rebuilding arch above first floor window. Photo by Julie Cannon Markham. *Left bottom:* Restored brick work on north gable. Note the template removed from the arch above main window, leaning against the wall. Photo by Lee R. Cowan. *Right:* Elaborate scaffolding needed to provide access. Photo by Lee R. Cowan.

Left: Quartzite sandstone niches on southeast tower. Note niche shape mimics windows. *Top right*: Niche being repaired. *Middle right*: Original water table seen on the north east tower. *Bottom right*: New quartzite used to rebuild the temples water table. Photos by Lee R. Cowan.

Ornamental tower niches were also restored. While the originals were covered with stucco, the material was now upgraded to quarzitic sandstone. This same stone, quarried in the Heber Valley, formed the "watercourse" along the base of the walls as well as other features of the building's exterior and the surrounding grounds.

Top left: A gablet adorns each gable. Such gablets were typically used as a means of venting attics. Note detail of the woodwork and the lightning rod. *Top right:* Temple wrapped in order to continue work during coldest weather. *Bottom:* Woodwork detail of turret and gable eaves. Photos by Lee R. Cowan.

Where original stone was chipped, it was not replaced but repaired. A "dutchman," or carefully matched piece, was attached so as to appear to be part of the original. During the winter of 2014, the whole building was wrapped in white fabric so temperatures could be kept warm

enough for this work to go forward and for the mortar and paint to cure without freezing.

A brass finial surmounted the tip of each corner turret. Interestingly, the first of these was being installed on the northeast tower as runners crossed the finish line in the second annual "Temple to Temple Run" on Pioneer Day, July 24, 2014. The finial was constructed around the section of log extending up from the top of the turret roof.

A feature which was not part of the original tabernacle was the stone bearing the familiar inscriptions, "Holiness to the Lord, the House of the Lord." Like the figure of Moroni atop the tallest tower,

Top left: Original center log extending out of the turret cap. Photo by Julie Cannon Markham. *Top right*: Copper sleeve fastened to center log to receive finial parts. Photo by Lee R. Cowan. *Bottom left*: Finial base slid into place. Photo by Lee R. Cowan. *Bottom middle*: Finial top being lifted manually. Photo by Julie Cannon Markham. *Bottom right*: Finial complete. Photo by Lee R. Cowan.

Opposite: The restoration of the central spire involved elaborate woodwork. Photo by Lee R. Cowan.

Left: Temple's east gable. *Right top:* Wood, then water barrier being attached to corrugated metal. *Right bottom:* Template used to mark location for heated line for melting ice. Photos by Lee R. Cowan.

these phrases clearly identify the building as a temple. The stone bearing these words in gold lettering was added to the temple's east gable façade early in August. These phrases would also appear adjacent to the temple's main entrances on the south. Adding and painting exterior wooden trim also went forward during the fall of 2014.

One of the final steps in completing the temple's steel structure was to cover the roof trusses and rafters with the corrugated steel sheets to which the roof would be attached. Completing the roof occupied most of the year 2014. Instead of replacing the original wooden shingles, the roof was upgraded to fireproof and more durable slate. Despite the cold weather in the East, needed supply continued to arrive in Provo so work could progress without interruption. Individual slate pieces were cut to match the shape of the earlier wooden shingles. They were attached to the thin wooden subroof with special copper nails. Copper tubing was embedded in the

Top left: Plywood routed to receive ice-melt tubing. Courtesy of Doug Fallon. *Top right:* Copper sheeting molded into routed line to protect tubing. Courtesy of Doug Fallon. *Middle left:* "Pitch hitter" nailing slate shingles to steep pitch of east gable. Photo by Lee R. Cowan. *Center:* Removing scaffolding from steeple base allowed slating to be finished. Photo by R. Cowan. *Middle right:* Waterproofing ridge cap for final slate installation. Photo by Lee R. Cowan. *Bottom left:* Finishing slating around central spire. Photo by Lee R. Cowan. *Bottom right:* Slating turret cap. Photo by Lee R. Cowan.

Finished product. Shiny copper will acquire a softer patina over time. Photo by Lee R. Cowan.

Opposite: Andrew Kosorok instructing Richard Cowan about varieties of stained glass and how pieces are leaded together on top of the blueprint pattern provided by the architects. Photo by Lee R. Cowan.

subroof under the slate shingles to heat them and prevent the buildup of snow and ice on the roof. Copper strips covered ridgelines and places where different surfaces of the roof came together such as on the octagonal towers. Beginning in September, this shiny metal presented a rather startling sight; over time, however, it would weather and take on a softer patina that would blend nicely with the slate roof.

The Temple's Windows

Ordinary window glass is formed by heating sand to 2,000 degrees and then pouring it onto a smooth tin surface to cool. Stained glass, also known as art glass or leaded glass, is heated to 2,400 degrees so minerals or oxides can be added to produce different colors. Centuries ago, only a few colors were used—red created with gold oxide, blue with cobalt, and green with copper. Now a wide variety of colors are available. Furthermore, this glass may be stirred during cooling to produce a swirl pattern, or it may be poured between carved steel rollers to produce different textures which add vibrancy and sparkle to the glass.

Since the 1917 renovation of the Provo Tabernacle, beautiful stained-glass windows had been a beloved feature of the building. Because it was heated by coal, the windows gradually became quite dirty. Furthermore, over the years, some panes were damaged by BBs, and a few pieces of stained glass had actually been picked out by children. From 1995 to 1996, therefore, a local company, Glass Images and Creations, made a thorough renovation of the windows. Before disassembling the windows, the company made rubbings to record the precise design of each one. Craftsmen then thoroughly washed the glass, replaced lead which had oxidized, and refurbished or replaced the wooden frames as needed. Only a few of the windows survived the 2010 fire, so Utah Valley Saints were grateful to learn

Andy Kirby had described the tabernacle as a "handmade building," lovingly created by our pioneer ancestors. Therefore, the dimensions of the designs had to be adjusted for each individual window.

that similar windows would be part of the new temple's design. Glass Images obviously was interested in the possibility of re-creating the beautiful windows.

After this local company succeeded in winning the contract for the new temple's art windows, it assembled a highly qualified team to do the work. Of over three hundred persons in the area who had received stained glass training, only a few had the level of craftsmanship and professional background to enable them to join the team. The dozen or so involved with this project each had as much as thirty years of experience. Early in the spring of 2014, Jerry Lynn, temple projects manager, and Andrew Kosorok, special projects manager, both at Glass Images, began working closely with David Brenchley of FFKR Architects, and Mark Robins of Jacobsen Construction along with committees in the Temple Department at Church headquarters in planning for the windows.

Over half of the windows would be recreations of those which had existed in the tabernacle. In these cases, the 1990s rubbings made by Glass Images were crucial. Other windows, such as those inside the temple, were designed by the architects and were "very heavily inspired by the original windows." Kosorok reviewed these designs, assuring that they were technically consistent with the Victorian or Gothic styles of the original windows. He also checked for their "constructability and survivability," making minor adjustments where necessary. All his suggestions were carefully reviewed and approved by the architects and Church committees.

Kosorok described the style of the windows as "Americanized Victorian," featuring abstract or stylized designs inspired by vines and flowers, set onto a geometric grid and border. Early Victorian abstractions of the fleur-de-lis, lily, lotus, or iris would be seen throughout the building. Kosorok thought of these floral designs as "reminders of eternal growth and the vibrancy of life." The large windows along the main exterior walls also alternatingly depicted beehives and open scriptures.

One interesting challenge was the fact that no two window openings were exactly the same size. Andy Kirby had described the tabernacle as a "handmade building," lovingly created by our pioneer ancestors. Therefore, the dimensions of the designs had to be adjusted for each individual window. Even these refinements needed to be approved. Fortunately, computerized design programs made creating, communicating, and adjusting plans for each window easier to accomplish.

In addition to all the art glass which would be an important part of the interior, there would be three notable examples of stained-glass in the new temple that had not existed in the tabernacle. The transom above the main ground-level entrance would proclaim "Holiness to the Lord, the House of the Lord" in vibrant gold letters. This would be the first temple to proclaim these phrases in glass rather than only in stone. Creating the serifs in the elegant script was a definite challenge even for the most experienced glass technicians. The skylight of the brides' room would be a second example. It featured vine and flower designs like those discovered in the stencil painting following the tabernacle fire. Third, the celestial room's

Left: William Jackman (left) and Andrew Kosorok (right) showing Richard Cowan the window for the transom of the South entrance. *Right top:* Richard Cowan examines serifs. *Right bottom:* Richard Cowan fits a piece of art glass into place. Note corresponding numbers written on glass and found on blue print. Photos by Lee R. Cowan.

Opposite: Richard Cowan examines construction of stained glass. Photo by Lee R. Cowan.

Kosorok was convinced that the craftspeople working on the windows had divine assistance. . . . During his twenty years of work, he has not seen this happen with other kinds of orders. These experiences on temple projects evidenced for him the importance of this work.

ceiling would include a backlit octagon formed by eight triangular panels of stained glass.

Approximately twenty-five stained glass colors and textures had been approved for the temple project. In a few cases, colors were more subdued and stately than those used in the tabernacle to be more suitable for use in a temple. For example, the green candles in the turret windows were changed from lime green to evergreen. Similarly, areas in transom windows became amber rather than "bubblegum pink." Rather than being crystal clear, beveled panels in exterior windows had to be "opalescent" to protect the sacred environment of the temple.

None of the sheets of art glass for the windows was produced locally, but rather came primarily from three companies elsewhere in the United States. The main supplier was Kokomo Opalescent Glass of Indiana, interestingly, where Louis Tiffany had developed his glass-making techniques. Craftsmen at Glass Images in Utah then cut the pieces of glass to the exact shapes, fit them together with lead strips which they soldered into place. Lead strips received a patina so they would appear black like the originals rather than silver.

Some of the assembly was farmed out to two factories in China and another in Mexico. In these cases, Andrew Kosorok traveled to China, and Jerry Lynn traveled to Mexico to carefully instruct the local workmen about the quality expected to meet temple standards.

Completed windows were then encased in layers of tempered glass that is many times more break resistant than ordinary glass. Exterior windows were protected by laminated glass a half inch thick on the outside and three-eighths of an inch on the inside. This made the window about two inches thick. The edges of this assembly were sealed together to become a single unit. This thickness provided insulation from changes in temperature and also from unwanted outside noise. Interior windows did not need to produce this kind of insulation, so they were enclosed by layers only an eighth of an inch thick; still this resulted in the window being over an inch thick.

Kosorok was convinced that the craftspeople working on the windows had divine assistance. More than once when they were facing tight deadlines, they were able to complete projects in far less

Opposite: Top left: West gable window installation at different stages. *Top middle:* West gable window casing being leaned into place. Most windows were installed from the inside. *Top right:* Window casing being secured in opening. Photos by Lee R. Cowan.

Left: The first step is to line the window openings with boards then sealed between the board and bricks with insulating foam. *Middle:* Stainless steel flashing being installed around window opening. *Right top:* Window sashes being lifted to second floor opening on east side. *Right bottom:* Window casing with preinstalled stained glass. Note the Gothic arch. Photos by Lee R. Cowan.

than the normal time. On one occasion, the shipment from one of the foreign companies came back totally destroyed, so Glass Images and Creations had to do it all over again. Kosorok gratefully acknowledged that they were able to complete about six weeks of work in just a few days. During his twenty years of work, he has not seen this happen with other kinds of orders. These experiences on temple projects evidenced for him the importance of this work.

The exterior windows were then crated and shipped to Re-View, the nation's premier historic window framing company, located in Kansas City. They then encased the glass in window frames. Most of the original windows had sashes that could be opened for ventilation. Even though the new windows have this appearance, they were sealed closed because the temple has a central air-conditioning system.

The company in Kansas City then trucked the completed windows back to Provo and sent workmen to install them. The first arrived on October 30, and the installation of exterior windows went forward during the next several months. The first were installed on the eight sides of the central tower. The next were in the octagonal turrets, and finally in the main body of the building. Work on all these projects went forward around the clock; at night, workmen wearing headlamps could be seen working high up on the scaffolding. Although the first windows were put into place from the outside, most were installed from inside. As this was accomplished, people

passing the temple in the evening could once again appreciate the beauty of the windows illuminated from within.

Because the beauty of stained glass is revealed only when light passes through it, Andrew Kosorok believes its use in a place of worship such as a temple is particularly appropriate. In such places, "we

Bottom left: First night of stained-glass illumination from within, November 24, 2014, just days before Thanksgiving. *Middle right*: Top tier turret windows being installed form the outside. *Bottom right*: Thickness of window casing seen from its side profile. Photos by Lee R. Cowan.

are invited to remember our connection with the Spirit that is all around us."

The Temple's Surroundings

Grounds of the Provo City Center Temple occupied the majority of two city blocks. In addition to the temple itself, there were to be two other structures. One was a mechanical building measuring 20 by 60 feet. Located just northwest of the temple, it housed heating, ventilation, and other utilities, allowing them to function without disturbing the quiet and reverent atmosphere within the temple itself. Its sandstone base, brick walls, and roof matched those of the temple.

The other building was to be a pavilion located in the gardens south of the temple. Patterned after a Victorian garden gazebo, this octagonal structure was about forty feet wide. Construction started during the summer of 2014. It was provided primarily for the

Opposite: Top left: Passing casing through the opening to be uprighted from inside. *Top right:* Preparation for installation of main west gable window. *Bottom:* Window installation moves forward. Photos by Lee R. Cowan.

West gable windows complete January 6, 2015. Photo by Lee R. Cowan.

convenience of groups waiting for wedding parties to emerge from the temple. Large picture windows afforded views of the temple and surrounding gardens. It could be entered either at ground level or from the underground parking garage.

Excavation for the 269-stall parking facility had taken place earlier in the year. The high standards seen in the temple itself were also evidenced in the careful construction of the garage's floor with its extensive web of rebar and thick layer of concrete. The roof over the area was constructed in the summer of 2014, and the curving ramp from 200 South was finally put in place early in 2015.

Preparations for landscaping also went forward during 2014. Walls for planter boxes were the first indications of the shape of the future gardens.

Top left: Pavilion taking shape. *Top right*: Preparations for exterior surface and windows. *Bottom*: Nearly completed pavilion. Photos by Lee R. Cowan.

Opposite: Top left: Mechanical building. *Top right*: Pavilion construction, June 2014. *Middle left*: Steam seen rising from the mechanical building after it came on line. *Middle right*: Roof over underground parking at half mark. *Bottom*: Status of construction of pavilion, underground parking, and temple, June 5, 2014. Photos by Lee R. Cowan.

Top left: Under advancing roof, note thickness. Photo by Lee R. Cowan. *Top right*: Prefabricated forms expedited the progression of walls. Photo by Lee R. Cowan. *Middle left*: Securing heating tubes to rebar on south ramp to underground parking. Photo by Lee R. Cowan. *Right*: South ramp to underground parking poured. Photo by Lee R. Cowan. *Bottom left*: Temple underground parking seen from Nu Skin entrance. Photo by Julie Cannon Markham.

Most of the gardens would be located over temple-related structures—dressing rooms on the north and parking to the south. A layer of "geofoam" several feet thick was placed directly atop the roofs of these facilities. This polystyrene material was lighter than dirt and rocks, provided drainage aided with waterproofing, and prevented settling. Geofoam under walks was of a higher density than that under gardens. Deeper spaces were left in specific places to accommodate roots of trees. Large white blocks of geofoam were carefully shaped to fit tightly together and provide the desired contours.

During the fall of 2014, soil and sprinkler system pipes were added. As the year 2014 drew to its close, decorative metal fencing began to replace the green tarps that had surrounded the construction site for two years.

The first evergreens were put in place west of the temple during December 2014. Surprisingly, the best time to plant trees is the winter when their root systems are dormant. As they "awake" in the spring, they can become established in their new setting.

Of particular interest was the large Victorian fountain constructed in the south garden between the temple and the pavilion.

Top left: Forms and rebar begin to shape the planters to the west of the temple. Photo by Doug Fallon. *Top right*: West planters fabricated, ready for geofoam to be placed. Photo by Doug Fallon. *Middle left*: Geofoam is strong but relatively light. Photo by Lee R. Cowan. *Middle right*: Blocks were cut to exact elevation and area specifications. Photo by Lee R. Cowan. *Bottom left*: Substructure waterproofed before geofoam blocks placed on top. Photo by Lee R. Cowan. *Bottom right*: Geofoam blocks were numbered for placement. Photo by Lee R. Cowan.

Top left: After sidewalks were poured, fill dirt and sprinkler lines marked the beginning of the landscaping. Photo by Lee R. Cowan. *Top right:* Decorative fencing receiving a cement foundation. Photo by Lee R. Cowan. *Middle left:* Applying primer and final coat to fencing. Photo by Lee R. Cowan. *Middle right:* West entrance to temple grounds. Photo by Lee R. Cowan. *Bottom left:* Trees delivered to site ready for planting. Photo by Shawn Wilson. *Bottom right:* Tree provides backdrop along west side of south garden. Photo by Shawn Wilson. *Opposite:* Arborist caring for one of the five original trees north of the temple. Photo by Lee R. Cowan.

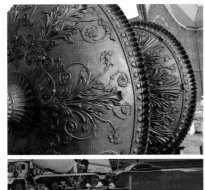

Top left: Victorian architecture was known for detail. Photo by Julie Cannon Markham. *Top right*: Splash rings to be added to the fountain base. Photo by Julie Cannon Markham. Middle left: Victorian fountain seen from a wing of the Nu Skin building. Photo by Julie Cannon Markham. *Bottom*: The view from 100 South. Photo by Lee R. Cowan.

Fabricated in bronze by Metal Art of Lehi, Utah, its surfaces were covered with Victorian designs of flowers and vines. Water coming from the fountain's finial fills and spills over two successive large bowls into a circular pond. It was situated even with the center line of 100 South, so motorists approaching the temple on that street either from the east or the west would see the beautiful fountain directly in front of them.

Opposite: *Top left*: Variety of foliage stockpiled for landscaping. Photo by Lee R. Cowan. *Top right*: Progress of landscaping. Photo by Lee R. Cowan. *Middle left*: Victorian fountain for the south garden arrived on the site on April 21, 2015. Photo by Julie Cannon Markham. *Middle right*: An unusual view inside the fountain. Note the reinforcing ribs. Photo by Julie Cannon Markham. *Bottom left*: Fountain being lifted into place. Photo by Julie Cannon Markham. *Bottom right*: Fountain finial being added. Photo by Julie Cannon Markham.

The Temple's Interior

While work was progressing outside, work on the temple's interior was also moving forward. As soon as a concrete floor was poured, work could commence on that particular level. Hence, during the fall of 2013 construction started in the basement and then progressed upward. As partitions were formed for the temple's rooms, "MEP" (mechanical, electrical, and plumbing) work took place. Ventilation ducts needed to be put into place, electrical wiring needed to be connected, and water pipes needed to be installed within walls before sheetrock and plastering could be completed. Then the interior stone and woodwork could be added. The beautiful woods came from many parts of the world. Even though many details reflected the work by pioneer Utah craftsmen, most of the woodwork in the new temple was milled in China. After painting was done, the interior stained glass could be put in place. Glass Images installed the temple's interior windows during 2015.

The baptismal font was a significant project. The original Provo Temple's font was a large single unit of stainless steel, so it had to be put into place even before reinforced floors and walls were constructed around it. At the City Center Temple, on the other hand, the font was to be of concrete, with a polished granite façade. Creating the forms for the font's oval shape posed a significant challenge. A plumbing package was put into place earlier, but the font itself was not poured until March 2014. When this was completed, the font was filled to assure that it was watertight. Andy Kirby noted that some workers good-naturedly wondered if they weren't trying a little too hard to "hasten" the work.

As walls began to be formed on the top floor, an unusual sight was created. The sealing rooms located in the temple's southern and northern extensions each would be illuminated by triple Gothic windows, a large one in the center with smaller ones on each side. This same pattern of three windows was repeated across the room on the wall between it and a hallway. The three windows were repeated once again between the hall and the celestial room in the building's center. Hence at least some natural light would enter this interior

Some workers good-naturedly wondered if they weren't trying a little too hard to "hasten" the work.

room through its south and north walls in addition to that coming through the stained glass in the ceiling. This was just one example of how the Gothic style of the tabernacle's upper exterior windows could be reflected in the interior on that floor in the new temple. This same three-window pattern was also found on the opposite side of the building. Hence, before stained glass filled these windows, a person could stand against the outside wall in one sealing room and see the triple-window pattern repeated five times, the final one being the outside windows clear across the temple.

Some recent temples present the endowment in a series of two rooms. In many cases, murals on the walls of the first room provide a visual setting for the endowment teachings given in that room. Murals for the two main floor instruction rooms of the Provo City Center Temple were painted at the Church's motion picture studio on the north edge of Provo. They were delivered to the temple on May 18, 2015, as canvas rolls and were installed on the rooms' walls during the next several days.

In the summer of 2015, a myriad of interior details needed to be completed. This included touch-up painting, laying carpets, hanging chandeliers, and installing seating in the chapel and instruction rooms. Because the temple's interior includes many features from

Left: Interior stained glass will mimic the Gothic shape of the exterior windows. *Right:* Temple's interior will feature extensive stained glass. Photos by Lee R. Cowan.

Central windows on south of temple seen through opening on north. Note the repetition of arches through intervening walls. Photo by Lee R. Cowan.

the original tabernacle, those who are familiar with the historic building will feel at home in the new temple. In the baptistry, they will see columns similar to those which supported the tabernacle's balcony. Window moldings will seem familiar. The newel posts and railings of the grand staircase will remind them of similar features that graced the tabernacle's rostrum and balcony. Those speaking in the temple's chapel will be standing behind the actual pulpit of the original Provo Tabernacle. Other features, such as artwork on ceilings, were part of the original tabernacle but did not survive the remodelings of later decades so will not be as familiar.

As summer transitioned into fall, final touches were put on the temple and its grounds. The Provo City Center Temple became ready for its open house, scheduled for January 15–March 5, 2016, and dedication on March 20, 2016.

Notes

1. Most of the material in this chapter is based on personal observations of the authors as well as repeated conversations with the contractor, John Emery; the site manager, James Bruce Hansen; and the construction missionaries, Jay and Silvia Newitt. Many details of chronology are confirmed by the blog "New Temple in Provo" created by Julie Markham.

2. Statement by John Emery, May 12, 2015

3. Andy Kirby, remarks at the Provo City Library, June 13, 2014, notes in possession of Richard O. Cowan.

4. Jay Newitt, remarks at Sharon Park Stake fireside, July 20, 2014, notes in possession of Richard O. Cowan.

CHAPTER 12
Some Reflections

Opposite: Top: Observing steel framework from Nu Skin balcony. *Bottom:* Richard Cowan comparing models of Provo's two temples built to the same scale. Model of the Provo City Center Temple was created by Jake Lattin using a 3D printer. Photos by Lee R. Cowan.

Left: Author Richard Cowan checks on temple progress. *Right:* Project manager John Emery discusses construction with Richard Cowan. Photos by Lee R. Cowan.

Over the years, the Latter-day Saints in Utah Valley had maintained a high level of religious activity and devotion. Therefore they were understandably shocked and saddened at the destruction of the Provo Tabernacle by a devastating fire only a few days before Christmas in 2010. Having made the Provo Temple the most productive in the Church, these Saints were certainly elated by President Thomas S. Monson's 2011 announcement that their beloved tabernacle would be painstakingly restored to become Provo's second temple. During the next few years, witnessing the unique steps in this process proved to be a favorite activity and moving experience. Following the progress in this reconstruction stimulated even more interest in temple service.

Provo's two temples were built during the time when significant strides were being made in Latter-day Saint temple history. When the original Provo Temple was dedicated in 1972, it became the fifteenth operating temple in the Church. The original four temples in Utah had been dedicated nearly one hundred years earlier, during the later nineteenth century. The first half of the twentieth century witnessed a remarkable geographical expansion, with temples in Hawaii, Canada, Arizona, and Idaho. The first "overseas" temples then came during the 1950s—in Switzerland, New Zealand, and England. This decade also brought the first temple in California, the largest built to that point in the Church.

Then the pace of temple building continued to increase after the Provo Temple was dedicated, including the first temples in Latin

America, Asia, and Africa. As the twentieth century drew to a close, Church President Gordon B. Hinckley received inspiration to make temples more available to Saints around the world by building them much smaller. As the twenty-first century dawned, over sixty of these smaller temples had been completed or were under construction at locations on every continent. Larger temples were being built once again as the new century entered its second decade.

The dedication of the Provo City Center Temple on March 20, 2016, made it the 150th in the Church. Hence during the forty-plus years between the dedications of the two Provo temples, there was a remarkable tenfold increase in the number of these sacred houses worldwide. Truly temples are dotting the earth as the prophets have foretold.

Feelings about the New Temple

Those who were involved in transforming the former tabernacle into the new Provo City Center Temple often expressed gratitude for this opportunity. A common theme was admiration for the original pioneer builders. Andy Kirby, the Church's project manager, for example, marveled at their sacrifice and craftsmanship which he believed "represented their dedication to God." He therefore felt that "it is such an honor to work on this building" and affirmed that "we hope to show respect for what they have done."[1]

Andrew Kosorov, who supervised the production of stained-glass windows for the Provo City Center Temple, recalled Brigham Young's statement that even our best is not quite good enough for a temple. "If that is true for most temples," Kosorov reflected, "we have to do even better for this one. We have been finding out that there is a lot more scrutiny with the construction of every aspect of this building than there is on most other temples." He believed this was true because the Provo City Center Temple means so much to so many people. "We are essentially resurrecting a monument to a group of people who died a hundred years ago."[2]

Sister Sylvia Newitt, one of the special construction service missionaries assigned to the temple building project, regarded the early builders as "people of great faith" who were "committed to their God." As a result, they freely gave their time and worked hard. Consequently, she concluded, "I honor these people for who they

Comparing the replica to the real thing. Photo by Lee R. Cowan.

were and for what they have given us." Sister Newitt had a similar regard for the modern craftsmen among whom she was currently serving. She believed that if the pioneer workmen could be here now,

Construction missionaries Jay and Sylvia Newitt. Courtesy of Jay and Sylvia Newitt.

they would be "proud of what they would see," because the work of
today's craftsmen is a "worthy" reflection of the pioneers' original
efforts and devotion. She reported having heard many working on
the temple assert that this was "the crowning jewel of their professional careers."[3]

Her husband, Elder Jay Newitt, similarly affirmed that the
workers "really care because they know they are building a temple."
He was aware of many who had "made significant sacrifices" to have
the privilege of working on this building. For example, some left an
employer for whom they had worked many years, and went to work
for a competitor in order to have this special opportunity. Even
though some were not active Latter-day Saints, they felt something
special. Elder Newitt referred to one of them who acknowledged that
while working on this project he had "felt the Spirit." He decided
that he and his wife "should be one of the first couples sealed for
eternity in the new temple." He therefore contacted his bishop to
know what he needed to do to get his life in order and be prepared to
achieve this goal.[4]

Andy Kirby indicated that he met frequently with architects,
engineers, contractors, or craftsmen. Each of these meetings started
with a prayer. He said that often he thanked Heavenly Father for "the
team He had given us to build this temple."[5]

Not all of the special feelings concerning this building came
from those intimately involved in rebuilding it. For example, about
one year before the fire, a family attended a holiday musical program
in the Provo Tabernacle. As they enjoyed the presentation, they also
admired the qualities of the pioneer building with its beautiful woodwork and stained-glass windows. As they were leaving, their preschool
daughter unexpectedly announced, "I am going to be married in this
building." Despite her parents' explanation that the tabernacle was
used only for church conferences and programs like the one they had
just attended, the little girl stuck to her affirmation that she would be
married there. One can imagine the sorrow she must have felt a year
later when she heard that the structure had been almost completely
destroyed by a terrible fire, then the reassuring joy she felt when

President Thomas S. Monson announced that the tabernacle would be rebuilt as a beautiful temple.

Preparing for Temple Service

As the Provo City Center Temple moved toward completion, local Church leaders in the area employed various means to raise temple consciousness among their members. For example, Elder and Sister Newitt were authorized and even encouraged to give firesides. Almost every weekend during the final months of construction, they visited stakes throughout the district to give these inspiring presentations. In these very popular events, they shared their intimate view of the building project in their richly illustrated talks. Along with interesting facts about the building process, they offered lessons they had learned related to gospel principles.

The leaders of the Provo South Stake, within whose boundaries the tabernacle had been located, noticed how much interest there was in the reconstruction project. With the cooperation of the contractors, they established a small information booth on the University Avenue side of the construction site. They prepared a fact sheet to hand out and recruited stake members to staff the booth. They also invited other stakes to provide volunteers and arranged with the Utah Provo Mission to have full-time missionaries take part. The stake placed about a dozen large photographs of the tabernacle's history along the security fence. Being aware of the great interest in the temple's construction, the contractors graciously left openings in the fence's green plastic cover where the public could view what was being accomplished. Visitors came from almost every state and from more than two dozen foreign countries.

On Pioneer Day 2013, the Provo South Stake sponsored a "temple to temple run." This five kilometer (just over three miles) event underscored that Provo's two temples would be closer together than any other two temples in the Church. Those registering for the run received attractive white t-shirts bearing an orange circle enclosing a silhouette of the angel Moroni. They also received a number to wear to enable their running time to be clocked accurately. The course began at the Provo Temple on the hill and ended on the grounds of the Utah County Courthouse, across University Avenue from the City Center building site. Along the way were exhibits featuring locations on the Mormon Pioneer route between Nauvoo and Salt Lake Valley. In addition to those who actually ran the course, hundreds of others walked at a slower pace, including young parents pushing baby strollers or holding the hands of their young children. This was an experience they wanted their young families never to forget.

After participants completed the course, many walked across the street to have a closer look at construction progress. In July 2013 the temple still was on "stilts" as the basement walls were being built up to reach the original brick structure above. When the event was repeated in 2014, participants witnessed the first finial being installed on the pinnacle of the northeast turret as they crossed the finish line. Observers were amazed at how much had been accomplished since the year before. By the time of this run in 2015, the temple and its beautiful grounds appeared to be almost finished.

In connection with these events, the Provo South Stake held well-attended firesides in which Andy Kirby presented illustrated reviews of construction progress. Like the Newitts, he too saw ways to make application to personal lives.

In 2013, A. LeGrand "Buddy" Richards, then president of the Provo South Stake, organized the first temple to temple run as a stake activity. However, there was such community interest in the event that they opened it to the public and it has become an annual event with thousands of participants. *Top:* Participants were invited to identify ancestors in whose memory they would run the 2015 race. *Bottom:* The finish line for the 2015 race was across the street from the Provo City Center Temple. Photos by Lee R. Cowan. *Next page:* Photo by Brent Nordgren.

Other stakes used different means to emphasize temple activity. In 2015 the presidency of the Provo East Stake challenged its members to become involved in family history and temple activity. Specific goals included holding a current temple recommend, attending the temple regularly, and identifying at least one ancestor for whom they could perform ordinances. Throughout the year, high councilors were assigned to treat specific temple-related topics as they spoke in the wards.

Completion of the temple in nearby Payson during 2015 naturally heightened interest in the Provo City Center Temple. As the open house attracted thousands during late April and May and the dedication took place on June 7, members just to the north looked forward to participating in these same events in connection with their own temple.

Creation of temple districts also helped to focus attention. At the groundbreaking for the City Center Temple on May 12, 2012, Church leaders had announced that the district to be served by the new temple would include the eight Provo and eight Springville stakes. Later, the area further south was assigned to the new Payson Temple, and the Orem area was transferred from the Mt. Timpanogos to the Provo Temple.

Gospel Lessons Pointed Out

As Andy Kirby, the Newitts, and others spoke about the new Provo City Center Temple, they pointed out significant lessons that could be drawn. For example, they likened the decision to rebuild the tabernacle into a temple to the gospel principles of rebirth and conversion.

In his fireside presentations, Elder Jay Newitt invited his listeners to contrast two photographs—one showing the charred tabernacle walls filled with rubble, and the other depicting the architect's rendering of the building as a beautiful temple. As we go through life, Elder Newitt suggested, we may encounter some difficulty or problem that "totally devastates us, or brings us to our knees." We may feel that all is lost. Likewise, many of us, following the fire, thought the tabernacle was lost. "Now it is being repurposed into a glorious temple, a building that will potentially impact the lives of millions of families for good eternally." Therefore, Elder Newitt concluded "as you drive by the building, apply this lesson to your life and gain more hope and faith by realizing that maybe the Lord is similarly repurposing you to make you better and stronger."[6] The Book of Mormon prophet Moroni explained that the Lord allows us to experience difficulties and have weakness so that we may grow. The Savior promised, "If they humble themselves before me, and have faith in me, then will I make weak things become strong unto them" (Moroni 12:27).

Andy Kirby directed attention specifically to the temple's carefully constructed foundation and pointed out that we might think of ourselves as temples and need an equally strong spiritual foundation in our personal lives. He referred to the Master's parable about a faithful man's house which successfully withstood the pounding of wind and rain, "for it was founded upon a rock" (Matthew 7:24–27). In a physical foundation, he explained, the concrete may develop cracks. The internal steel rebar, however, keeps the cracks from opening too widely. He taught that through such practices as regular church attendance, holding family home evenings, searching the scriptures, and heartfelt prayer, we similarly build our foundations on our Savior, Jesus Christ. We will have the reinforcing power of the Spirit which will give strength to keep our gospel foundations solid.[7]

From despair came hope, illustrating the principle of conversion. Photo courtesy of Doug Fallon. Rendering © Intellectual Reserve, Inc.

Elder Newitt likened the ground water surrounding the temple's basement to the corrosive temptations we face in life. Just as the builders carefully followed a painstaking process to waterproof the temple, we need to put into place a spiritual barrier to shield us from the harmful influence of the world and sin.

The Anticipated Dedication

Temple dedications and related events have become spiritual high points in the lives of the Latter-day Saints (see the discussion in chapter 5). Open houses have enabled more and more members of the community, whether Latter-day Saints or not, to visit and admire the quality and beauty of the completed temple. Open houses along the Wasatch Front since 1980 have been particularly well attended, attracting at least 400,000 visitors each. In fact, the Bountiful Utah Temple, dedicated early in 1995, received 870,000 visitors, more than any other temple open house in the history of the Church. Nearly a half million attended the Payson Utah Temple open house in 2015. These have also been occasions when basic gospel principles can be shared. Church leaders were aware of the large interest in the Provo City Center Temple, so they planned the unusually long six-week period early in 2016 to accommodate the anticipated large open house crowds.

A "cultural celebration" became a meaningful feature of temple dedications beginning about three decades after the Provo Temple was dedicated in 1972. When the Accra Ghana Temple was dedicated in 2004, such a commemoration was held for the first time at the request of President Gordon B. Hinckley. In a nearby sports stadium on

Open House Participation

Year	Temple	How Many Attended
1956	Los Angeles	662,401
1972	Provo	246,201
1974	Washington, DC	758,238
1981	Jordan River	>550,000
1993	San Diego	720,000
1995	Bountiful	870,000
1997	Mount Timpanogos	679,217
2009	Draper	684,721
2009	Oquirrh Mountain	<600,000
2012	Brigham City	404,500
2014	Ogden (rebuilt)	550,000
2015	Payson	>475,000

the evening before the dedication, nearly two thousand youth participated in a folkloric presentation of West African traditions and dances. This was the largest Latter-day Saint youth activity in Africa so far.[8] Following the success of this event, similar celebrations have accompanied all temple dedications since that time. While most are held in large arenas or stadiums, the 2010 celebration at Kiev, Ukraine, was held in a beautiful old castle. The purpose is to help the youth connect with the temple. "I am an advocate for such events," affirmed President Thomas S. Monson. "They enable our youth to participate in something they truly find unforgettable. The friendships they form and the memories they make will be theirs forever."[9]

The celebration accompanying the 2009 dedications of the Draper and Oquirrh Mountain Temples in the southern part of the Salt Lake Valley was held in the Conference Center adjacent to Temple Square on two successive evenings, May 29 and 30. Youth from the 25 stakes in the Draper Temple district made their presentation the first evening, while those from the 26 stakes in the Oquirrh Mountain Temple district performed the next night. The sets and storyline were identical both nights, but each group had its own costumes and choreography. A total of fourteen thousand youth participated.[10] Similarly, the cultural celebration linked to the 2014 rededication of the Ogden Temple included two performances with a different cast in each, allowing sixteen thousand youth to participate. The celebration accompanying the June 2015 dedication of the Payson Temple was planned around the theme "Fill the World with Love" and was held in LaVell Edwards Stadium on the BYU campus. The committee was charged with the goal of "involving every young member of the Church living within the temple district age 12 to 18 plus any of their friends of other faiths who wish to take part." About thirteen thousand participated. A secondary objective was "to depict in the celebration something of the geography, history, and culture of the Payson Temple District."[11] A similar celebration for the Provo City Center Temple was scheduled for March 19, 2016.

In June 2015, Church leaders appointed Steven J. Lund to take charge of the open house, cultural celebration, and other logistics related to the Provo City Center Temple's dedication. He was the

Elder Steven J. Lund, former Area Seventy. Courtesy of Steven J. Lund.

executive chairman of Nu Skin Enterprises, which he had helped
found years earlier. He also had served as an Area Seventy from 2009
to 2014. He would be responsible for an array of significant areas
including audio visual arrangements, the cultural celebration (including the script and production), dedication recommends, finance, historical record and cornerstone box content, housing and hospitality,
member missionary efforts, music, physical facilities, public affairs,
safety and security, translation, and transportation/parking. Under
his direction, subcommittees were formed to carry out each of these
functions.[12]

Temple dedications in recent years have taken place in three sessions on a single Sunday. Proceedings have been carried to locations
outside of the temple in order to accommodate the large number of
Latter-day Saints who are interested and who are worthy to attend.
In such cases, the buildings where the dedication were viewed have
been treated as extensions of the temple. Those attending, including
youth, needed to have temple recommends or special invitations
issued following an interview with ecclesiastical leaders. Sometimes
the area covered by such overflow broadcasts has been quite broad.
The dedications of temples at significant historic sites—Palmyra,
Nauvoo, and Winter Quarters—were carried to stake centers throughout North America. Proceedings at the recently dedicated Oquirrh
Mountain, Brigham City, and rebuilt Ogden Temples in Utah were
made available throughout the state. Dedication of the Payson
Temple, on the other hand, was available only within that temple's
district. The First Presidency announced the dedication of the Provo
City Center Temple on March 20, 2016, would once again be seen
throughout the state.

Rather than being a separate earlier event, as was the case when
the Provo Temple was dedicated in 1972, the cornerstone-laying
ceremony has been incorporated into the first session of temple dedications since the early 1980s. Near the beginning of this session, the
General Authorities and a few other designated persons left the celestial room where the service was being conducted. They went outside
to the location where the cornerstone was to be placed. A separate
outside choir provided music. The member of the First Presidency

Opposite: Youth cultural celebration on
the eve of the Payson Temple dedication.
Photos by Angie Clayson.

Left: Place for temple cornerstone (note the Victorian fountain in the background). Photo by Lee R. Cowan. *Right:* Space provided for commutative time capsule. Photo by Lee R. Cowan. *Opposite: Top:* The temple in its Provo city center. Photo by Dane Christensen. *Bottom:* View of Provo's temples from the freeway, May 18, 2014. Photo by Lee R. Cowan.

Allen and Nancy Ostergar. Courtesy of Allen Ostergar.

who was presiding, and other dignitaries, placed mortar to seal the cover closed. This symbolized the completion of construction on the temple. A favorite moment was when even children from the onlooking group were invited to participate. A space in the east face of the Provo City Center Temple's southeast turret was prepared for the commemorative metal box and cornerstone plaque.

When the first Provo Temple opened in 1972, approximately a month was allowed following dedication to commence the full performance of ordinances. In more recent years, by contrast, ordinance work has typically started the day after the temple was dedicated. This certainly was a blessing to those who had traveled long distances to reach the temple. Even though such extensive travel would not be a major factor at the Provo City Center Temple, Utah Valley Latter-day Saints certainly anticipated being blessed by the prompt inauguration of temple service.

In July 2015, Allen C. Ostergar Jr. was named as the Provo City Center Temple's first president. Born in Blackfoot, Idaho, he served a mission in Brazil and earned a master's degree in public administration at Brigham Young University. His wife, the former Nancy S. Farnsworth, will become the temple's first matron. They are the parents of nine children. His life has been extraordinarily full of service to the Church. President Ostergar

Views of the Provo City Center Temple taken from a drone. Photos by Dane Christensen.

was one of the first teachers at what would become the Missionary Training Center in Provo, becoming director in 1970 and serving as administrative director of all MTCs worldwide until 2003. He also has served as a bishop and as president of a young single adult stake. He presided over the Kentucky Louisville Mission from 1984 to 1987 and over the Brazil MTC from 2003 to 2006. He became president of the Oak Hills Stake in northeast Provo in 2007 and was serving in that position when he was called as temple president.

Conclusion

Provo's two temples have some characteristics in common, but they are unique in other ways. Both serve the large and very faithful population of Latter-day Saints in Utah Valley and beyond. On the other hand, both have distinctive designs; The Provo Temple's rounded corners are unique as are the City Center Temple's red brick walls and Victorian/Gothic design.

Thus the new Provo City Center Temple joins its cross-town companion as a unique member of the Church's worldwide family

Opposite: View of Provo's two temples from the hills of northeast Provo, March 7, 2015. Photos by Lee R.Cowan.

of temples. It too is an appropriate symbol of the strong faith of the Utah Valley Saints, and it is a powerful spiritual beacon to all living in or traveling through the area.

Notes

1.   Andy Kirby, remarks at Provo Library, June 13, 2014, notes in possession of Richard O. Cowan.

2.   Andrew Kosorov interview, March 5, 2015, notes in possession of Richard O. Cowan.

3.   Jay and Sylvia Newitt, Sharon Park Stake fireside talk, July 20, 2014, notes in possession of Richard O. Cowan.

4.   Newitts, fireside, 2014; young single adult stake fireside talk, March 29, 2015. Notes in possession of Richard O. Cowan.

5.   Andy Kirby, remarks at Provo South Stake fireside, July 21, 2013, notes in possession of Richard O. Cowan.

6.   Newitts, fireside, 2014.

7.   Kirby, remarks, 2013.

8.   Gerry Avant, "Bright Day for Youth in Ghana: Program Was Opportunity for Youth to 'Have Some Fun,'" *Church News*, January 17, 2004, 8–9.

9.   Thomas S. Monson, "Welcome to Conference," *Ensign*, November 2009, 6.

10.   Sarah Jane Weaver, "Temple Celebrations," *Church News*, June 5, 2009, retrieved from http://www.ldschurchnewsarchive.com/articles/57434/Temple-celebrations.html

11.   The Payson Temple Cultural Committee, "Committee's Message—O Youth of the Noble Birthright," www.filltheworldwithlove.org, April 20, 2015.

12.   Steven J. Lund to stake presidents, June 10, 2015.

Appendix A

Additional Images

Provo Temple

Photo by Bruce Nordgren.

Top: Photo by Reinhard Franz. *Bottom*: Photo by Jessleetrevi. *Next page*: Photo by Reinhard Franz.

Photo by Bruce Nordgren.

Provo City Center Temple

Charred remains of west side. Photo by Lee R. Cowan.

Top: Laser target mounted on wall for detecting any movements while temple was on stilts. *Left, middle right, and bottom right:* Water was an ongoing concern. It was continually pumped from the excavation inside of the water-barrier walls. A major concern was the upward pressure that would result when the water table was allowed to return to its normal level. The building was anchored to keep it from "floating" as the water level came back up (see pages 221–23). Photos by Julie Cannon Markham.

Top: Courtesy of Doug Fallon. *Bottom:*
Photo by Juliana G. Cox.

Top left: Signatures were found on the original beams from those who worked on the original tabernacle. Photo by Lee R. Cowan. *Top right*: Temple construction workers signed their names on beams in the spire. Photo by Lee R. Cowan. *Bottom left*: Copy of painting which survived the fire. Note how figure of Christ was undamaged. Courtesy of A. LeGrand "Buddy" Richards. *Bottom right*: Harry Anderson's painting *The Second Coming*. © Intellectual Reserve, Inc.

Top left: Burnt gable. Photo by Donna Coleman. *Top right:* Restored gable. Photo by Lee R. Cowan. *Bottom left:* Damaged southwest tower cap. Photo by Lee R. Cowan. *Bottom right:* Restored tower cap. Photo by Lee R. Cowan.

Photo by Lee R. Cowan.

Photos by Julie Cannon Markham.

Photo by Lee R. Cowan.

Photo by Brent Nordgren.

Photo by Julie Cannon Markham.

Top: Photo by Julie Cannon Markham.
Bottom: Photo by Brent Nordgren.

Photo by Brent Nordgren.

Photo by Kazumasa Aoyama. *Next page:*
Photo by Brent Nordgren.

Photo by Lee R. Cowan.

Top: Photo by Lee R. Cowan. *Bottom:*
Photo by Julie Cannon Markham.

Photo by Brent Nordgren.

Photo by Brent Nordgren.

Richard Cowan at the Nu Skin building
overlooking the Provo City Center
Temple. Photo by Lee R. Cowan.

Top: Photo by Kazumasa Aoyama. *Bottom*: Photo by Julie Cannon Markham.

Photo by Lee R. Cowan.

Photo by Lee R. Cowan.

Above: Committee assigned to plan the open house, cultural event, dedication, and related events for the Provo City Center Temple. Elder Steven J. Lund, the committee chair, is at the left. The one in the middle with the temples tie is Richard Cowan (one of the authors to this volume), who chairs the subcommittee assigned to prepare the history for and identify other items to be placed in the cornerstone box. *Right*: Sylvia and Jay Newitt showing the cornerstone box to Richard Cowan, who has the responsibility of choosing what artifacts should be placed within it. Photos by Lee R. Cowan.

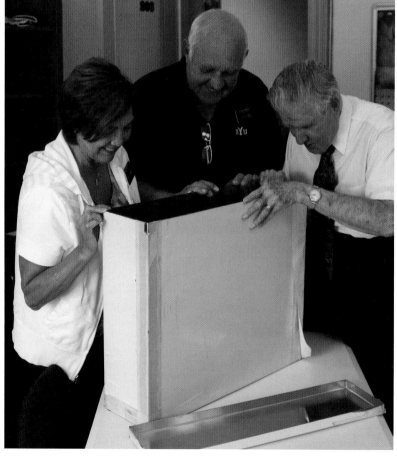

APPENDIX B

Milestones

1776   Spanish explorers praise Utah Valley

1830   Church of Jesus Christ organized in New York State (April 6)

1836   First LDS temple dedicated at Kirtland, Ohio

1840   Baptisms for the dead inaugurated at Nauvoo

1849   Fort Utah founded

1860s   Brigham Young and others prophesy of a temple on a hill north of Provo

1867   Meetinghouse or "Old Tabernacle" dedicated (August 24)

1877   Endowments for the dead inaugurated at St. George Temple

1883   Cornerstone laid for larger Provo Tabernacle (April)

1886   April general conference convenes in the uncompleted Provo Tabernacle

1893   Salt Lake Temple dedicated (April 6)

1898   Provo Tabernacle dedicated by President George Q. Cannon (April 16)

1909   US President William Howard Taft speaks in Provo Tabernacle (September 24)

1911   BYU's Maeser Building dedicated on Temple Hill

1917   Central tower removed from tabernacle, stained glass added to tabernacle

1919   Old Tabernacle torn down

1940   LDS population in Utah Valley reaches nearly 45,000

1950s   Proposals for training missionaries at BYU revive idea of temple in Provo

1955   Swiss Temple presents endowment in one room using film

1956   Los Angeles Temple (largest in the Church) dedicated

1960s   Seventies quorum in Provo inaugurates tabernacle tours

1964   Oakland Temple (last before Ogden and Provo Temples) dedicated

1965   Emil Fetzer becomes Church architect (July 1)

1966   Latter-day Saint population in Utah Valley passes 107,000

1967   First Presidency announces plans to build Ogden and Provo Temples, would follow Swiss pattern (August 14)

Provo Temple site announced (September 2)

Fetzer appointed to design Ogden and Provo Temples

During his flight, Fetzer envisions arrangement of temple rooms (August 30)

1968   First Presidency approves temple design (January 24)

1969   All stakes raise their allotted funds (by August)

Ground broken by President Hugh B. Brown (September 15)

Hogan and Tingey submit low bid (October)

1970   Ground-floor walls and higher steel framework completed (by October)

1971   Cornerstone laid and temple presidency announced (May 21)

Temple presidency and recorder set apart (June 4)

Tower completed (July)

1972   Public open house held (January 10–29)

Temple dedicated (Tuesday, February 9)

First ordinances; baptisms for the dead done (February 23)

Endowments inaugurated (March 14)

1974   Waiting/meeting room created in basement

Special sessions offered in Spanish, for hearing impaired, and so forth

1976   Record of 76,000 endowments performed in a single month (January)

Missionary training complex dedicated nearby (September 27)

1978   All missionaries being trained in Provo (beginning October 26)

1985   Expanded parking opens across the street from the temple

1997   With opening of Mount Timpanogos Utah Temple, Provo Temple no longer the most productive

2000   Escalators removed (May)

2003   Statue of angel Moroni added to temple tower (May 12)

2009   More ordinances done at Provo than in any other temple during a single year

2010   Stake Christmas fireside, last event in the Provo Tabernacle (December 12)

Dress rehearsal for *Gloria* (December 16)

Tabernacle destroyed by fire (December 17)

Gloria performed at UVU (December 19)

Stabilizing tabernacle walls commences (December 20)

2011   Final report sets loss at $15 million (March 31)

Church buys property on block to the south of the tabernacle (August)

Plans announced to rebuild the tabernacle as a temple (October 1)

Foundation of first tabernacle located by ground-penetrating radar (November)

2012   Student archaeologists excavate first tabernacle (winter)

Name selected for Provo City Center Temple (spring)

Ground broken for Provo City Center Temple (May 12)

Octagonal turret roofs removed and placed on ground to the north (August)

Reinforced concrete applied to inside of brick walls (September and October)

Support piles driven ninety feet into the ground (November and December)

2013   Excavation for lower floors to depth of about forty-five feet (January and February)

Foundation, five feet thick, put into place (spring)

Existing walls supported by piles while ground is excavated (March–April)

Pouring of mat footing marks beginning of new construction (May 24)

Basement walls engage with brick walls above; support piles are removed (summer)

First steel beam placed in temple's interior structure (August 20)

Central spire lifted into place, completing steel structure (December 5)

2014   Final turret roof put back into place (January 20)

Statue of angel Moroni placed atop central spire (March 31)

"Holiness to the Lord" stone placed on east gable (August)

Stained-glass windows installed in temple's exterior (November and December)

2015   Three-tiered bronze Victorian fountain set in place (April 21)

First trees planted (December)

Dedicatory Address of Provo Temple

By Joseph Fielding Smith
February 9, 1972

President Smith, who presided at the temple dedication, gave this address at the beginning of the afternoon and evening sessions.

*M*y dear brothers and sisters, I welcome you to these dedicatory services for the Provo Temple of The Church of Jesus Christ of Latter-day Saints, and I pray that the Lord will pour out His Spirit upon us in great abundance.

Today is the 172nd anniversary of the birth of my grandfather, the Patriarch Hyrum Smith, and I am pleased that we are celebrating that occasion by presenting to the Lord another holy temple, wherein those keys and powers, held jointly by him and the Prophet Joseph Smith, may be used for the salvation and exaltation of many of our Father's children.

Hyrum Smith, an older brother of the Prophet, was born Feb. 9, 1800, at Tunbridge, VT. He stood at the side of the Prophet through all his trials, and together they sealed their testimony with their blood, so that all things might be established in the mouths of two witnesses.

Of him the Prophet said: "My beloved brother Hyrum . . . possesses the mildness of a lamb, and the integrity of a Job, and in short, the meekness and humility of Christ; and I love him with that love that is stronger than death."

In announcing their martyrdom to the world, the formal proclamation of the church said: "In life they were not divided, and in death they were not separated. . . . And henceforth their names shall be classed among the martyrs of religion. . . . They lived for glory; they died for glory; and glory is their eternal reward. From age to age shall their names go down to posterity as gems for the sanctified."

President David O. McKay and those associated with him sought the Lord in mighty prayer and were guided by the spirit of inspiration in arranging for the construction of this house of the

Lord. It is now our purpose to present it to the Lord, as one of His holy houses, as a place where His Spirit may dwell in the hearts of all those who come here to worship Him in spirit and in truth.

In this holy house we are entitled to receive revelation and guidance from on high. The Lord is anxious to reveal His mind and His will to us, and to give us counsel and direction and doctrine as rapidly as we are able to receive them.

We believe all that God has revealed, all that he does now reveal, and I testify to you that there are many great and important things yet to be set forth in the days that are ahead.

It is my prayer that we shall use this holy temple for the performance of the ordinances of salvation and exaltation, for both the living and the dead; that the saints in this area will come here to find peace and the spirit of inspiration; and that through our work here many more souls shall be saved in our Father's kingdom.

I ask the Lord to bless and prosper all who have contributed in any way to the construction of this temple and that He will bless those who labor in it for the salvation of the children of men.

When we dedicate a house to the Lord, what we really do is dedicate ourselves to the Lord's service, with a covenant that we shall use the house in the way He intends that it shall be used.

The dedication is performed in a prayer of thanksgiving and praise and petition for the blessings of the Lord. In this prayer, acting in the power and authority of the holy Melchizedek Priesthood and in the sacred name of the Lord Jesus Christ, whom we serve and whose agents we are, we present the temple to the Lord as one of His houses on earth. Our other public prayers are simple and short and offered as guided by the Spirit of the Lord.

Dedicatory prayers for temples, however, are formal and long and cover many matters of doctrine and petition. This pattern was set by the Prophet Joseph Smith in the dedication of the Kirtland Temple. The prayer given on that occasion was revealed to him by the Lord; all prayers used since then have been written by the spirit of inspiration and have then been read by such of the Brethren as have been appointed to do so. The prayer I have prepared for the dedication of this Provo Temple is no exception.

I have asked President N. Eldon Tanner to conduct these services and President Harold B. Lee to read this dedicatory prayer for me at the conclusion of the session. President Lee and President Tanner are spiritually attuned and the Lord will bless them as they participate in these responsibilities as they are blessed in all other matters in their ministry.

I bear testimony to the truth and divinity of the great work in which we are engaged and leave my blessing with you in the name of the Lord Jesus Christ, Amen.

("Hyrum Smith Honored By Pres. Smith," *Church News*, February 12, 1972, 3–4)

Dedicatory Prayer of Provo Temple

Read by President Harold B. Lee
February 9, 1972

O God, the Eternal Father, the Creator of heaven and earth and all things that in them are; thou Man of Holiness who hast created us, thy children, in thine own image and likeness and endowed us with power and agency to follow thee; thou who knowest all things and hast all power, all might, and all dominion; thou who created the universe and ruleth with justice and equity and mercy over all the works of thy hands—hallowed be thy great and holy name!

We come before thee in the name of thine Only Begotten Son, even the Son of Man, in whose sacred name thou hast ordained that we shall have access to thee, the Lord; and we plead with thee to pour out thy Holy Spirit upon us as we raise our voices in praise and thanksgiving and seek blessings under thy hands.

We know that thou art our Father and that we are the workmanship of thy hands, the sheep of thy pasture, the saints of thy congregation; and we thank thee for life and being and for the privilege of receiving our mortal probation in a day when thou hast given the fullness of thine everlasting gospel to men on earth.

Our hearts are filled with gratitude that this thy gospel is the plan of salvation for all men, and that thou didst choose thy Beloved and Chosen One to be the Redeemer and Savior and to put into full effect the provisions of thy great plan. We thank thee for the atoning sacrifice of thy Beloved Son; that he came into the world to die upon the cross for the sins of the world; that he has ransomed us from temporal and spiritual death; that by his stripes we are healed. And we covenant before thee to walk in the light of revealed truth so that we may have joyous fellowship one with another and so that the blood of Jesus Christ, thy Son, may cleanse us from all sin.

And so now, with thy grace attending, may we shout praises unto the Holy One of Israel, and say: O Jehovah, thou God of our fathers, Abraham, Isaac, and Jacob; thou who "wast slain, and hast redeemed us to God by thy blood out of every kindred, and tongue, and people, and nation"; thou who shalt make us "unto our God kings and priests" that we may live with thee a thousand years—thou art "worthy . . . to receive power, and riches, and wisdom, and strength, and honour, and glory, and blessing."

And may we, O God, our Heavenly Father, be numbered everlastingly with that mighty congregation of the righteous which acclaims with one voice: "Blessing, and honour, and glory, and power, be unto him that sitteth upon the throne, and unto the Lamb forever and ever."

Our Father, we have no power of expression to ascribe unto thee the gratitude in our hearts for thy love and mercy and condescension unto us, thy children. We are overwhelmed by thy grace and goodness in sending thine Only Begotten Son, that whosoever believeth in him might have eternal life; and we rejoice and praise thee for restoring in this dispensation, through thy servant Joseph Smith Jr., the fullness of thine everlasting gospel.

We thank thee that thou didst appear with thy Beloved Son in the spring of 1820 to usher in this final gospel dispensation; that thereafter thou didst send Moroni to reveal the Book of Mormon; that John the Baptist, and Peter, James, and John ministered to Joseph Smith and Oliver Cowdery; that Moses and Elijah and Elias and Gabriel and Raphael and divers angels came from the courts of glory, "all declaring their dispensation, their rights, their keys, their honors, their majesty and glory, and the power of their priesthood; giving line upon line, precept upon precept," until the whole plan of salvation, in all its beauty and glory, is now again on earth.

O Lord, we thank thee for the saving truths revealed anew in our day and for the noble and great spirits sent to earth to carry forward thy great work in these last days. We rejoice in the mission and ministry of the Prophet Joseph Smith and the Patriarch Hyrum Smith, who together held the keys of this final dispensation and who sealed their testimony with their blood. We thank thee for the faith and devotion of all those who have worn the prophetic mantle, and of all thy faithful saints, and we pray for strength to be even as they are.

We thank thee that thou didst reveal unto us thy priesthood, even the sealing power, by the hand of Elijah the prophet, so that in this temple and all thy other holy houses, thy faithful Saints may be endowed with power from on high and may enter into those everlasting covenants which open the door to the receipt of all of the blessings of Abraham, Isaac, and Jacob, and all the holy prophets.

O our Father, we seek to be like thee; we seek to pattern our lives after the life of thy Son; we desire righteousness for ourselves and our children and our children's children; we turn our faces to this holy house; and we plead with thee to make us worthy to inherit the fullness of those blessings found only in thy holy temples, even those blessings which grow out of the continuation of the family unit forever.

Thou knowest, O Father, that we seek these blessings, not only for ourselves and our descendants, but also for our forebears; for thou hast said that we, as saviors on Mount Zion, have power to save and redeem our worthy dead. We seek so to do, and we plead for thy guidance and directing light as we go forward in this work—one of the greatest ever revealed to the children of men in any age of the earth.

We look forward to the day, O our God, when thou wilt reveal unto thy servants where other temples shall be built in all the nations where thy saints increase in numbers and serve thee in righteousness. We know that all men are thy children, and we pray for the day when all who will come may come and partake of the waters of life freely and gain for themselves the fullness of the blessings that thou hast in store for all those who love and serve thee with all their hearts.

Incline thine ear, O Lord; look down upon us in mercy; hear us in these our petitions; and grant us the desires of our hearts in righteousness, as we plead with thee for the welfare of Zion and all her interests and concerns. This is thy church; thou hast established it and hast "brought it forth out of obscurity and out of darkness, the only true and living Church upon the face of the whole earth." Wilt thou now cause it to "shine forth fair as the moon, clear as the sun, and terrible as an army with banners," that all men everywhere may know that this is thy work; that it is thy will that they should come unto thy Son and live his laws and gain salvation in thine eternal kingdom.

O may the interests of Zion prevail and triumph in all the earth! May thy kingdom, which is thy church, "go forth, that the kingdom of heaven may come, that thou, O God, mayest be glorified in heaven so on earth, that thine enemies may be subdued; for thine is the honor, power and glory, forever and ever."

O God, our Father, in this day of turmoil and evil, when Satan has power over his own dominion and when his forces seek to destroy thy work, we are strengthened and comforted and given courage by thy decree that thy Son "shall have power over his saints, and shall reign in their midst." And we testify before thee that we know that he does reign in our midst, for which blessing we praise thy holy name forever.

We remember with soberness and subdued souls thy promise that no weapon that is formed against thy saints shall prosper; and that if any man lift his voice against them, he shall be confounded in thine own due time.

We thank thee, O our God, that thou didst ordain and establish the Constitution of the United States by the hands of wise men whom thou didst raise up unto this very purpose. We thank thee for the freedoms and rights and privileges which are guaranteed to us in this sacred document and pray that they may be established forever. We beseech thee to put into the heart of the chief executive of this nation the desire and determination to preserve our free institutions for us and our posterity. Wilt thou bless the executive, legislative, and judicial branches of our government, that each may function wisely and courageously in its respective field, for the preservation of our constitutional form of government.

Now, O Father, thy faithful saints are and shall be in all the nations of the earth. We have deep concern for their temporal and spiritual well-being. We pray that the rulers of all people, under the guidance of the Holy Spirit, may be constrained to adopt forms of government which will assure to all men those freedoms which rightly belong to them and which are justifiable before thee.

Wilt thou, O Lord, put into the hearts of thy saints everywhere, a desire and a determination to follow implicitly the declaration, "We believe in being subject to kings, presidents, rulers, and magistrates, in obeying, honoring, and sustaining the law." May they strive to further the cause of righteousness by the election to office of good and righteous men, and to "be subject to the powers that be, until he reigns whose right it is to reign, and subdues all enemies under his feet."

Our souls are troubled and we weep because of the wickedness of the world and the evils that abound on every hand. Out of deep concern, therefore, we pray for the youth of Zion, for the young and rising generation, for those who must now prepare themselves to bear up the kingdom in their time and season.

Keep them from evil; hedge up the way so they may not fall into sin and be overcome by the world. O Lord, bless the youth of Zion and us their leaders that we may guide and direct them aright.

We know that thy kingdom shall roll onward and that hosts of the young and rising generation shall yet stand forth in power and great glory as witnesses of thy name and teachers of thy law. Preserve them, O our God; enlighten their minds and pour out upon them thy Holy Spirit, as they prepare for the great work that shall rest upon them.

Let that great temple of learning, the Brigham Young University, and all that is associated with it, and all other Church schools, institutes, and seminaries be prospered to the full. Let thy enlightening power rest upon those who teach and those who are taught, that they may "seek learning, even by study and also by faith."

Bless us, O Lord, that we may "teach one another the doctrine of the kingdom," as thou hast commanded. May we do so with such diligence that thy holy grace shall attend, so that we may "be instructed more perfectly in theory, in principle, in doctrine, in the law of the gospel, in all things that pertain unto the kingdom of God."

May those who teach and study in all academic fields have their souls enlightened with spiritual knowledge so they will turn to thy house for blessings and knowledge and learning that surpass all that may be found elsewhere.

We are grateful, O our Father, that it is thy purpose to provide for thy saints and are mindful of the command thou hast given us to care for the needy and unfortunate among them. We know thou hast commanded us and all men to subdue the earth and to earn our bread in the sweat of our face, but our hearts go out to those among us who have been overtaken by misfortune and who are not able at all times to care for their own needs.

We are most grateful, therefore, that thou didst inspire thy servants to institute the welfare program of thy church so that the poor and unfortunate may be provided for without the forfeiture of their self-respect. And now, with the rapidly expanding number of stakes and missions throughout the world, we earnestly pray that thy servants may continue in thy favor, that they may merit thy inspiration to develop this welfare program of thy church until it becomes perfect in all respects, for the care and blessing of thy people wherever they may be gathered together.

We seek thy guidance and Spirit, O Holy Father, so that thy saints may be cared for in thine own way. We desire to follow those principles thou hast given, which are:

That those who are in distress shall use their own individual efforts to the full;

That those who are rich in wisdom, in leadership, and in the material things of the world shall contribute of their talents and means;

That all of us shall unite together in the bonds of true brotherhood in caring for the fatherless and the widows;

And that we shall keep ourselves unspotted from the sins of the world—all of which, as thou hast said, is pure religion and undefiled before thy holy face. O Lord, bless thy servants with revelation in this and all things pertaining to the growth and development of thy work on earth.

And now, O God, the Eternal Father, accept from our mouths these words of praise and thanksgiving and petition. Hear our cries; read the thoughts and intents of our hearts; and be pleased to grant us all that we need.

We acknowledge Thy hand in all things and desire to serve thee and keep thy commandments, that we may have place with thee in thy kingdom.

It has been our privilege, as guided by the whisperings of thy Spirit, to build unto thee this temple which we now present unto thee as another of thy holy houses.

Wherefore, according to the pattern thou hast given, and in harmony with the course pursued by thy servants who have been before, and acting in the authority of that priesthood which is after the order of thy Son and in His holy name, we dedicate this temple to thee, the Lord.

We dedicate it as a house of baptism, a house of endowment, a house of marriage, a house of righteousness for the living and the dead.

We humbly pray that thou wilt accept this edifice and pour out thy blessings upon it as a house to which thou wilt come and in which thy Spirit will direct all that is done, that it may be accepted unto thee. Let thy Spirit and blessings attend and guide all who officiate herein, that a feeling of holiness will prevail in every room of this, thy holy house.

May all who enter have clean hands and pure hearts, and may they be built up in their faith and depart with a feeling of peace and praising thy holy name.

We dedicate the grounds on which it stands and which surround it. We dedicate the font and ordinance rooms and especially the sealing rooms, that they may be kept holy and that thy protecting care may be over them, and that thy spirit may ever be present to enlighten those who attend.

We dedicate all the structural parts from its foundation to the tower. Protect it, we pray thee, from any devastating influence, holocausts, hurricanes, storms, or destruction of any kind.

We dedicate the walks, the ornamental landscaping, the trees, plants, flowers, and shrubbery which will subsequently be added. May they add beauty and give fragrance to the surroundings.

Protect all the mechanical parts to the end that there might be a harmonious operation of this holy temple from day to day.

May all that is done herein be with an eye single to thy glory and to the building up of thy kingdom here upon the earth.

And now finally, we dedicate this temple as an abode for thee and thy Son and thy Holy Spirit and ask that thou wilt place thy ratifying seal of approval upon this dedicatory ordinance and upon all that we have done and shall do in this, thy holy house, which we now give unto thee, the Lord.

O Lord God of our fathers, who sitteth upon thy throne, and who liveth and reigneth over all things, blessed be thy holy name both now and forever!

In the name of the Lord Jesus Christ, thine only Son, even so. Amen and amen.

(*Ensign*, April 1972, 26–32; see also "Dedication Prayer of Provo Temple," *Church News*, February 12, 1972, 4–5)

Provo Temple Leaders

Presidents and Counselors, Matrons and Assistants

Provo Temple Leaders

President and Counselors	Matrons and Assistants
Harold Glen Clark (1971–76)	**Mary Deane Clark**
Joseph Y. Toronto	Fern M. Gardner
O. Wendle Nielsen	
Orville C. Gunther (1976–80)	**Betha Allred Gunther**
Joseph T. Bentley	Kathleen B. Bentley
Herald H. Holley	Leah C. Holley
J. Wallace Boswell	Ada F. Wipple
A. Theodore Tuttle (1980–82)	**Marne Whitaker Tuttle**
Phil D. Jensen	Lillian M. Bendio
A. Herald Goodman	Irva P. Andrus
Leland F. Priday (1982–86)	**Thelma Farnsworth Priday**
Sanford M. Bingum	Lillian M. Bendio
Calvin H. Swensen	Irva P. Andrus
	Edna A. Bingum
	Ila S. Swensen
Arthur J. Sperry (1986–89)	**Carol J. Sperry**
Walter D. Talbot	Dorleen W. Talbot
James H. Polve	Dorothy T. Polve
J. Elliot Cameron (1989–92)	**Maxine Petty Cameron**
Vernon J. Finch	Kathleen T. Finch
Herald J. Anderson	Gloria S Anderson
Arthur S. Anderson (1992–95)	**Janice Jacobsen Anderson**
William B. Green	Iona N. Green
Dee V. Sharp	Carol C. Sharp
Robert J. Smith (1995–98)	**Lola Nielson Smith**
Vernon J. Finch	Kathleen T. Finch
Max R. Cannon	Elsie S. Cannon
Dean L. Larsen (1998–2001)	**Geneal Johnson Larsen**
Richard D. Matthews	Faye H. Matthews
A. LaDue Scovill	Roanna V. Scovill
Angus H. Belliston	Jenny J. Belliston
Rulon S. Francis	Geraldine Y. Francis

President and Counselors	Matrons and Assistants
Jay M. Smith (2001–4)	**JenaVee Cordon Smith**
Rulon S. Francis	Geraldine Y. Francis
R. DerMont Bell	Linda B. Bell
Stewart R. Ivie	Patricia F. Ivie
Carl W. Bacon (2004–7)	**Carolyn Bacon**
Raymond E. Beckham	Janette Beckham
Richard M. Obeson	Alix Obeson
Neal E. Lambert	Anne Lambert
Merrill J. Bateman (2007–10)	**Marilyn Bateman**
Robert H. Daines	Janet Daines
Clyde R. Hicken	Bonnie Hicken
Robert H. Daines (2010–)	**Janet Lundgren Daines**
Larry E. Dahl	Roberta Dahl
Stanley R. Riding	Karen Riding

Temple Recorders

Dates	President
1972–78	J. Wallace Boswell
1978–80	Kenneth F. Soffe
1980–86	J. Wallace Boswell
1986–91	Jack E. Purser
1991–2002	Gaylan S. Gallacher
2002–	Kurt J. Jensen

Biographies of Provo Temple Presidents

Harold Glen Clark (1971–76)

Born June 11, 1902, in Lehi, Arizona, he and his wife, Virginia Driggs, became the parents of six children. Following Virginia's death, Harold married Mary Deane Peterson Gilbert in 1950. After teaching in Mesa public schools, he earned his PhD at George Washington University and accepted education-related assignments with the Department of Agriculture. He then joined the BYU faculty and eventually became dean of Continuing Education. He served as bishop of two wards and as a general board member of the Young Men's Mutual Improvement Association. Following his tenure as Provo Temple president, he served a mission to Sri Lanka and died March 2, 1984.

Orville C. Gunther (1976–80)

Born January 1, 1912, in Lehi, Utah, he married Betha O. Allred, and they had six children. A businessman, he served as president and chairman of the board of the Bank of American Fork. He was a member of the state House of Representatives and chaired the State Tax Commission. He served as bishop, mission president, and regional representative. He died January 13, 2007.

A. Theodore Tuttle (1980–82)

Born March 2, 1919, in Manti, Utah, he attended Snow College, earned a bachelor's degree at BYU, and earned a master's degree at Stanford. During World War II, he served with the Marine Corps in the Pacific theater. After teaching seminary and directing the institute at the University of Nevada, Reno, he supervised seminaries and institutes until becoming a member of the First Council of the Seventy. In this latter calling, he supervised missions and members in South America for several years. He and his wife, Marne Whitaker, had seven children. He died November 28, 1986.

Leland Forbes Priday (1982–86)

Born December 4, 1914, in American Fork, Utah, he received his BA from Brigham Young University. He married Thelma Farnsworth in 1942, and they became the parents of eight children. He owned and operated an office supply store in American Fork, presided over the Alpine and American Fork North Stakes, served as stake patriarch, and directed the Independence Missouri Visitors' Center. He died October 23, 2004.

Arthur J. Sperry (1986–89)

Born in Salt Lake City in 1919, he and his wife, Ruby Carol Jones, had three children. He received both bachelor's and master's degrees from the University of Utah and became a teacher and school administrator. He served as bishop and mission president.

J. Elliot Cameron (1989–92)

Born February 9, 1923, in Panguitch, Utah, he attended Branch Agricultural College (now Southern Utah University) in Cedar City. He was active in athletics and student government. After serving in the US Army during World War II, he received bachelor's, master's, and eventually doctorate degrees at BYU. After working in education all his life, he became the dean of students and vice president at BYU, president of BYU–Hawaii, regional representative, and Commissioner of the Church Educational System. He served as bishop, stake president, and member of the Sunday School general board. He and his wife, Maxine Petty, were the parents of four children and one foster son. He died February 27, 2011.

Arthur S. Anderson (1992–95)

Born January 17, 1923, in Boise, Idaho, he married Janice Jacobsen. He served as bishop, mission president, and regional representative. As a marketing executive, he served on the board of Deseret Book Company and as board chairman for Primary Children's Medical Center.

Robert J. Smith (1995–98)

Born December 25, 1920, in Snowflake, Arizona, he and his wife, Lola Nielson, became the parents of eight children. After graduating from BYU, he earned an MBA at Northwestern University and DBA at Indiana University. He became financial and administrative vice president at BYU and served as stake president, district president, and bishop.

Dean L. Larsen (1998–2001)

Born May 24, 1927, in Hyrum, Cache County, Utah, he and his wife, Geneal Johnson, had five children. After graduating from Utah State University, he taught seminary and institute and became secretary of the Church's Indian Committee. He served as a bishop, mission president, member of the Sunday School general board, secretary of the adult correlation committee, regional representative, director of instructional materials, and editor of the Church Magazines. He was ordained a member of the First Quorum of the Seventy in 1976 and later became one of the seven presidents of the Seventy. He was designated as an emeritus General Authority in 1977.

Jay M. Smith (2001–4)

Born June 14, 1932, in Denver, Colorado. After earning his PhD in accounting at Stanford, he taught at the University of Minnesota before joining the BYU faculty, where he helped to develop the Junior Core in accounting. He and his wife, JenaVee Cordon, became the parents of eleven children. He served as bishop and mission president.

Carl W. Bacon (2004–7)

Born in Hollywood, California, he married Carolyn Schade. He served as a bishop, stake and mission president, and Area Authority Seventy. As a land developer, he has directed Provo's Freedom Festival and BYU's Development Office.

Merrill J. Bateman (2007–10)

Born June 19, 1936, in Lehi, Utah, and raised in American Fork, Utah, he and his wife, Marilyn Scholes, had seven children. He received his PhD in economics at the Massachusetts Institute of Technology. He taught in Ghana and the Air Force Academy before coming to Brigham Young University, where he became dean of the School of Management. He presided over two stakes and became a member of the Second Quorum of the Seventy in 1992 and the Presiding Bishop of the Church in 1994. Then he was called to serve as president of BYU from 1996 to 2003, during which time he was also sustained as a member of the First Quorum of the Seventy.

Robert H. Daines (2010–13)

Born May 30, 1934, in Logan, Utah, he and his wife, Janet M. Lundgren, had seven children. Served as bishop, stake president, and mission president. He was a BYU professor of finance in the School of Business.

Alan C. Ashton (2013–present)

Born in Salt Lake City in 1942, he and his wife, Karen Jackman, are the parents of eleven children. After earning a PhD in computer science at the University of Utah, he taught computer science at Brigham Young University for fourteen years. A businessman and entrepreneur, he was one of the founders of WordPerfect and established Thanksgiving Point. He has served as a stake and mission president.[1]

Note

1. "Entrepreneurship Founders: Alan Ashton," *Centers for Entrepreneurship and Technology*, BYU Marriott School, 2013.http://marriottschool.byu.edu /advisoryboard/detail.cfm?mem=1045&group=3.

Groundbreaking Prayer of Provo City Center Temple

Given by Elder Jeffrey R. Holland
May 12, 2012

Our beloved and Holy Father in Heaven, we gather today on this historic site to dedicate already-sacred ground for an even more sacred purpose—the construction of the Provo City Center Temple. This day is beautiful in every respect, as these hills and this valley have been beautiful since our pioneer ancestors settled here a century and a half ago. We are enjoying another magnificent May morning within the shadow of Y Mountain and against the shores of Utah Lake. As the hymn says for us too, there is springtime in our souls today. . . . The dove of peace sings in our heart, and the flowers of grace appear.

Father, thou knowest the history of this location. Thou knowest the faith of the members of The Church of Jesus Christ of Latter-day Saints who have cherished it for many years. How grateful we are that the First Presidency of thy Church has determined to not only save this space, but sanctify it further by building a house unto thee—a house of the Lord, inviting holiness unto the Lord where so many, including many of those gathered here today, met to worship weekly. Now we can meet and be sanctified daily, even hourly, to make covenants and perform ordinances essential to eternal life.

Today our purpose, Father, is to break the ground and begin the construction, which we're only too eager to do. So in the name of the Lord Jesus Christ, thy Beloved Son, and by the authority of the Holy Melchizedek Priesthood, acting today with apostolic authority under the direction of the prophet and president of this Church, we dedicate this ground and all the attendant property around it for the construction of the Provo City Center Temple—with all the ancillary buildings, beautiful grounds, other services, and systems that we'll obtain here.

We bless the architects, the construction companies, the designers and suppliers and workers, all who labor in any way on this beloved project; we bless them that they will be both inspired and safe, edified and protected. That not only will each life be in thy care and keeping, but each act will be a consecrated one, consecrated to all that a temple means to thee and to this people. We protect the site and the people who work here against violence, danger, natural calamity, and vandalism of man. May there be no accidents, nor carelessness, nor sorrow in our efforts here, and may no unhallowed hand nor force of nature mar this project nor bring grief to these holy purposes.

May the workmanship of this house of the Lord be worthy of thy Beloved Son, the best that mortal labor can provide. May the beauty resemble in its own way the original beauty of Solomon's Temple of old, with the added benefit today of a pioneer facade that will forever recall for us those faithful early Saints who made this day possible. May angels attend us while we wait, and the laborers while they work, that in a proper time and without undue delay this completed house may be dedicated unto thee. May we all in this extended community see it as our temple and take pride in keeping the clean and worthy structure that we ourselves are supposed to be.

Lastly, we note with gratitude that it is only through the faithful tithes and offerings of thy Saints—the widow, the student, the economically distressed as well as the financially prosperous—that this and every other temple goes forward. Bless those who contribute not only out of their abundance, but in more difficult circumstances continue to contribute of their means in times of want. Surely such faithfulness is part of the wonder of this work, part of the marvelous devotion the Saints of the Most High have always and will always show. To them as well as to thee we are indebted for this new structure about to rise in the heart of our city. We close this prayer of site dedication and groundbreaking service in the name of Jesus Christ, whose perfect life and atoning sacrifice make this day, and this temple, and our very lives the hopeful, happy realities that they are. We express gratitude to him and to thee, who as Father and Son gave so much and continue to give so much that we might have peace in this world and eternal life in the world to come. In the name of Jesus Christ our Savior, amen.

(Transcribed by author from video recording.)

About the Authors

Richard O. Cowan. Courtesy of
Richard O. Cowan.

Richard O. Cowan

Richard O. Cowan is a professor emeritus of Church history and doctrine, Brigham Young University. Unable to see well for most of his life, he became totally blind several years before retiring. He served a Spanish-speaking mission in Texas and New Mexico from 1953 to 1956. He enrolled at Occidental College in Los Angeles, graduating Phi Beta Kappa before going on to Stanford University for his master's and doctoral degrees. After earning his doctorate in history at Stanford in 1961, he taught Church history at Brigham Young University for fifty-three years. His research focus has been on Latter-day Saint history during the twentieth century with emphasis on LDS temples.

Justin R. Bray. Courtesy of Justin R. Bray.

Justin R. Bray

Justin R. Bray is a coordinator of oral histories in the Church History Department of The Church of Jesus Christ of Latter-day Saints. He received a bachelor of arts in history from Brigham Young University and is pursuing a master of arts in history from the University of Utah. Justin has coedited two books: *Exploring Book of Mormon Lands: The 1923 Latin American Travel Writings of Mormon Historian Andrew Jenson* (with Reid L. Neilson) and *Rediscovering the Sites of the Restoration: The 1888 Travel Writings of Mormon Historian Andrew Jenson and Edward Stevenson* (with Reid L. Neilson and Alan D. Johnson).

Index